THE
COMPLETE
BOOK
OF
WORD
PROCESSING
AND
BUSINESS
GRAPHICS

THE COMPLETE BOOK OF
WORD PROCESSING
AND
BUSINESS GRAPHICS

Walter Sikonowiz

Micro Text Publications, Inc.
Prentice-Hall, Inc., Englewood Cliffs, New Jersey O7632

Library of Congress Catalog Card Number: 82-60431

ISBN 0-13-158659-9 [pbk.]
ISBN 0-13-158667-X

Prentice-Hall International, Inc., *London*
Prentice-Hall of Australia Pty. Limited, *Sydney*
Prentice-Hall of Canada Inc., *Toronto*
Prentice-Hall of India Private Limited, *New Delhi*
Prentice-Hall of Japan, Inc., *Tokyo*
Prentice-Hall of Southeast Asia Pte. Ltd., *Singapore*
Whitehall Books Limited, *Wellington, New Zealand*

This Spectrum Book is available to business and organizations at a special
discount when ordered in large quantities. For information, contact Prentice-
Hall, Inc., General Publishing Division, Special Sales, Englewood Cliffs, N.J.
07632

Micro Text Publications, Inc. for Prentice Hall, Inc.
Englewood Cliffs, New Jersey 07632

ISBN 0-13-158659-9   {P}

ISBN 0-13-158667-X   {C}

To Jake and Elwood

CONTENTS

PREFACE

Conceivably, there are a number of different ways in which a book of this sort could have been written. For instance, it might have been aimed at the clerical worker, for whom a how-to book with few technical details would have been sufficient. Or, it might have been intended for the designer of office-automation systems, and in that case it would have been concerned with nuts and bolts, and little else. In writing this book, I took the middle ground. Although the book is undeniably technical, it does not require that the reader have previous experience in electronics or computer programming to understand it. Quite the contrary; sufficient introductory material is included so that no one interested enough to be reading this preface should feel uncomfortable with the rest of the book. At the same time, persons with a technical bent should feel equally at home, since important concepts have not been reduced in scope for the sake of simplicity. The underlying philosophy of this book is that the buyer of office-automation equipment must understand how things work before making a purchase. This is the only way to be sure of getting the right equipment for the job.

The material here has been divided into three principal sections. The first of these, Basic Concepts, is an introduction to computers and how they are used in word processing and business graphics. Chapter One explains what word processing and graphics are all about. Chapter Two takes a look at the insides of a computer, mass storage of information is discussed in Chapter Three, and local networks are examined in Chapter Four. Readers already comfortable with computers may find some familiar information here and there in Chapter Two, but the remainder of Section I should present exciting new territory.

Section II, Word Processing, takes a good look at the equipment and software needed to process text. Chapter Five tells how to select the correct printer, special ancillary hardware is discussed in Chapter Six, editing procedures are covered in Chapter Seven, and Chapter Eight tells all about the printing and formatting of text. It should be pointed out that Chapters Five and Six are mainly concerned with hardware (machines), while Chapters Seven and Eight deal with the features found in word-processing software (programs).

The final section, Business Graphics, concentrates on those aspects of computer graphics most useful in business. Chapter Nine looks at some of the special devices that enter graphical information into a computer; Chapter Ten examines the various electronic displays and recording instruments used in graphics; general features of graphics software are the topic of Chapter Eleven; and, finally, Chapter Twelve takes a look at some of the interesting applications for graphics in business. Again, the first two chapters in this section are concerned with hardware, while the latter two focus on software.

A glossary and a directory of manufacturers round out the book. Every effort has been made to define a word before using it in the text, but it makes no sense to define a word each time it comes up. Since this book makes use of technical language, it is inevitable that an occasional word will trip you up. When this happens, just look the word up in the glossary. The directory of manufacturers serves as a quick reference to who is selling what. For convenience, the directory is divided into individual product categories, and in each category the names, addresses, and telephone numbers of various manufacturers are listed. The directory could be the most valuable part of this book, because manufacturers of exotic equipment advertise only in technical and special-interest publications, to which the general reader may not have access.

Finally, special thanks are extended to all those persons who supplied photographs and technical information used in the preparation of this book: Margaret Barnes (Diablo Systems Inc.), Lee Benedict (Image Resource Corp.), Douglas K. Blackwood (Hewlett Packard/Desktop Computer Div.), James Busby (Datasouth Computer Corp.), Daniel Byford (PrintaColor Corp.), Patricia Compton (NEC Information Systems), Bruce W. Friesen (The Keyboard Co.), Joan M. Green (TeleVideo Systems Inc.), Tamisie Honey (Advanced Business Technology Inc.), Valerie Maddox (Mannesmann Tally Corp.), Traci McDonnald (Videx, Inc.), Wendy Mitchell (MicroPro International), Sharon H. Nelsen (Tektronix Inc.), Dana Perkins (Hayes Microcomputer Products), Chris Ray (Morrow Designs), David Register (Comdec Inc.), Carol Sartain (Action Computer Enterprise Inc.), Ross H. Snyder (Hewlett Packard/Business Computer Group), Susan M. Storey (Lanier Business Products Inc.), and Maurie D. Wagner (Houston Instrument Inc.).

SECTION I
BASIC CONCEPTS

CHAPTER ONE
Processing Words
and Pictures

As a result of recent advances in solid-state technology, computers have undergone a profound transformation: no longer are they the expensive tools of a privileged few. Instead, small and economical machines known as microcomputers have taken the business world by storm. Most of these trim, compact computers are busy doing what their bulky forebears once did: they process financial data. Generating bills and invoices, balancing the books, and keeping tabs on inventory are the traditional jobs for which a business buys a computer. But once the books have been balanced and the bills have been printed out, the astute office manager often starts dreaming about what other tasks he can hand the computer.

One of the best ways to make an idle computer earn its keep is by having it assist in the preparation of documents. Familiar examples of business documentation include correspondence, financial or technical reports, contracts, graphs, charts, catalogs, and schematic diagrams. Not only does a computer generate these items faster than a person can by hand, it does a better job as well. This is especially true when appearance is important, since computer-generated documents are not marred by erasures or whiteouts.

It should be obvious that every document must consist of either words or pictures, or both. When a computer is used to prepare text, the operation is known as word processing. If that same computer can produce drawings and charts, it is said to have graphics capability. It takes special hardware (electrical or mechanical equipment) and software (computer programs) to enable a computer to process words and pictures. Hardware without software, or the reverse, will get the user nowhere. The need for a balance between hardware and software is reflected in the organization of this book: roughly equal amounts of space have been allocated to each.

Covering word processing and business graphics in one book makes sense for a number of reasons. For one, it is very likely that the person who needs word processing can also make use of graphics in his or her business. Generally, it is word processing that has the more widespread acceptance at the present time. However, considering the rate at which new business-graphics software has been proliferating of late, one hardly needs to be clairvoyant to see that computer graphics has a bright future. In the years ahead, business graphics should blossom just as word processing did in the past decade.

Another reason for treating word processing and graphics together is that they tend to require the same hardware resources, such as computers, terminals, and mass-storage devices. Because many readers will have no more than a passing acquaintance with equipment of this sort, the first section of this book provides an introduction to computer systems and their operation. This puts everyone on an equal footing, and paves the way for a serious assault on word processing and graphics in the sections that follow.

Word processing and graphics overlap not only in their reliance on computers for support, but also in their use of peripherals, or auxiliary pieces of equipment. For example, certain electronic printers are equally adept at handling text or graphics. Another peripheral device, the light pen, can be used to select letters or words on a CRT (cathode-ray tube) screen or to draw lines there. The behavior of the light pen is governed by the word-processing or graphics software currently running on the computer.

The techniques used in word processing are notably similar to those used in graphics. Text or drawings must first be created, usually by an operator working at a terminal. At first glance, a terminal looks like a cross between a typewriter and a television set. The operator types commands and data on the keyboard of the terminal and watches his text or diagram take shape on the display screen. In most cases, documents will need to be edited, either to modify their contents or to correct mistakes. Text is edited by deleting letters and words, rearranging them, or inserting new ones. Likewise, diagrams are edited by adding, deleting, or rearranging lines and changing colors.

Once the desired effect has been obtained, a document can be stored, printed, or transmitted to another computer. Magnetic disks and tapes are the most common storage media for text or diagrams. Documents may be stored for later use on the same computer or a different one. If suitable communications facilities are available, documents can be transmitted directly from computer to computer over a special cable or telephone line. In this way, several work stations can collaborate on the preparation of a document. Eventually, the user will want to produce hard copy, which is to say, a printed record of what he has done. There are a variety of peripheral devices for this purpose—some specialized, others equally at home with graphics or text.

APPLICATIONS OF WORD PROCESSING

The bulk of business communication takes place *via* the printed word. It is therefore understandable that word processing should enjoy a higher priority than graphics in most offices. The primary benefits of word processing are an increase in worker productivity and an improvement in the appearance of the printed copy produced. Industry sources cite an average productivity increase of 50 percent when word processing takes the place of conventional typing. The chief reason for such an increase in worker efficiency is that documents do not have to be retyped in their entirety when corrections or modifications must be made. The operator, who sits before a video screen, edits text electronically. Mistakes made during the initial keyboarding of a document can later be corrected without disturbing the good parts of the text. New words or sentences can be inserted, awkward old ones can be deleted, and paragraphs can even be rearranged, if necessary, to improve the structure and coherence of the text.

Once all the corrections and modifications have been made, and the text on the video screen meets with the operator's approval, the document is printed on paper. Assuming that the operator has been conscientious, the final copy will be devoid of mistakes: no crossouts, whiteouts, or holes gouged in the paper from overzealous erasing. In short, the document will look impressively neat and precise. To some people, this may be reason enough for switching to word processing. However, there are other advantages. For example, ten copies of a document can be printed just as easily as one. And each copy will have the look of an original, which can be an advantage to lawyers, writers, and others who care about such things.

We would be remiss not to take note of one of the most valuable applications of word processing: the production of form letters. Properly executed, a form letter appears to have been prepared expressly for its recipient, when in fact the very same information is being sent to hundreds or thousands of other people. The trick, of course, is that the word processor automatically inserts vital statistics like names and addresses into the letter at selected points. Producing form letters requires that the text of the letter be imbedded with special characters that mark the points where insertions are to be made. Once the text of the complete letter has been prepared, the operator instructs the system to begin cranking out the desired number of form letters. Word-processing software automatically fetches names, addresses, and other data from storage (usually on magnetic disk) and inserts them where necessary in the letters being printed. Worker productivity can be increased strikingly using word-processing software that can print form letters.

Another word-processing function that goes hand in hand with the production of form letters is mailing-list generation. In this application, the word processor prints mailing labels based on customer data that it retrieves from magnetic disk or tape. The same stored data that were used to print form letters could be used to produce mailing labels. Names can be added or deleted as necessary so that mailing-list data remain up to date. As one would expect, having a computer print mailing labels is much faster and less tedious than doing it by hand. Mailing lists are usually compiled from business records, but in some instances they may be purchased from other firms in the same line of work.

APPLICATIONS OF GRAPHICS

Computer graphics can be used in a seemingly limitless number of ways. One of the most popular business applications of graphics is in the production of charts and graphs. Pie charts, line graphs, and bar graphs are very useful means of expressing financial or technical data. Producing charts manually requires the services of a graphic artist in most cases. Granted, most of us can plot a readable graph ourselves, but producing artwork good enough for a company report or advertisement requires more skill (and patience) than the average person can muster. A computer outfitted with the right peripherals can eliminate the need for a graphic artist. Hard copy in the form of photographs or printed material can be created very quickly, and multiple copies can be produced if necessary. If a company makes extensive use of charts and graphs, it can quickly recoup its investment in graphics hardware and software from the money saved in artist's fees.

Even more important, a computer eliminates the inevitable delays that occur when artwork is prepared outside the company.

Technical drawings such as schematic diagrams, architectural layouts, maps, flowcharts, and chemical-process diagrams can also be produced efficiently with computer assistance. Once a draftsman gets used to working with a computer and a digitizing tablet instead of a pencil and a T-square, his output increases significantly. (A digitizing tablet makes it easy for an operator to enter graphical information into a computer system; more on this in Chapter Nine). Another less obvious benefit is that traditional graphical skills are no longer necessary with a computer. In fact, the computer draftsman does not even have to be able to draw a straight line; the computer does it for him after he specifies the line's endpoints. Diagrams can be produced on vellum, paper, mylar (for overhead projection), or photographic film. With the right peripherals, even color copy can be obtained. Anyone who has ever attempted to produce camera-ready diagrams by hand will appreciate yet another benefit of computerized drafting: No corrections or erasures mar the artwork, because mistakes are edited out electronically before the diagram is printed.

The difficult task of visualizing a three-dimensional object can also be made easy with computer graphics. Once an object has been defined on a 3-D graphics system, it can be rotated about three axes, moved around, and expanded (or contracted) on the viewing screen of the computer terminal. What an observer sees on a flat TV screen is actually a two-dimensional projection of a three-dimensional object. If more realism is needed, expensive display systems based on vibrating mirrors or laser projection can be used to simulate the depth relationships in a 3-D scene. Most of us will never have occasion to use such devices; nevertheless, 3-D projection equipment is one indication of just how sophisticated computer graphics has become.

We are all familiar with the old saying that a picture is worth a thousand words. The ability of pictures to convey information quickly and succinctly can be of great importance in many fields. For instance, in education the use of computer-assisted instruction is a technique that is slowly gaining acceptance as teachers become familiar with low-cost microcomputers. Used intelligently, graphics can expand the power of computer-assisted instruction and enhance an otherwise dull presentation. Another field that can benefit from computer graphics is that of industrial process control. Displaying the current status of a manufacturing process graphically on a CRT screen makes it easy for the person monitoring the process to spot trouble in the system and correct it. For example, a computer might be hooked up to monitor various strategically placed pressure, flow, and fluid-level sensors in a chemical plant. Based on what it senses, the computer could generate a graphic display of tanks, pipes, and fluids for the benefit of the operator in charge of the process.

There are some applications of computer graphics too specialized to be of use in the average business, but deserving of mention, nonetheless. One of the more complex graphical applications is flight simulation, a technique that allows rocket and airplane pilots to train without ever leaving the ground. Not only is simulation the safest way to train, it is also the most economical, since no fuel is consumed in the process. Moreover, a pilot can be quickly exposed to a wider range of flying and landing conditions than would be feasible in actual flight. The simulator produces a graphical display of runways, houses, clouds, and other aircraft; as the pilot operates his flight controls, the display changes in response to his actions. The system must respond quickly enough so that no lag is apparent; as a result, complicated and expensive high-speed hardware is needed to generate the display.

Science and engineering have been the breeding grounds for many esoteric applications of graphics. Molecular modeling is used to give chemists a close look at proteins, carbohydrates, and other complex macromolecules. The raw data gleaned from the heavens by radiotelescopes is transformed, with the help of computer graphics, into multi-colored maps that astronomers can comprehend. In electronic and mechanical engineering, the automated design methods that have become so essential today rely heavily on computer graphics for their success. All things considered, scientists and engineers have generally been the most active users of computer graphics. This trend may change as more non-technical persons become aware of the computer's aptitude for graphics.

FEATURES OF WORD-PROCESSING SOFTWARE

The goal of word processing is to make the preparation of text as quick and easy as possible. To attain this goal, word-processing systems offer certain convenience features that have become more or less standard regardless of who writes the software. For now, a quick introduction to some of these useful features should give the reader some idea of what word processing can do. More detailed descriptions of the features common to word-processing software will be found in Chapters Seven and Eight.

Because everyone makes mistakes, word-processing software offers a variety of ways to eradicate errors. Letters, words, lines, and large blocks of text can be made to vanish from a system's video display by touching the appropriate keys. Items to be deleted are usually singled out by means of a cursor, a small flashing rectangle or underline character that the user can position anywhere on the screen. (In Latin, cursor means runner.) The movable cursor acts as a general-purpose pointer. Most actions initiated by an operator occur at a point on the screen defined by the cursor. Thus, a single letter might be deleted by first moving the cursor, with the help of various cursor-positioning keys, until it came to rest on the unwanted letter. Then, hitting another key would obliterate the letter beneath the cursor, and cause all text to the right of the cursor to move left one space so that no gap remained. Different procedures are used to remove larger amounts of text.

Very often it is necessary to insert new material into text already entered into a word-processing system. Like deletion, insertion is guided by the cursor. Small amounts of text can be inserted in the middle of a line by first positioning the cursor, and then invoking the insertion function with the appropriate key. Subsequently typed text usually appears to the left of the cursor, and the cursor, together with all text to its right, is shifted to the right to make room for each letter inserted. When the insertion is complete, hitting some designated key cancels the insertion mode and returns the system to normal operation. If more than a few letters or words are to be inserted, the procedure is slightly more involved, but the principle remains the same: old text can be split apart at any point to make room for newly inserted material.

Suppose that a document has been typed into a word-processing system, and that the operator later decides that certain words need to be changed. One way to make these changes would be to carefully review the text, search out each occurrence of the word in question, and change the word using deletion and insertion. This approach is feasible, but there is an easier way. Most word-processing software offers a replacement function, which automatically replaces some or all instances of one word with another. For example, a writer might wish to change the name of a story's protagonist from Horace to Boris. By supplying the system with the two names and invoking the replacement function, he could swap Horace for Boris in a matter of seconds. Replacement can be done globally—that is, throughout a document—or it can be carried out only for certain instances of a target word. In either case, the process in much faster than if the operator had to search for words and change them himself. Replacement is often a handy way to revise a technical manual or instruction book in the wake of design changes.

Sometimes the structure of a document can be improved by rearranging sentences, paragraphs, or chapters. Without a word processor, a writer jots cryptic notes about rearrangement in the margins of his first draft, and hopes they can be deciphered later when the manuscript is retyped. Some people prefer to cut pages apart, rearrange the pieces, and glue them back together with rubber cement. The product still has to be retyped. With a word processor, rearrangements can be made effortlessly with a few key strokes, and nothing has to be retyped.

It has been said that a person must be lacking in imagination to spell a word just one way. Those who resort to this kind of rationalization are referred to charitably as creative spellers. Their editors, who are not inclined to be charitable, speak of them in more colorful terms. Using a word processor, even the most creative of spellers can turn out intelligible English. The feature that makes this possible is commonly referred to as a dictionary or a spelling checker. After a document is finished, an author can request that the system perform a spelling check. Every word in the document is compared with words stored in the system's dictionary. Words that do not match dictionary entries are identified so that the author can look them over. Some of the suspect words will actually be misspelled, while others will be perfectly good but absent from the dictionary. New entries can usually be added to the dictionary, but the larger the dictionary becomes, the longer it takes to perform a spelling check. The size of the dictionary is kept in check by including in it only those words that occur most frequently in the user's text.

FEATURES OF GRAPHICS SOFTWARE

With the aid of a ruler, most of us can draw a respectable straight line. And with a compass, we can produce an equally respectable circle. Easy as these two manual operations are, having a computer draw lines and circles is even easier. To draw a straight line, all that a person has to do is identify the endpoints of the line, hit the proper keys on his terminal, and watch as the system automatically draws the desired straight line on his video screen. In most cases, the operator picks the endpoints he wants with the aid of a digitizing tablet or joystick. Both of these graphical input devices are explained thoroughly in Chapter Nine. Suffice it to say for the present time that input devices like the joystick and digitizing tablet provide a convenient means by which a user can feed spatial information to a computer.

Circles are not much harder to draw than straight lines. The user specifies a center and a radius, invokes the circle-drawing function, and sits back as the system plots a circle on his video screen. The ellipse, squashed cousin of the circle, is similarly easy to draw. By performing most drawing operations automatically, graphics software allows a user to produce accurate drawings with a minimum of effort.

Once drawn, some lines will inevitably have to be erased. Fortunately, this is no more difficult than drawing them was in the first place. On some systems, features must be erased by redrawing them in the color of the background. Thus, a white line on a blue screen would be erased by redrawing the line in blue. Other systems offer a special erase or delete function. In this case, a line can be erased by positioning the cursor to lie on the line, and then hitting the proper combination of keys to perform the deletion. The cursor used in graphics often has the shape of a circle or a cross, which is useful for precisely locating points on the screen. Generally, an input device like a joystick, light pen, or digitizing tablet is used to move the cursor around on the screen.

One of the more fascinating aspects of computer graphics is the creation of three-dimensional images. Software with 3-D capability allows a user to draw an object on a CRT screen and then manipulate it. Rotating the object about three independent axes allows it to be viewed from the front, back, or side. At the same time, the object can be made to move toward the observer or to retreat into the distance. And the object's image can be shifted up, down, right, or left on the screen. Three-dimensional graphics makes an important contribution to mechanical engineering, where it helps in the design of everything from internal-combustion engines to airplanes. In chemistry, 3-D computer graphics allows a complex molecule to be studied from every conceivable angle.

Software designed to automatically plot charts and graphs has become a staple of the business-graphics market. All that the user of this type of program usually has to do is enter the data he wants plotted and indicate how the axes of the graph should be labeled. Graphs may be plotted in one of several forms, including conventional line graphs, bar graphs, and pie charts. The user selects which type of graph he wants, then relaxes while the software draws and labels the axes of the graph and plots the data. If the results that appear on the CRT screen are not quite right, some of the parameters can be changed and the graph can be quickly replotted. Once suitable results have been obtained, the graph can be printed on paper, drafting vellum, or clear mylar. If the user's hardware and software permit it, graphs can even be plotted in color. Automatic graph plotting eliminates the need for a graphic artist and provides camera-ready artwork very quickly. More information on graph-plotting and other aspects of graphics software will be found in Chapters Eleven and Twelve.

EQUIPMENT OPTIONS

Thus far little has been said about the computer equipment needed to implement word processing and graphics. Several options are available to the user. The general-purpose computer is the most versatile and cost-effective alternative, but in some circumstances specialized machines like dedicated word processors or graphics computers may be desirable.

Dedicated Word Processors

The dedicated word processor is a computer system that has been fine-tuned to provide the utmost convenience and efficiency in word processing. Generally, dedicated word processors are conceived as integrated packages consisting of a computer, some form of mass storage, a printer, and software. One advantage of an integrated system is that the buyer does not have to waste time searching for compatible components. Everything he needs can be purchased from one source. Another benefit of integration is that it usually implies optimized performance and a certain degree of harmony within the system. The strongest selling point of a dedicated word processor is its software, which can generally be expected to offer many refinements and convenience features. That the manufacturer of a dedicated word processor offers superior software should come as no surprise: In order to compete with general-purpose computers, a dedicated word processor must be more convenient to use.

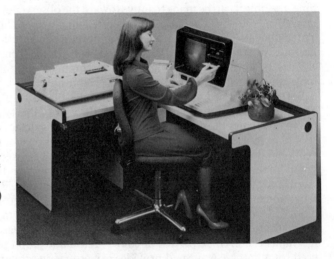

Fig. 1-1. Of the various ways in which word processing can be implemented, the one that generally provides the most refinements and convenience features is the dedicated word processor. (Courtesy of Lanier Business Products Inc., Atlanta, GA)

The chief disadvantage of a dedicated word processor is that its use is limited to word processing. In response to competition from general-purpose microcomputers, some manufacturers have begun to endow their word processors with limited mathematical capabilities, but this may be no more than window dressing in many cases. Older word processors, which can still be found on the used-equipment market, were not software-driven. These early machines had circuits that were completely hard-wired, which is to say that their operation was essentially unmodifiable. Later models were controlled by firmware, integrated circuits containing the programs that ran the system. Firmware-driven machines could be updated by a technician who swapped new ROM (read-only memory) chips for old. The current crop of word processors is software-driven, which means that the user himself can make performance updates when improved software is developed by the manufacturer. At the present time, a bare-bones word processor costs $7,500-$10,000; extras like mass storage and networking capability raise the price considerably.

General-Purpose Computers

Unlike a dedicated word processor, a general-purpose computer can perform a wide variety of different tasks. Accounting, word processing, graphics, inventory control, and financial forecasting are just a few of the things a computer can do when given the proper software. In addition, the cost of adding new capabilities is often quite low, since in many cases all that has to be purchased is new software. On microcomputers, the software is purchased outright, while on large computers (mainframes) it is usually leased by the month. As far as word processing is concerned, the best software is available for the smaller computers. Granted, a few of the word-processing packages available for microcomputers seem poorly conceived, but as a general rule word-processing software written for micros is much "friendlier" and easier to use than large-system software.

Fig. 1-2. When word processing is implemented on a general-purpose computer instead of a dedicated word processor, the buyer sacrifices some refinements but gains operational flexibility. (Courtesy of Hewlett-Packard/Business Computer Group, Cupertino, CA)

Computers come in all shapes and sizes. Large mainframes offer the high-speed operation and large storage capacity that big jobs demand. At the other extreme, microcomputers are very affordable, and they are capable of handling a surprising number of jobs in the office. A third type of computer, the minicomputer, is intermediate between micros and mainframes in terms of cost, speed, and memory capacity. In theory, the micro is easily distinguished from the mini, because the micro's CPU (central processing unit) is contained on one integrated circuit, known as a microprocessor, whereas the mini's CPU comprises many separate chips. In terms of performance, however, it is becoming increasingly difficult, as micros gain higher speed and larger memory capacity, to tell the difference between a high-end micro and a mini. This augurs well for micro users who want graphics, since many graphical applications demand large quantities of memory and high-speed computation.

Graphics Computers

Some computers come equipped with special features that enable them to excel at graphics. Included among these features are a large bit-mapped display (explained in the next chapter), a high-speed processor, and a large amount of semiconductor memory. As a result, such machines are capable of generating high-resolution (i.e., finely detailed) images in black and white, gray levels, and color. High-speed

Fig. 1-3. When an application makes extensive use of complex, high-resolution graphics, the purchase of a graphics computer like this HP 9845 may be warranted. (Courtesy of Hewlett-Packard/Desktop Computer Div., Fort Collins, CO)

operation is an advantage in that it allows pictures to be updated rapidly—a must for animation. Graphics computers usually interface readily with such essential graphical accessories as light pens, digitizing tablets, and plotters. Even more important is the graphics software that the manufacturer makes available for the system, since nothing gets done without it. In contrast to a dedicated word processor, a graphics computer is not limited to use in one special application. With the proper software, a graphics computer can do anything that a general-purpose computer can do. The high-resolution display and large memory capacity of a graphics computer necessarily make it more expensive than its general-purpose counterpart. For the relatively simple requirements of business graphics, a graphics computer is rarely necessary.

Making a Choice

The easiest and most cost-effective way to implement word processing and graphics is by means of a general-purpose computer. If such a machine is already in use for accounting or some other similar application, the cost of adding word processing or graphics is minimal: the only things that will have to be purchased are software and perhaps a few peripherals. Bear in mind, however, that when one computer has to do everything, chaos reigns if that machine breaks down. Minis and mainframes can usually be serviced quickly on the premises if a maintenance contract has been purchased. Having to buy such a contract may seem like extortion, but even the best-engineered computer breaks down. Some microcomputer manufacturers offer maintenance contracts, but they are not for on-site service. The ailing machine must be taken to a factory-authorized service center, or be shipped there by common carrier. The total turnaround time for repairs can be anything from one day to three weeks, depending on the nature of the trouble and the competence of the service organization. Therefore, while it is certainly economical to do everything on one computer, the practice is nevertheless a precarious one.

The business that can afford to supplement its general-purpose computer with a dedicated word processor gains several advantages. For one, the main computer will not be bogged down with word-processing duties, so it will be better able to handle other tasks without delay. Another advantage is that all work will not come to a standstill when one machine—either the computer or the word processor—breaks down.

A graphics computer makes sense only for the user who makes extensive use of high-resolution graphics in his work. Engineers and scientists are prime candidates for this type of machine. A graphics computer is just as versatile as a general-purpose computer, since it can run all sorts of programs in addition to graphics. But few applications in everyday business warrant the extra expense of a graphics computer.

A NOTE ON WHAT FOLLOWS

The next three chapters cover computer theory, mass storage, and local networks, in that order. Much of this material is essential to the chapters on word processing and graphics that follow. Readers familiar with computers may want to skim through these chapters, but most should be patient and read the introductory material. It makes the remainder of the book much easier to understand.

CHAPTER TWO
Computer Fundamentals

People tend to regard the computer with an unwarranted measure of bewilderment and awe. Perhaps if computers were mechanical rather than electronic, they might seem less intimidating. Gears and levers are taken in stride by most of us, but considerable study is required before we feel comfortable with transistors and logic gates. Nevertheless, one need not become an electronics engineer to understand the workings of a computer. By regarding the machine as a collection of logical function blocks that work together to process information, it is possible to gain considerable insight into computer operation. The same approach works well when applied to computer systems; that is, groups of interacting computers and peripheral devices. One chapter is hardly enough to do justice to computers and computer systems, but it should prepare the non-technical reader for what lies ahead. If more information is desired, there are a number of good introductory computer books on the market. Some deal with general theory; others are dedicated to the operation of specific computers, like the Apple or Radio Shack machines. Both types of book may be helpful, but neither is required for an understanding of word processing or graphics.

INSIDE THE COMPUTER

Data Representation

The smallest unit of data in a digital computer is the bit; the name is a contraction of the words binary digit. Being binary, a bit can have one of two values: 0 or 1. Physically, 1 is often represented by a high voltage in the computer, and 0 is represented by a low voltage. Sometimes, however, the situation is reversed. To represent data other than 0 or 1, bits must be combined into words. The more bits there are in a word, the more data values the word can represent. A two-bit word can have one of four unique values: 00, 01, 10, or 11. Similarly, a three-bit word has eight possible values: 000, 001, 010, 011, 100, 101, 110, or 111. In general, the number of possible values that a word of n bits can have is given by the n-th power of two, that is, two multiplied by itself n times.

A word of eight bits is an entity important enough to warrant the special name of byte. Since bytes run rampant in computer literature, it would be well to memorize the foregoing definition here and now. Thanks to someone with a sense of humor, four-bit words are commonly known as nybbles. For our purposes, however, the nybble is not nearly as important as the byte. Computers may be categorized according to the size of the word they use to represent data. At the present time, most microcomputers use eight-bit data words, though micros with 16-bit data words are becoming more common. Minicomputers use data words of 16 or 32 bits, while mainframes typically use 64-bit words. The size of the data word is roughly indicative of a computer's speed. Larger words convey more information and do the work of several smaller words. A machine that uses large data words can do a given amount of work in fewer steps (and less time) than a machine that uses small words. This explanation may be oversimplified, but the reasoning is essentially correct.

Data words can represent several different kinds of information. Naturally, a computer must be able to handle numerical data. The decimal number 15 might be represented in an eight-bit computer as the binary number 00001111. Other codes besides pure binary can be used, but in all cases, a number is represented in terms of ones and zeros.

The letters and symbols that make up ordinary English text can also be represented by ones and zeros in the computer. The most popular method of encoding letters and symbols is in the ASCII (American Standard Code for Information Interchange) format. ASCII uses seven bits to represent 96 printable characters and 32 non-printable control characters. The 96 printable characters include uppercase and lowercase letters, punctuation marks, and the digits 0-9. The control characters cannot be printed, either on a video screen or on paper. They are interpreted by computers and peripheral equipment as commands that initiate various actions. The sequence A, B, C would be encoded in ASCII as 1000001, 1000010, 1000011. In a microcomputer, which uses byte-size data words, one bit of a byte can be ignored or used for some other purpose when seven-bit ASCII codes are in use.

Yet another type of information that a computer must encode is truth or falsity. In most cases, a true condition is represented by a 1, a false condition by a 0. Logical decisions are made by the computer on the basis of true/false data, and the results of those decisions are likewise in the form of logical ones and zeros. A single byte can hold eight separate pieces of true/false data.

Words may also be used to represent computer instructions. These instruction codes tell the computer what to do. A sequence of instructions that describes some useful task is known as a program. Instructions are distinctly different from data in their function, yet both data and instructions are stored in the same way inside the computer.

One may wonder whether there is some physical characteristic that can be used to distinguish whether a word is an instruction or some form of data. There is none. A word is interpreted by the computer according to what the computer expects that word to be at a given instant. Thus the byte 01000001 might be interpreted as the number 65, the letter A, six falses and two trues, or an instruction that causes two numbers to be added. This may seem to be a confusing state of affairs, but in fact it allows for considerable freedom in the computer's operation.

The Bus

Figure 2-1 illustrates the internal organization of a computer in greatly simplified form. What we have are various function blocks connected together by means of a bus, or set of parallel conductors. The bus may be thought of as a multi-lane expressway, congested with digital data instead of automobiles. In itself, the bus is nothing extraordinary, just a bunch of electrical conductors. What makes it interesting is the way in which the bus is used by the function blocks as a communications pathway. The chief function block, which more or less coordinates the operation of everything else, is the CPU or central processing unit. The CPU is the place where the actual business of computing is performed. In a typical instance, data might be sent to the CPU from memory to be operated on. Later, the results of that operation might be transferred out of the CPU and sent back to memory. Data transfer into and out of the CPU takes place *via* the bus.

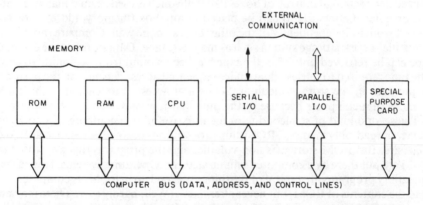

Fig 2-1. The internal organization of a computer consists of certain function blocks which communicate over a bus, or set of electrical conductors. Three different kinds of information—data, address, and control signals—are transmitted over the bus.

The lines of the bus can be logically separated into three groups: a control bus, a data bus, and an address bus. Control-bus lines carry signals that guide the interaction between the various modules of the system. For example, the CPU uses one line of the control bus to tell memory that it wants to extract (read) stored data, and another line to indicate that it wants to enter (write) new data into storage. The data written or read would be conveyed back and forth between the CPU and memory over the data bus, which has as many lines as there are bits in a data word. Whenever data are transferred between the CPU and memory, the CPU must inform memory of the exact address, or location, where each data word should be read or written. It sends this information by way of the address bus.

The number of lines comprised in a bus varies greatly. As noted above, the data bus always has as many lines as there are bits in a data word. Thus, the data bus of a typical microcomputer will have eight bidirectional lines capable of carrying data back and forth between the CPU and any other module of the system. The size of the address bus depends on how much memory the computer can handle. The more memory it has, the more address lines it will need. If the number of address lines is represented by n, the number of unique memory locations is given by two to the n-th power. The typical microcomputer has a 16-line address bus and a maximum of 65,536 bytes of memory. The number of lines in a control bus is determined by a computer's manufacturer and is not generally predictable.

Semiconductor Memory

There are two major kinds of semiconductor memory inside a computer. The first kind is known as RAM, or random-access memory. RAM is volatile, which is to say that any data or programs stored in RAM will be lost when the computer is turned off. For long-term storage, therefore, RAM is useless. The distinguishing characteristic of RAM memory is that stored data can be recalled in any order. Furthermore, the time required to retrieve a data word, or store it, is independent of the location (address) of the word in memory. RAM may conveniently be visualized as a rectangular array of boxes like that which is used to hold mail in an office or hotel. Letters (data) can be placed in any box (memory address), or removed from it, independently of the other boxes on the wall. Compare this with a sequential-access storage system such as magnetic tape. Data stored at the end of a tape can be retrieved only after the tape has been wound from beginning to end. The time required to retrieve data under sequential access depends on the position of the data in the storage medium. Sequential access is untenable in the main memory of a computer because of the time that it wastes.

The second kind of semiconductor memory found in a computer is known as ROM, or read-only memory. ROM chips are random-access devices, just as RAM chips are. But ROM storage is non-volatile, and the programs that are stored in ROM are put there by a computer's manufacturer. Operating systems, languages, and utility programs are typical of the things that end up in ROM. A computer can read the contents of ROM, but never alter them. (Well, hardly ever. There is a new form of ROM known as EAROM, electrically alterable read-only memory, whose contents can be changed by a computer. But this is a special product that is not intended for the same functions as standard ROM.) As a rule, ROM storage is reserved for important programs necessary to the operation of a computer system. Application software, like a word-processing or accounting program, is not imbedded in ROM, but loaded into RAM from disk or tape. In this way, only the software currently in use takes up valuable space in memory.

Any form of random-access memory will have address inputs that allow the CPU to select a memory location (*via* the address bus, of course). Data inputs and outputs will also be present, and these will connect to the CPU through the data bus. In addition, RAM must have a pair of control inputs that connect to the control bus and allow the CPU to specify a read or write operation. Since ROM can only be read, it needs no control inputs.

External I/O

To be effective, a computer must be able to interact with the world outside its cabinet. It does this through various I/O ports, special circuits that provide two or more electrical conductors over which two-way (input/output) communication can occur. An I/O port may be referred to equivalently as an interface. Figure 2-1 shows a system in which the CPU communicates with I/O ports over the same bus it uses to "talk" to memory. Ports connected in this manner are said to be memory-mapped. In microcomputers, memory-mapped I/O is quite common, but larger machines often have a special I/O bus to handle communication between the CPU and I/O ports. In the case of memory-mapped I/O, a port has its own unique address and looks just like memory to the CPU. By reading data from a port's address, the CPU can fetch information that was received by the port from external equipment. Alternatively, the CPU can send data to an external device just by writing to the address of the proper port. The operation of systems having a separate I/O bus is similar, except that ports and memory are kept distinct.

There are several types of ports, but most are variations on just two themes: the parallel port and the serial port. If memory-mapped, a parallel port is little more than a buffered extension of a system's data bus. All the bits of a data word are transmitted simultaneously by a parallel port. Hence, there will be as many lines connecting the parallel port to external equipment as there are bits in a data word. Some parallel ports are unidirectional, capable only of sending or receiving. Ports designed to drive a printer, for example, are required only to transmit data. Bidirectional ports designed for two-way communication may have lines that can alternately send and receive, or they may use separate sets of lines for outgoing and incoming data. In addition to data lines, a parallel port must have several handshaking lines. These coordinate the flow of information and ensure that a sender does not transmit until a receiver is ready to accept data. The speed of parallel data transmission varies but is usually very fast.

The serial port divides up data words and transmits them bit by bit over a single wire. Since the bits are transmitted one after another rather than simultaneously, serial transmission is slower than parallel. Usually, separate wires are used for incoming and outgoing data. Lines similar to the handshaking lines of the parallel port will be present also, but these are not needed in every application. In one form of serial communication, both parties are synchronized with respect to a common clock signal. This allows relatively high transmission rates, but for most purposes the simpler technique of asynchronous serial communication is adequate.

The most popular form of asynchronous serial transmission is the RS-232C standard, which is used by virtually every computer and terminal now on the market. Asynchronous serial transmissions begin with a start bit that alerts the receiver to the fact that data is on its way. Next comes a sequence of data bits. In most cases, the data will be a seven-bit ASCII code, but there is nothing that says it has to be. As long as both parties agree on a data format, any code within reason can be used. The data is followed by an optional parity bit, which is used as a means of error detection. If odd parity has been selected, the transmitting device always adjusts the value of the parity bit so that the total number of 1's contained in the parity and data bits is odd. For example, if three data bits are 1's, the parity bit will be 0, but if two data bits are 1's, the parity bit will be 1. The receiving device checks the incoming data; if it encounters a character in which the total number of 1's in the parity and data bits is not odd, it sends an error message or a request for retransmission to the sending device. If even parity is selected, the sender adjusts the parity bit so that the total number of 1's in the parity and data bits is even.

Parity checking is an effective way of dealing with single-bit errors. These can be produced by electrical interference if the distance between communicating devices is large. For transmission over short lengths of wire, parity checking is not necessary and can be turned off. One or more stop bits signal the end of a character transmission.

The rate of asynchronous serial transmission is measured in baud, or bits per second. The standard rates are 50, 75, 110, 134.5, 150, 300, 600, 1200, 2400, 3600, 4800, and 9600 baud. Both parties must be using the same transmission rate, which can be set with a switch. If one start bit, seven data bits, one parity bit, and one stop bit (a total of ten bits) are used for each character transmitted, the transmission rate in characters per second (cps) can be found by dividing the baud rate (bits per second) by ten. Thus, a 4800-baud transmission would be equivalent to 480 cps. The relatively slow transmission rate provided by a serial port limits its range of application. Nevertheless, serial data transfer is widely used because of its convenience—it requires only a few wires. Serial ports can talk only to other serial ports, while parallel ports are similarly restricted to talking only amongst themselves.

The CPU

Most internal computer operations are controlled by the CPU, or central processing unit. Microcomputers use a one-chip CPU called a microprocessor, while larger computers have CPUs that comprise hundreds of integrated circuits. Using a microprocessor reduces the cost of a computer but results in slower operating speed. Nevertheless, microprocessor-based computers are sufficiently fast to be of use in a wide range of applications.

In addition to orchestrating the flow of data along a computer's bus, the CPU performs all the computations called for by a computer program. It does this with only a small repertoire of primitive operations: shifting, complementing, and adding. Complementing changes a bit from 1 to 0, or vice versa; shifting moves all the bits of a word sideways one space; and adding performs binary addition on two words. Other more complex mathematical operations can be performed by combining primitive operations in some way. For instance, binary multiplication can be accomplished by alternately shifting and adding. All of the logical decisions that a computer must make are also the responsibility of the CPU.

The CPU takes its instructions from a stored program that resides either in ROM or RAM. A program is stored so that the logical order of its instructions is reflected in the physical order of their storage. This means that a given instruction will be stored at an address one higher than that of the preceding instruction, and one lower than that of the next instruction. Thus, given the address of the first instruction in memory, the CPU can easily find the rest, since they are stored one after the other. When a program is being run, the CPU first fetches an instruction from memory, and then executes it. The pattern of alternate fetching and execution continues until the last instruction has been executed, at which point the program is finished.

In order for the CPU to run a program, the instructions that make up the program must somehow be stored in memory first. Programs in ROM present no problem, since they are already in place. Other programs must be loaded into RAM before execution. The CPU itself will see to it that a program is properly stored, but the program must originate with a source outside the computer. Getting the program into the computer requires an interface circuit of some kind. If the source of the program is a data terminal, a standard RS-232C serial port will couple the terminal to the computer. If the program is on a magnetic disk, a special interface circuit will be used to connect the disk drive with the computer's internal bus. This interface will also work in reverse, so that programs fed into the computer from a terminal can be transferred from RAM to disk. Peripherals like magnetic disk and tape allow programs and data to be stored permanently. They are known as mass-storage devices, since their storage capacity greatly exceeds that of computer RAM.

There are principally two types of computer program: system software, and application programs. System software is necessary to get a system running; without it, a computer can do very little. Operating systems and high-level languages are the two most important examples of system software. An operating system manages computer input and output, controls the storage of data and programs on magnetic disk or tape, and creates an environment within which application programs can work. The latter is very important, because by creating a standard environment, an operating system insulates an application program from a computer's hardware idiosyncrasies. Thus, if two physically different computers are equipped with the same operating system, an application program developed for one computer should run on the other with little or no modification. Microcomputer manufacturers have botched things up to some extent by failing to adopt a standard format for data storage on 5.25-inch disks. Fortunately, eight-inch disks adhere to the IBM 3740 standard, which means that programs recorded by one machine can be loaded and run by another—provided, of course, that both use the same operating system.

High-level languages are designed to make the process of program development easier. Instead of having to speak the computer's primitive language of ones and zeros, the programmer using a high-level language can think in terms of statements composed of English-like words and mathematical symbols. This makes programs easier for humans to write and read. Not only is it more convenient to program in a high-level language, it is faster too, since one statement may do the work of several dozen primitive machine-language instructions. (Machine language is the set of binary instructions understood by the CPU.)

Application programs are designed to do such useful things as word processing, accounting, graph plotting, and data-base management. In most instances, application software is written with the aid of system software, and it may require the support of system software when it is run. Whereas system software is designed to make the computer function smoothly, application software is concerned with solving the problems of the user.

Special Modules

There are numerous special modules that can be added to a computer to extend its capabilities. These modules typically take the form of printed-circuit boards, or cards, that plug into the computer and mate with its bus. The disk and tape interface circuits discussed earlier are two common types of add-on module. Another is the time-of-day clock, which allows the computer to keep track of the date and time. Often, the clock is used by an operating system to mark files with the time and date of their creation or revision. (In computer parlance, a file is a set of related data stored under one name on disk or tape.) The clock circuit has its own unique address in the memory space of the computer. To fetch the time, the CPU performs a read operation using the address of the clock, just as though the clock were an element of memory.

A computer must often interact with electronic devices that are analog in nature, which is to say they encode information in the magnitude of a voltage. For example, an analog transducer might convert temperature to voltage in such a way that a rise in temperature of one degree produced a 0.1-volt increase in output. This stands in sharp contrast to the operation of a digital circuit, where only two values of voltage are recognized. In order to read an analog signal, a computer requires a special module to translate foreign analog information into familiar digital form. Such a translation is performed by an analog-to-digital (A/D) converter. The reverse process of changing a digital signal into analog form is required when the computer transmits information to an analog device. The module that performs this translation is called a digital-to-analog (D/A) converter. The joystick, a popular graphics peripheral, interfaces with its host computer through an A/D converter.

There are a great number of other special-purpose modules that can be fitted to a computer. We will have occasion to discuss some of them later in this chapter.

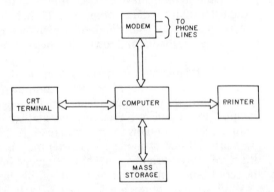

Fig. 2-2. A complete computer system consists of a computer and various peripherals. The most common of these are a CRT terminal, some form of mass storage, a printer, and a modem.

COMPUTER SYSTEMS AND PERIPHERALS

Figure 2-2 illustrates a simple computer system made up of a computer plus certain peripherals: a printer, a CRT terminal, some form of mass storage, and a modem. A terminal or modem interfaces with a computer through a standard RS-232C serial port. A printer will usually have a standard serial or parallel port, but a special interface may be used in some instances. Mass storage requires high-speed data transfer and uses a special interface for this purpose.

A terminal is necessary so that an operator can communicate with a computer. In some instances, the terminal and the computer are incorporated in the same package. This technique is popular in the world of personal computers because it saves space and money, but large machines always make use of a separate terminal. A printer is essential when hard copy is produced, as in word processing or accounting. Some printers are capable of reproducing diagrams and are thus well suited for use in graphics. In many instances, however, graphical applications call for the use of special peripherals like plotters and film recorders to produce hard copy. At the same time, graphics usually requires that special input devices like light pens or digitizing tablets be added to a computer system.

A modem is essential when a computer must communicate with a terminal or another computer located a great distance away. By converting digital signals into audio tones, the modem allows inter-computer communication to take place over the telephone lines. Mass-storage devices allow a computer to make a permanent record of important data or programs. Words and pictures can be stored with equal ease.

Fig. 2-3. A conventional all-in-one package design is embodied in the Model 910 terminal from TeleVideo Systems. The typewriter-style keyboard and CRT screen permit a convenient dialogue to take place between man and computer. (Courtesy of TeleVideo Systems Inc., Sunnyvale, CA)

Terminals

Figures 2-3 and 2-4 show the two styles of CRT terminal in use today. By means of a terminal a person can issue commands to a computer and observe the machine's response. The basic CRT terminal, often referred to as a dumb terminal, consists of little more than a keyboard, a video display, and a serial interface. Whatever the operator types on the keyboard is sent to the computer, which digests the information and acts upon it. As a rule, dumb terminals do not directly display information typed by the operator. It is up to the computer to echo this information back to the terminal's display. In addition, the computer must send along any results it obtains together with prompts for the operator. Terminals that rely on a computer to echo back information typed on their keyboards are said to be operating full-duplex.

Smart terminals come equipped with native intelligence in the form of a microprocessor. As a result, they can do many things independently of the computer. For one, they can put text on their own display screens without computer assistance; this is known as half-duplex operation. If desired, smart terminals can also be operated in the full-duplex mode. Other features of a smart terminal include the ability to format text, highlight it, and edit it before transmission. By editing off-line and then transmitting text in one continuous block, the user of a smart terminal wastes less computer time and saves money, especially on long-distance telephone hook-ups. Of course, if a terminal and a computer are linked by telephone, modems must be used at both ends of the line. A built-in modem can be installed in many smart terminals as an option. Smart terminals usually have enough internal memory to store several pages of text, which can be off-loaded to a printer or mass-storage device through the appropriate built-in ports.

Fig. 2-4. The Model 950 smart terminal from Tele-Video Systems displays text as 24 lines of 80 characters using a 14x10-dot character cell. A detachable keyboard and a tiltable screen help to minimize operator fatigue. (Courtesy of TeleVideo Systems Inc., Sunnyvale, CA)

Smart or dumb, the conventional terminal is primarily intended for the display of text. Graphics capability, if available, is likely to be primitive and limited to the display of simple line drawings. For the person with a serious interest in graphics, there are three practical options. The first is to use a computer with built-in facilities for the display of graphics. If modest resolution will suffice—as it will in most business applications—a personal computer with graphics capability is the most economical way to go. Applications demanding higher resolution may call for a graphics computer, as described in Chapter One. The second possibility is to use a graphics terminal along with a general-purpose computer. A graphics terminal, like the one illustrated in Fig. 2-5, will display high-resolution graphics as well as standard text. Naturally, the cost of a graphics terminal is higher than that of a conventional terminal. The third way to obtain a graphical display is by equipping a general-purpose computer with a special graphics board, and feeding the output of the board to a video monitor. (Monitors are similar to conventional television sets, but they lack the detection and conversion circuits necessary to receive commercial broadcasts.) Graphics boards are available for many of the popular computer buses, such as the ubiquitous S-100 bus and Digital Equipment's Q-bus. Displays of medium to high resolution can be generated with a graphics board, but a conventional CRT terminal must still be used for general input and output.

Before CRT terminals became so popular, the Teletype machine with its printer and keyboard was commonly used for computer input and output. Terminals with built-in printers are still around today. For the person who dislikes staring at a CRT, or who wants a written record of his work as it progresses, these tubeless terminals are ideal. However, they are of little use in word processing, since it is impossible to edit text conveniently without an electronic display.

Yet another variety of terminal is shown in Fig. 2-6. Personal computers that display 40 columns of text in uppercase only are at a severe disadvantage in word processing, since they cannot display a document exactly as it will appear on paper. The Apple II is one such computer. To remedy this, various manufacturers offer terminal boards that plug into the Apple II and take over the job of generating a video display. Generally, these boards produce an 80-column display consisting of uppercase and lowercase letters. The output of such a terminal board is fed directly to a video monitor. It would seem that such a board is really only half a terminal, since the built-in keyboard of the personal computer is retained as an input device. But many boards, such as the Videoterm, manufactured by VIDEX, Inc. for the Apple II, intercept and modify input data, so that lowercase letters and extra characters can be typed from the keyboard. Thus, they qualify as full-fledged terminals.

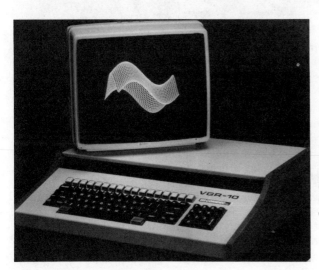

Fig. 2-5. For high-resolution graphics applications in which a conventional CRT terminal would prove inadequate, a graphics terminal like this VGR-10 from Comdec is necessary. The raster-scan display comprises 256,000 individually addressable pixels. (Courtesy of Comdec Inc., Ann Arbor, MI)

The Raster-Scan CRT

At the heart of every terminal and video monitor is a cathode-ray tube, or CRT. It is worthwhile to examine the construction and operation of the CRT, because by doing so we can gain an appreciation for the different display requirements of text and graphics. Figure 2-7 is a side view of a typical cathode-ray tube. An electron-gun assembly located at the rear of the tube is responsible for generating a finely focused beam of high-velocity electrons. This beam of electrons can be steered by means of two pairs of deflection coils. Currents flowing in these coils set up an electromagnetic field that deflects the electron beam horizontally and vertically. Wherever the beam impinges on the phosphor-coated viewing screen of the tube, a bright luminous spot appears. By controlling the beam's intensity electronically, it is possible to adjust the brightness of the spot. The beam may even be turned off, so that no visible spot is produced. An image can be displayed by simultaneously deflecting the beam and varying its intensity. Because images fade quickly, they must be retraced on a regular basis. This process is known as refreshing the display; it must take place at least 60 times a second so that no flicker will be apparent.

Fig. 2-6. The Videoterm 80-column board from Videx, Inc. (Corvallis, OR) converts an Apple II computer from its original 40-column, uppercase-only display format to a full 80 columns, with lowercase letters as well as uppercase.

There are two distinct ways in which an image can be drawn on a CRT display. The most versatile and popular method is known as raster scanning. The other method, called random scanning, is used exclusively for certain applications in graphics. Random scanning will be discussed in Chapter Ten; for now, we will concentrate on the raster-scan display process, depicted in Fig. 2-8. Here, we see that the electron beam is being made to scan the screen in a zig-zag pattern or raster. As the screen is scanned, the intensity of the electron beam is modulated (varied). Figure 2-8 shows how this technique might be used to draw a vertical line. The beam is cut off most of the time, but turned on once in each horizontal scan line. This produces the image of a vertical line consisting of closely spaced dots. The smallest dot that a system can display is known as a pixel, a term derived from the words "picture element."

The scanning of a complete image, or frame, is usually done in two steps: First the even-numbered lines are scanned, then the odd-numbered lines. Each set of lines is referred to as a field. Scanning that alternates between even and odd fields is said to be interlaced. The advantage of interlaced scanning is that it allows a picture to be refreshed at a slower rate. Remember we said earlier that a picture must be continuously refreshed (retraced) in order to keep the image from fading away. Interlaced scanning allows a picture to be refreshed 30 times a second—half as often as would be necessary with a non-interlaced scan. We can get away with it because interlacing makes it hard to detect the fact that a line in one field is starting to fade when an adjacent line in the other field has just been refreshed and is bright. Why should it be desirable to refresh at a lower rate? The answer is that it allows the use of less expensive video circuitry with a narrower bandwidth.

The average video monitor is capable of displaying 480 scan lines, while high-resolution systems display 1,000-2,000 lines. Personal computers with low- to medium-resolution displays need so few scan lines (240 or less) that they forego interlacing altogether. In this case, there is no difference between a field and a frame. A non-interlaced frame must be refreshed 60 times a second so that image flicker will not be apparent. General-purpose video monitors, which can display conventional television pictures as well as text and drawings, use CRTs with white phosphors. But data terminals and computer-display monitors use CRTs with green or amber phosphors instead, since these induce less eyestrain.

The single-gun CRT we have been discussing can display only black, white, and shades of gray. However, its principle of operation adapts readily enough to the display of color. The special tube that allows colors to be displayed is known as a shadow-mask CRT. Three separate guns are used, one for each of the three additive primary colors: red, green, and blue. The inner surface of the viewing screen is coated with special phosphors that emit a red, green, or blue glow when struck by an electron beam. Tiny dots of these three phosphors are arranged in triads on the screen. The shadow mask, a metal sheet pierced by thousands of tiny pinholes, is interposed between the phosphor-coated screen and the electron guns; it ensures that each of the three electron beams strikes only dots of the proper color. All three beams are aimed by the same set of deflection coils, but their intensities are independently controlled. By varying the relative intensities of the three beams, a broad spectrum of colors can be produced. Compared to a conventional CRT, the shadow-mask tube offers inferior resolution and brightness. In most applications, however, these are not serious limitations.

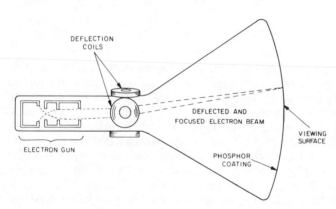

Fig. 2-7. Side view of a cathode-ray tube (CRT). The electron gun emits a focused beam of electrons, which can be deflected horizontally and vertically by means of two pairs of current-carrying coils. Wherever the beam impinges on the phosphor-coated viewing screen, a luminous spot appears.

The builder of a raster-scan display system must decide how data appearing on the screen will be stored in RAM. The most versatile approach is to bit-map the display. Let every pixel (dot) on the screen be represented by at least one bit of memory, and possibly more. Consider a black-and-white display of medium resolution: 256 pixels wide, and 256 high. There are a total of 65, 536 pixels that must somehow be represented in memory. If one bit is allocated to each pixel, a total of 8,192 bytes of RAM will be needed to hold a full screen of data. Since a single bit can have only two values, it follows that each pixel must be limited to two states: on (white) if its bit is equal to 1, off (black) when that bit equals 0. If gray levels are desired, the display must be designed so that the intensity of each pixel is determined by a group of bits. Suppose, for instance, that a nybble (four bits) is used to encode the intensity of each pixel. We can now display 16 intensity levels ranging from black to white, with 14 levels of gray in between. The total amount of RAM needed to hold a full screen of data under this new mapping arrangement is 32,768 bytes.

It should be obvious from the foregoing that a bit-mapped display has a voracious appetite for RAM. Large memory requirements notwithstanding, the bit-mapped display is tremendously important in graphics. Since the intensity of each pixel on a bit-mapped display can be independently adjusted, any image can be drawn just by turning on the right combination of pixels.

Fig. 2-8. A raster-scan pattern, as it might be seen from the front of a CRT. The raster is the path taken by an electron beam as it sweeps over the screen. In this case, the pattern consists of two interlaced scans, or fields, one of which contains odd-numbered lines, the other even lines.

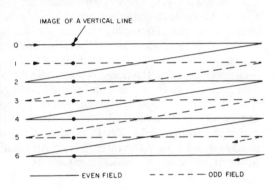

For text displays, however, bit mapping offers more than we really need. It makes sense, therefore, to take advantage of a simpler technique that uses less memory. For this, we need an integrated circuit known as a character generator. To get an idea of how this new system works, first imagine an 8x8 matrix of pixels. Letters can easily be represented by turning on various combinations of pixels within the matrix. This is done by the character generator, a ROM that remembers which pixels to turn on for any printable ASCII character. If we feed the ASCII code for a letter to a display system containing a character generator, the right dots will automatically be put on the screen (at a point defined by the cursor). A seven-bit ASCII code fits comfortably in one byte of RAM, yet it controls 64 pixels with the aid of a character generator. The simplest bit-mapped display would encode 64 pixels in eight bytes of RAM. Thus, using a character generator has reduced the size of display memory by a factor of eight in this example.

Conventional CRT terminals, which are primarily intended for text, make use of character generators. Graphics terminals, graphics computers, plug-in graphics boards, and many of the more popular personal computers have bit-mapped displays for graphics, and character generators for text. This does not mean that bit-mapped displays cannot represent text, just that character generators are easier to use. High-priced office-automation systems based on minis use bit-mapped displays for graphics and text. This allows letters to be generated in a wide range of fonts (type styles) and sizes. With character generators, letters are usually generated in just one font and size, though occasionally a system will offer an extra font for the sake of variety. Simple graphics are possible on a character-generator display. The trick here is that the manufacturer programs his character generator to produce short line segments and symbols (hearts, diamonds, etc.) in addition to the usual letters. Simple images can be created by plotting these pre-programmed lines and symbols on the screen just as though they were letters. However, character-generator graphics cannot compete with the images produced on a bit-mapped display, where every single pixel is addressable.

Color displays can be bit-mapped just as easily as black-and-white. For example, if eight bits are available for each pixel, two bits could be assigned to green, leaving three bits each for red and blue. In this way, a total of 256 colors could be generated, including black and white. More colors could be obtained if more bits were allocated to each pixel. Another way to get more colors is by means of color mapping, a technique that makes a given number of bits do the work of more. If a system allocated 24 bits of storage to each pixel, it could generate 16,777,216 different colors; unfortunately, the cost of such a system would be prohibitive in many instances. With the proper hardware and software, however, it is possible to use only eight bits of storage per pixel, but to map these eight bits into 24. The result is that the system can now display more than 16.7 million colors, but with one catch: no more than 256 different colors can be displayed simultaneously. Maps can be redefined by software to produce a new set of output colors suited to the application at hand. Not only does color mapping extend the range of colors produced, it also allows any color to be specified with greater precision. The only drawback of a color map is that the number of simultaneous colors is limited by the amount of memory assigned to each pixel. As the cost per bit of semiconductor memory continues to drop, system designers will be able to build displays having more bits per pixel, and the need for color mapping will diminish.

We have established how a raster-scan CRT display might be represented in memory, but have said nothing about how information gets from memory to the CRT. In essence, screen data is simply read bit by bit from memory, and then translated into a form acceptable to the display. The circuit responsible for doing this is known as a display processor. Since a CRT display must be continuously refreshed, the display processor reads and translates all of the data in screen memory 30 or 60 times a second, depending on whether the scan is interlaced or not. Screen memory is often said to be dual-ported, which means that the display processor and the CPU can independently gain access to this block of memory. The CPU deposits new data into screen memory whenever a pixel or set of pixels must be changed. At other times, the CPU can ignore display memory completely, since the display processor does the tedious work of refreshing the display with the contents of memory. Thus, the CPU is not bogged down by the refresh process and is free to do other things.

Modems

It is often necessary that computers and terminals separated by long distances be able to communicate with one another. The use of a special cable is obviously impractical for distances much greater than several hundred feet. Since the entire world is now linked by telephone lines, it would be nice if the phone lines could transmit digital data in addition to voice. But the frequency response of standard telephone circuits is limited to 3,000 Hz, which is too low to accommodate digital data directly. Therefore, a special device known as a modem or data set is used to translate digital data into audio tones that can be transmitted over the telephone lines. A modem must be used at each end of a two-way telephone hookup. Each of the communicating devices feeds its modem through a serial port. In most instances, a standard RS-232C asynchronous port is used, but certain high-speed modems may make use of special synchronous ports. The modem acts as a modulator/demodulator, a device capable of encoding information in a new form and decoding it as well. In this case, audible whistles and chirps are used to convey digital information. Other styles of modem, designed for use with broadband-bus networks rather than the telephone system, convert digital data into radio-frequency signals. These RF modems will be discussed in Chapter Four, which deals with local-area networks.

Fig. 2-9. Because it connects directly to the telephone lines, the Hayes Smartmodem™ permits long-distance data communication without awkward, error-prone acoustic couplers. (Courtesy of Hayes Microcomputer Products, Norcross, GA)

Two different styles of modem are in common use: direct-connect and acoustic-coupled. The latter have rubber cups into which a standard telephone handset can be inserted. The receiver of the handset is coupled to a microphone in the modem, while the transmitter of the handset mates with a speaker. The rubber cups provide a degree of isolation from ambient room noise, which can interfere with the exchange of audio tones between the handset and the modem. Acoustically coupled modems suffer from occasional errors induced by the compaction of carbon granules in the handset's transmitter. Loud room noises are another possible source of data errors.

The shortcomings of the acoustically coupled modem are eliminated with a direct-connect unit, which interfaces to the telephone lines through a transformer. It used to be that modems could be directly connected only though a data-access arrangement (DAA), which had to be rented from the phone company. The DAA is still used, but recent changes in regulations allow customers of the phone company to buy and use their own equipment, and that includes the interface required by a direct-connect modem. As a result, the manufacturers of direct-connect modems now provide the necessary interface circuits; there is no longer any need to pay a monthly charge for the use of a DAA. Figure 2-9 illustrates a modern direct-connect modem.

There are several different methods of modem operation. The simplest, known as frequency-shift keying (FSK), is used on low-speed modems having a maximum transmission rate of 300 baud (30 cps). FSK transmission makes use of four different audio frequencies. The originating modem (the one that initiates two-way communication) uses 1070 Hz to represent a 0, and 1270 Hz to represent a 1. The answering modem uses 2025 Hz to signify a 0, and 2225 Hz to signify a 1. Modern modems can be operated either as originating or answering devices simply by flipping a switch. The use of four transmission frequencies might seem odd at first, since only two entities—0 and 1—need to be transmitted. Four frequencies are used so that modems can be operated full-duplex, which is to say that two separate transmissions going in opposite directions take place simultaneously. It is also possible to operate half-duplex, in which case transmissions are sent alternately in opposite directions, so that only one transmission is carried at a time by the telephone line. Receiving circuits at both ends of the line separate the correct tones from all the rest by means of electronic filters. The originating modem transmits on 1070 and 1270 Hz, but listens on 2025 and 2225 Hz. The situation is exactly reversed for the answering modem. More complex transmission schemes are used by high-speed modems, which may operate at speeds greater than 9,600 baud on specially conditioned telephone lines.

CHAPTER THREE
Mass Storage

Mass storage is a non-volatile means of storing large quantities of data and programs. The capacity of mass storage greatly exceeds that of computer RAM, yet the cost of storage is much less on a per-bit basis. Data are usually stored in a magnetic medium, but the future now looks bright for optical storage as well. The various mass-storage systems generally make use of random access for the sake of speed, though magnetic tape and bubble memories store data in sequential fashion. All mass-storage devices are much slower than RAM when it comes to accessing data, but this is not a serious handicap in most applications. Before information in mass storage can be used, it must be loaded into computer RAM.

At the present time, the most important forms of mass storage are floppy disks, hard disks, and magnetic tape. The first two of these are commonly referred to as secondary storage, while the latter may be called tertiary. This terminology reflects the way in which large computer systems make use of disk and tape. Disks are random-access devices that enable data to be stored and retrieved relatively quickly, while tape labors under sequential access but stores data at a lower cost per bit. As a result, tape is often reserved for archival storage. When needed, the data on the tape can be transferred to disk or RAM for use by the computer. Tape is not always relegated to tertiary status, however. Very small computer systems may make use of cassette tape as their primary storage medium. Most business applications require at least floppy disks, and very often hard disks as well.

Optical discs and bubble-memory devices are two new forms of mass storage that will become more prevalent in the future. Bubble memories are available today, but they are relatively expensive. The chief virtues of bubble memory are its ruggedness and light weight. Whereas all other forms of mass storage are electromechanical in nature, magnetic-bubble devices are electronic. Thus, bubble memories tend to be faster and more reliable than other mass-storage devices. As bubble-memory technology matures, it is finding its way into a variety of new products—such as a portable word processor that fits comfortably inside a brief case.

Optical discs can store an astonishing amount of data in a small space. At the present time, the primary application of optical-disc technology is in video playback equipment; mass-storage systems based on optical discs will not be available until 1984 or 1985. Although the first optical-disc storage systems will be relatively expensive in terms of hardware, the cost of storing a bit of data will be vanishingly small. Optical discs will thus make it possible to store huge amounts of data economically. Some readers may be wondering what the difference is between a disk, as in magnetic disk, and a disc, as in optical disc. It is only the result of a spelling convention, and if a "c" sometimes gets substituted for a "k", no one will protest.

FLOPPY DISKS

Figure 3-1 illustrates a floppy disk and a typical disk drive. The disk itself, which may be 5.25 or eight inches in diameter, is housed within a square protective jacket. The eight-inch units are properly called disks, while the 5.25-inch units are known as diskettes or mini-disks. Most people prefer to call them both disks, since it is simpler and rarely causes confusion. Every disk jacket has an oblong cutout through which the read/write head of the disk drive can make contact with the surface of the disk. Floppy disks have a flexible substrate of mylar, onto which a thin layer of iron oxide has been deposited. Iron oxide is a magnetic material capable of storing data in the form of reversals in the orientation of a magnetic field. In conventional disks, iron oxide is applied in the form of a slurry and allowed to dry. Newer disks designed to hold a greater amount of data make use of a thin film of metal instead of iron oxide, and are more expensive than conventional disks. Special disk drives are needed to take advantage of the higher data capacity of thin-film disks. At the present time, most floppy-disk recording is done on conventional disks coated with iron oxide.

Fig. 3-1. A floppy disk is shown here resting on top of a typical disk drive. Once the small trapdoor on the front of the drive has been raised, the disk can be inserted through the slot and clamped in place by closing the door. The elongated hole in the disk's protective jacket allows the read/write head of the drive to make contact with the surface of the disk.

The disk drive clamps a floppy disk by its central hub and spins it at 300 rpm (5.25-inch disks) or 360 rpm (eight-inch disks). These relatively slow rates of rotation are necessary to minimize wear on the disk and the read/write head of the drive, which is pressed into direct contact with the disk's iron-oxide layer. Floppy-disk drives use a ferrite head, that is, a tiny electromagnet with a ceramic core consisting of the oxides of iron and other metals, such as nickel and zinc. Driving the head with pulses of current magnetizes areas of the disk as they pass under the head. Later, stored data can be read with the same head. This is possible because of the phenomenon known as magnetic induction: spinning a magnetized disk beneath the head induces a voltage pulse in the head each time that a magnetic-field reversal is encountered. These pulses are sensed and converted to digital data. Some drives are designed to accommodate special double-sided disks. Two read/write heads are required to read both sides of the disk, which has head-access slots cut in the front and back sides of its jacket. The advantage of a double-sided disk is that it stores twice as much data. Both 5.25- and eight-inch double-sided floppies are available.

Data are recorded on a floppy disk in numerous concentric rings or tracks. Each track forms a closed circle that is not connected to any of the other tracks. This stands in contrast to a phonograph record, where the tracks form one large, continuous spiral. The number of tracks on a floppy disk is subject to some variation. Most 5.25-inch disks have 35 tracks, while eight-inch disks typically have 77. More tracks may be used on systems that record data at very high density. Each track is divided into a number of circular arcs or sectors. The sector is the fundamental unit of data storage on a disk. There are two methods of dividing a disk into sectors: hard sectoring and soft sectoring. A hard-sectored disk has a ring of tiny holes punched close to its hub. These holes, which are spaced at regular intervals, can be detected by means of a photocell and a light source. Each time that a hole passes before the photocell, it allows light to strike the cell's sensitive face. This signals the start of a new sector to the disk system. A soft-sectored disk has just one hole punched near its hub. Sectoring is performed by the computer's operating system, which uses the single hole as a reference point. Hard-sectored and soft-sectored disks are not interchangeable.

A single-density 5.25-inch floppy disk holds about 100 kilobytes of data, while an eight-inch disk holds about 250 kilobytes. Double-density disks, which record data more densely, have a larger capacity. For instance, the typical double-density 5.25-inch disk will hold about 160 kilobytes, 60 percent more than a single-density disk. The density at which data are recorded is determined by the characteristics of the disk drive and the operating system used by a computer. Current honors for putting the most data on a disk go to Micropolis and Percom, both of whom offer drives capable of storing more than two million bytes. Recording at very high density requires the use of special disks designed to expand or contract very little in the face of changing temperature and humidity. This is necessary to keep the closely spaced tracks from shifting out of position. Expansion is not a problem on standard disks because track positioning is less critical. High-density disk recording is desirable whenever large quantities of data must be stored; for instance, high-density floppies are useful for Winchester backup (explained shortly). High-density disk drives are more expensive than their low-density counterparts, and the special disks they require cost about five times as much as conventional disks.

Convenient as it is, floppy-disk storage is not without shortcomings. In applications that require the storage of extremely large amounts of data, floppy-disk capacity may be inadequate. Likewise, the rate at which data can be accessed by floppy-disk systems may be too slow in certain applications. Another factor to consider is the open construction of the floppy disk and its drive: environmental debris can easily contaminate a disk and render all or part of it useless. Most of the foregoing handicaps can be overcome with a hard disk.

HARD DISKS

Hard disks are capable of storing larger amounts of data than floppy disks; in addition, the data can be accessed much more quickly. Although the initial cost of a hard-disk system is high, the cost per bit of storage is less than it is with a floppy. Hard disks have rigid substrates of aluminum and rotate about ten times faster than floppy disks. To avoid an inordinate amount of wear on the disk, a hard-disk system's read/write head is aerodynamically designed to float just above the surface of the disk. A cushion of air generated by the rapidly spinning disk supports the lightweight head.

Removable-Cartridge Systems

One type of hard-disk system makes use of disks that are removable. These disks are enclosed in cartridges that protect them from dirt and physical damage. Usually, a cartridge holds several disks that share a common spindle. Openings in the cartridge allow the read/write heads of the drive to gain access to the disks. Removable-cartridge systems are convenient because they allow data recorded on one drive to be transported to another. And since removable disks can be replaced when full, drive capacity is practically unlimited.

Nevertheless, as designers struggled to increase the density of hard-disk storage, it became obvious that the removable cartridge was an impediment to progress. The reason was simple: Recording data at higher density required that the read/write head be brought closer to the surface of the disk. Unfortunately, at such close distances even the tiniest bit of debris on the disk would cause the head to crash. Imagine hitting a two-foot boulder while driving a car at 100 mph; the ensuing collision would approximate what happens when a low-flying read/write head crashes into a speck of dust. Since removable cartridges had to have access holes for the heads, it was inevitable that some debris should get inside. For this reason, the low-flying heads that would be needed for higher recording densities were simply not compatible with removable cartridges. So, while removable-cartridge systems were not scrapped, they had to be supplemented by something new in order to obtain higher storage density.

Winchester Drives

The solution to the problem of obtaining higher storage density came in the form of the Winchester drive, introduced by IBM in 1973. In a Winchester drive, the heads, disks, and head-positioning apparatus are all contained in a hermetically sealed enclosure. The air within this enclosure is filtered and recirculated so that it remains free of contaminants. This allows the heads to fly low without risking a collision with airborne debris. As a result, Winchester drives are able to store data more densely than conventional removable-cartridge hard-disk drives. Since Winchester disks are enclosed in a hermetically sealed chamber, they cannot be replaced when full. This is a limitation, but there are ways to get around it, as we shall see later. Figure 3-2 illustrates the interior of a typical Winchester drive.

The high storage density of the Winchester drive was achieved by lowering the flying height of the read/write head to a mere 20 microinches, and by using a thinner magnetic coating on the disks. Like removable-cartridge drives, Winchesters generally have several disks on a common spindle. This increases the storage capacity at very little added cost, since the expensive drive mechanism and electronics are shared by all the disks. Both sides of a disk are coated with magnetic material, so at least two heads are needed for each disk. High-performance drives often dedicate several heads to each disk surface. This minimizes the amount of head travel necessary to access a particular track, and speeds up the storage and retrieval of data.

Winchester disks are available with diameters of 5.25, 8, 10.5, and 14 inches. Storage capacities range from two to 675 million bytes. The smaller drives are no larger than a floppy drive, yet their storage capacity is ten times as great. Storing data on a Winchester disk is about 100 times less expensive per byte than storing it in RAM. Large Winchester drives are naturally more expensive than small ones, but they are generally more economical when the cost per byte is considered. Economy is not the only advantage of a Winchester. The user of floppies will be astounded by how fast a Winchester stores and fetches data. In many instances, the speed of program execution depends on how fast data can be shuttled between the computer and disk storage. Any program that transfers large amounts of data between RAM and disk on a regular basis will run faster with a Winchester.

Fig. 3-2. In this interior view of the Morrow Designs M-20 Winchester disk drive, four separate hard disks can be seen stacked on a common spindle. (Courtesy of Morrow Designs, Richmond, CA)

The storage capacity of Winchester drives promises to increase in the future. Aluminum disks are being plated with thinner magnetic films to boost the density of storage. Density can further be increased by substituting thin-film heads for the more common ferrite types. Thin-film heads dispense with the bulky coil of wire found in a ferrite head and use a tiny, flat spiral of plated metal instead. Many of the same techniques used to make integrated circuits are used in the fabrication of thin-film heads. The result is a smaller head that writes data in a more compact form. The combination of thin-film heads and thin-plated disks is expected to produce a tenfold increase in Winchester storage density by 1990.

Because Winchester disks cannot be removed from a drive, the user must provide some form of external backup, that is, a means by which data can be electronically transferred from a Winchester disk to some other storage medium—usually tape. Backing up a Winchester disk at regular intervals protects the user from head crashes and other failures of the drive mechanism, though these are rare.

More importantly, backup is a hedge against operator error, which may cause valuable data to be inadvertently deleted or overwritten. Another advantage of a good backup system is that it allows old information to be removed to make room for new. When needed again, the old data can always be transferred back to the Winchester disk from tape or some other storage medium.

The ideal backup device would operate very quickly and store the contents of an entire disk on one volume (reel, cartridge, or whatever). To see why the foregoing criteria are important, it is necessary to consider a poor choice of backup—for example, floppy disk. If we decide to backup a 10-megabyte Winchester drive with double-sided, double-density, 5.25-inch floppy disks, it will take about 50 minutes to do the job. Approximately 25 disks will be needed, and the total cost will be about $80. Not only is this system slow and expensive, it requires an excessive amount of operator support as well. (Someone has to load the disks into the drive and remove them.) A more practical solution would be to back the Winchester up with a ¼-inch streaming tape drive. Only one tape cartridge would be needed, and the entire 10 megabytes would be copied in about 5 minutes, at a cost of less than $30. (The prices quoted above are for storage media only; the necessary drive in either example is an extra, one-time expense.)

There are a number of practical backup devices on the market. Streaming tape drives that use ¼-inch cartridges are fast and relatively economical as Winchester backups. Reel-to-reel tape drives operated in the streaming mode are also excellent backup devices, though more expensive than cartridge drives. Removable-cartridge hard-disk drives are quite expensive, but they too will perform very well. One enterprising manufacturer (Corvus) offers a converter that allows a standard videocassette recorder to serve as a backup device. It is even possible to use one Winchester to backup another. Data are copied quickly by the second Winchester, but the information is no more portable than it was to begin with. In some applications, the ability to carry data from one computer to another does not matter; in others it does. A relatively new development that obviates the need for external backup is the removable-cartridge Winchester drive. It would seem that such a device should be less reliable than a conventional Winchester, since the cartridge cannot be hermetically sealed. However, the manufacturers of removable-cartridge Winchesters claim that the reliability of these devices is excellent. If this proves to be true, removable-cartridge Winchesters are likely to proliferate.

Why would anyone bother with a Winchester disk and the attendant nuisance of backing it up when there are removable-cartridge hard-disk systems on the market? The answer is that Winchesters are faster, and they store data at less cost per byte. Furthermore, Winchester drives are more reliable than removable-cartridge drives, so the cost of maintenance is less. Winchester drives are also less bulky than their removable-cartridge counterparts. Whereas a Winchester can fit unobtrusively on the user's desk, a removable-cartridge drive will have to sit on the floor or on a special table. It is not surprising, then, that Winchester drives have become so popular in recent years.

MAGNETIC TAPE

Magnetic tape consists of a long, thin strip of mylar coated on one side with iron oxide. Tape for digital recording is available on reels or in cartridges; the usual widths are ¼ and ½ inch. Digital tape recorders differ in several ways from the more familiar audio variety. Data are generally recorded by a digital tape deck in nine tracks, eight of which hold a byte of data, while the ninth contains a parity bit. All nine tracks are recorded simultaneously. When data are later retrieved from tape, parity checking is used to detect errors caused by tape defects.

In the conventional digital tape recorder, data are blocked into groups known as records, which are separated by blank gaps. Before laying down a record, the tape deck erases a short gap as the tape is accelerated to full speed. Next, all the data that make up the record are stored in a short, continuous block. Once all the data have been recorded, the tape is decelerated and another short gap is erased. Start/stop recording is convenient because it allows transactions to be stored in distinct records, which can later be retrieved from storage on an individual basis. But start/stop decks are expensive, and they fail to make efficient use of tape, since 20 to 80 percent of the available space may be taken up by interrecord gaps.

In applications where access to individual records is not necessary, a new type of tape deck, the streamer, can be used to store data more efficiently. A streaming tape deck operates at a continuous high speed of 30-100 inches per second. Since no interrecord gaps are used, more than 97 percent of the space available on tape is filled with data. This means that data can be stored at lower cost per byte. Streamers cannot replace conventional start/stop decks in every instance, but they are valuable for such applications as Winchester backup, where the ability to block data into records is not required. Because streaming decks are not as mechanically complicated as start/stop machines, they cost considerably less.

At the present time, magnetic tape is the most economical data-storage medium. For that reason, large computer systems use tape for the archival storage of large amounts of data. The low cost of magnetic tape is offset, however, by the relatively high cost of digital tape decks. Sophisticated start/stop decks cost in excess of $3,000 and are thus seldom encountered in small computer systems. Streaming tape drives cost about one-third to one-half as much, and have become quite popular for Winchester backup. The imminent arrival of optical-disc systems threatens to usurp some of tape's present domain, particularly in the area of archival storage.

BUBBLE MEMORY

Most forms of mass storage are electromechanical in nature; hence, they are not particularly rugged or reliable. But bubble-memory systems are solid-state devices with no motors, cams, or gears. This makes bubble-memory systems light and robust enough to go anywhere. Another benefit of bubble memory is that contamination is not a problem, as it is with disk systems, because bubble-memory devices are sealed against dirt and moisture. Better still, the purely electronic nature of bubble memories means that they can provide faster data access than magnetic disk or tape. In spite of the advantages of bubble memory, however, this technology is not likely to see widespread use for some time. The reason is that bubble memory is currently the most expensive means of mass storage. In fact, the only form of storage more costly than bubble memory is RAM. But as bubble-memory technology matures, its cost per bit will inevitably drop to a more economical level.

At the present time, bubble memory is used only in those applications that demand some combination of high speed, light weight, and ruggedness. Military and aerospace electronics consume about a third of all the bubble-memory devices produced annually. It goes without saying that military gear must be rugged. Telephone systems also make use of bubble memories to store various service messages ("The number you have dialed..."). Here, the speed of access and the reliability of bubble memories are desirable characteristics. In portable equipment, where light weight and small size are of paramount importance, bubble memories have become quite popular.

Bubble-memory operation depends on the tendency of garnet to form mobile magnetic domains ("bubbles") in the presence of a magnetic field of the proper strength. These cylinder-shaped bubbles are maintained in a thin slab of garnet by means of a small permanent magnet. Since the magnet is permanent, storage is non-volatile. A digital one is represented by the presence of a bubble, a zero by its absence. Electromagnets controlled by special electronic circuits shift magnetic bubbles around inside the garnet crystal, so that information can be encoded in a bubble pattern. Bubble memories are sequential-access devices, yet unlike magnetic tape, they provide rapid access to stored data. The reason for the high speed of bubble memory is that data are accessed electronically, not mechanically as on tape. Bubble-memory input and output are both handled serially. The capacity of current bubble-memory chips ranges from 64,000 to one million bits, with four-megabit chips on the way.

OPTICAL DISCS

When they become available in 1984 or 1985, optical-disc systems will revolutionize the world of mass storage. Although optical-disc hardware will be relatively expensive, it will store data at an almost infinitesimal cost per byte. In fact, storing information on an optical disc promises to cost one-tenth as much as storing it on magnetic tape, currently the cheapest form of mass storage. The first optical storage systems will probably record information in a pattern of micron-sized holes burned into a tellurium-coated disc. These tiny holes, gouged out by means of a laser, will enable data to be stored very densely. At the present time, it appears that ten to twenty billion bits of data will be stored on one side of a 12-inch optical disc. This translates into roughly one or two billion characters (i.e., bytes), the equivalent of 500,000 to 1,000,000 pages of text! The exact amount of data stored will depend on the number of errors incurred in the recording process.

Like magnetic disks, optical discs are random-access devices, which means that they will store and retrieve information very quickly. Optical discs are divided into tracks just as magnetic disks are; the only difference lies in the number of tracks used. While a hard disk may have several hundred tracks, the current crop of optical discs uses 54,000. (We should note that the 54,000-track figure was taken from consumer video-disc equipment, which is used to play back pre-recorded television programs. For reasons to be discussed later, it would be advantageous if at least some of the new optical storage systems were compatible with low-cost video-disc players. However, there is no reason to believe that this will be the prevailing sentiment in optical-disc design.) The combined advantages of very high storage density, fast data access, and low cost per byte make optical-disc systems very attractive for the archival storage of large amounts of data. If all goes well, optical discs should be the dominant form of archival storage in the 1990s.

Figure 3-3 illustrates the so-called direct-read-after-write (DRAW) method of optical-disc recording. Digital data fed to the recording system are used to modulate a high-power argon laser. In this case, the modulator is essentially a shutter mechanism that either passes or blocks the beam of the write laser. Modulation produces a chopped beam that burns tiny holes in a reflective film of tellurium on the optical disc. Since the disc is spinning all the while, a circular track of holes is inscribed in the tellurium film. These burned-out holes are about one micron in diameter and non-reflective.

To detect possible recording errors, the DRAW process reads information immediately after it has been recorded. By comparing what actually was recorded with what should have been, control circuits within the system can detect bad areas of the disc. The information contained in a bad area is recorded again on another part of the disc, and the bad region is ignored during subsequent read operations.

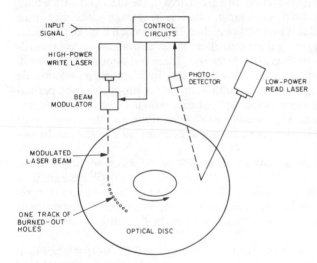

Fig. 3-3. The direct-read-after-write (DRAW) method of optical-disc recording. A high-powered laser beam, modulated by a digital signal, burns holes in a reflective tellurium film that coats the surface of the optical disc. Later, a low-powered read laser is bounced off the disc and picked up by a photo-detector, which converts light pulses into a digital signal.

Reading—whether it occurs immediately after writing, or later when information is retrieved—is done with a low-power semiconductor laser. The power of the read laser is deliberately kept low so that new holes are not burned into the tellurium film. A complicated optical system, which is not shown in Figure 3-3, aims the beam of the read laser at the proper track on the disc. The beam bounces off the reflective tellurium film and strikes the light-sensitive face of a photodetector. Since burned-out holes do not reflect light, they effectively chop the read laser beam. The photodetector converts this chopped beam into an electrical signal, which is subsequently decoded to yield digital data.

Current methods of optical-disc recording could stand improvement in several areas. The high-power argon-gas laser used for writing is an expensive, bulky device that must be water-cooled. Researchers would like to replace the gas laser with a semiconductor device, but diode lasers are not powerful enough for writing at the present time. Diode lasers are small, reliable, and inexpensive. Furthermore, they can be pulsed on and off electronically, so they do not require an external beam modulator. Eventually, high-power diode lasers will be developed, and the gas laser will no longer be needed.

The storage lifetime of optically encoded data also needs improvement. A tellurium film oxidizes and becomes useless in about ten years. To prevent data from being lost, the contents of an optical disc would have to be transferred to a fresh disc before ten years had elapsed. The storage lifetime might be extended by protecting tellurium with an overcoat, alloying it with other metals, or replacing it altogether with a new metal or an organic compound. We should note, however, that the storage lifetime of an optical disc is a significant improvement over that of magnetic tape. Data stored on tape must be rewritten every 3-5 years; furthermore, tapes must be stored under conditions of controlled temperature and humidity. In contrast, tellurium remains unaffected by humidity and tolerates a relatively wide range of temperatures.

Once burned into an optical disc, data cannot be erased. The only way to update a file is to record new information on a fresh area of the disc. Old data would remain in place but be ignored. Of course, this wastes storage space, but since there is plenty of that available on an optical disc, the approach is quite practical. Research is currently being conducted into alternative methods of optical recording which will allow data to be erased. However, there are some applications in which nonerasability is desirable. In archival storage, for instance, a nonerasable disc is eminently practical, since archived information is supposed to be permanent. And in banking, a nonerasable optical disc would provide an indelible record of every transaction. This would facilitate auditing and the detection of computer crimes, such as the loading of a bogus account with electronically pilfered funds.

At the present time, there appear to be at least two distinct applications for optical-disc systems. As noted before, optical discs will make possible the archival storage of huge amounts of information. Users will be able to store and later retrieve data with the same equipment. Because of the low cost and high density of optical storage, it is likely that optical discs will eventually dominate the field of archival storage.

The other likely application of optical-disc technology is in electronic publishing, that is, the dissemination of text on optical discs. Subscribers will be able to read these discs by means of a low-cost video-disc player, the same type of machine now used to play back pre-recorded movies. Electronic publishing is not likely to make books and magazines obsolete, because printed material is far too convenient to be abandoned entirely. But as a means of distributing large volumes of information at low cost, electronic publishing should prove invaluable. For instance, the reams of medical and technical information that take up so much library space could be stored handily on a few optical discs. Electronically published material will be recorded on a master disc, which will later be replicated economically in plastic, just as phonograph records are. As an added bonus, it should not be difficult to put text and video on the same disc.

Single-disc storage systems will probably cost in the vicinity of $10,000 when they first appear on the market. Larger systems comprising multiple discs, several access terminals, and a laser printer for hard copy should go for $100,000 to

$500,000. Obviously, equipment of this sort is not intended for the average office. Typical users might include the military and the IRS. RCA and Philips Laboratories are reportedly working on equipment capable of storing in excess of 25 trillion bytes.

CHAPTER FOUR
Local-Area Networks

The business that owns several computers or word processors may find it advantageous to connect individual machines together in a network. One benefit of a network is that it enables separate computers or terminals to communicate with one another. Thus, several workers can collaborate on an assignment by exchanging comments and data. Networks also allow the sharing of expensive resources, such as hard disks and printers. It is even possible for a network to be set up so that a central computer is shared by several terminals. However, since the speed with which a computer performs a given operation is diminished when the computer divides its time among several tasks, the current trend is to give each worker his own computer, usually a micro, and to share only such things as mass storage and peripherals. Response time is faster than it would be if a central computer were shared, and the low cost of microcomputers makes such a network economical. Of course, there are applications that demand more performance than a microcomputer can provide, and in such instances a mainframe can be shared by a network of users. (Mainframes are too big and expensive for each worker to have one of his own.) But even when a network is built around a central mainframe, the humble micro can still be a valuable asset. If each worker has his own microcomputer, which is linked by the network to a central mainframe, the burden on the large computer is diminished. A significant part of the processing is handled by the microcomputers, which call on the mainframe only when they need assistance.

Computer equipment in the same room or building can be joined together in a local-area network. Although local networks are primarily intended to link equipment separated by no more than a few thousand feet, the reach of such networks can be extended easily with modems. Two widely separated local-area networks communicating over the telephone lines form a new network with a wider scope. Local networks vary widely in architecture, number of workstations, and cost, which may range from $10,000 to well over $200,000. The size of a network is roughly correlated with its cost; inexpensive networks may be limited to less than fifteen users, while high-priced systems can, at least in theory, interconnect as many as 65,000 workstations. Regardless of a network's complexity, however, the cost of adding a new workstation is generally a relatively small part of the total network cost. This makes future expansion of the network economical.

At first glance, it might seem that networks are intended primarily for large businesses. The truth of the matter, however, is that even a small business can benefit greatly from a local network. By allowing several workers to share a common database, a network makes information processing more efficient. At the same time, hardware costs are reduced because expensive peripherals, such as hard-disk drives and printers, are shared among several workstations. As we shall see in this section, some types of networks are best suited to the small business, while others are practical only when the number of users is large.

TOPOLOGY AND CONTROL

One of the distinguishing characteristics of a network is its topology, that is, the way in which things are connected together. From a topological standpoint, it does not matter how the separate nodes (points) of a network are arranged in space; all that matters is how the nodes are linked together. For example, there is no topological difference between a square, a rectangle, and a parallelogram. All of these familiar figures consist of four nodes, each one of which is joined to two neighboring nodes by line segments. When a computer network is analyzed topologically, its nodes correspond to CRT terminals, computers, and other pieces of equipment. Internode electrical connections are established by means of coaxial cable, twisted-pair wiring, or fiber-optic cable. As noted above, the physical arrangement of a network's components has absolutely no bearing on its topology. Thus, if the components of a star network were arranged in a straight line, topologically the network would still be a star.

Fig. 4-1. A dedicated word processor will usually allow individual work stations to be interconnected in order to share a common database and printing facilities. The Lanier Cluster/ Shared system illustrated allows central mass storage of the equivalent of 70,000 pages of text. (Courtesy of Lanier Business Products Inc., Atlanta, GA)

Different topologies usually reflect different strategies of network control. On the one hand, control may be localized at one node, where a switching device determines which piece of equipment can transmit at any given instant. Star and loop network configurations have localized control. On the other hand, control circuits may be imbedded at every node of a network, so that responsibility for determining which node can transmit at a particular instant is distributed throughout the network. Ring- and bus-oriented systems employ some form of distributed control. The chief distinction between localized and distributed control is that a network with a single, central controller becomes totally disabled if that controller breaks down; but a distributed-control system, which does not rely on a single node for control, remains at least partially functional when any node fails.

Most networks designed for commercial and office use are not really fail-safe, regardless of whether control is localized or distributed. In theory at least, a distributed-control network should be more resistant to total, catastrophic failure than a network with centralized control. One cannot infer, however, that manufacturer A's network is better than manufacturer B's simply because A uses distributed control and B does not. It is one thing to advertise that a network is reliable because it uses distributed control, and quite another to build a network that lives up to expectations. Networks designed for industrial process-control or military applications, where reliability is of paramount importance, are usually redundant; when one part of the system fails, backup circuits cut in and assume control. For general office use, the need for reliability is seldom urgent enough to warrant the added expense of redundancy.

Most network traffic is time-division multiplexed; in plain English, this means that separate messages are divided up into small segments that are interleaved in time. For example, suppose that one user of a network wishes to transmit a simple alphabetical sequence, while another user wants to send a series of numbers. The two messages might be multiplexed as (a,1,b,2,c,3,d,4...) or (a,b,1,2,c,d,3,4...) and transmitted in this fashion over the network. The intended recipient of either message would have to pick out the proper message fragments when they were transmitted, and then combine them to recover the original message. Time-division multiplexing (TDM) is easily extended to accommodate any practical number of senders. The examples cited above use one- and two-byte message fragments, but fragment length is arbitrary and varies between networks. The virtue of TDM is that it allows several transmissions to take place in a seemingly concurrent fashion over a single pair of wires or a coaxial cable. In reality, of course, the messages are transmitted alternately rather than concurrently.

We are now ready to take a closer look at the characteristics of some popular network topologies. Figure 4-2 provides a graphical illustration of five different kinds of network topology. It should be noted that "terminals" (circles) and "terminal/distributed controllers" (squares) in Fig. 4-2 may represent CRT terminals, computers, printers, Winchester drives, or other kinds of peripheral equipment. Thus, a node where a circle or a square appears could be occupied by any one of the above-mentioned devices in a real network. Terminal equipment that incorporates its own control circuits is required in any network that uses distributed control. Table 4-1 summarizes some of the important characteristics of typical networks having the topologies illustrated in Fig. 4-2. In the discussion of network topology that follows, the reader should refer to Fig. 4-2 or Table 4-1 whenever necessary.

Stars

The star network makes use of a central switching device that routes data between the various nodes of the network. A point-to-point hookup links each terminal with the central controller. The old computer time-sharing systems were basically star networks in which one computer was shared by a cluster of data terminals. Modern office networks, whether they have the star configuration or some other, tend to share mass storage and peripherals, and to give each worker his own micro-computer. Low-cost star networks typically link tens of users; 16- and 32-user systems seem to be the most common. Digital PABX systems (private automated branch exchanges, i.e., interoffice phone systems with automatic switching) also use the star configuration. Since the new PABX systems are entirely digital, they can handle data as well as voice, though voice usually predominates. Hundreds, and sometimes thousands, of users can be linked by a large PABX system.

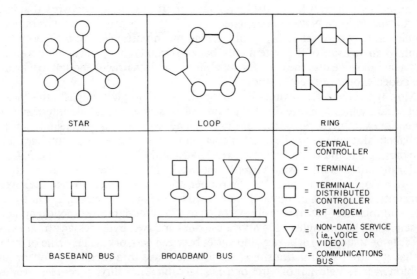

Fig. 4-2. A comparative look at network topology.

The Achilles heel of any star network is its central controller; once that breaks down, the entire system is out of commission. Nevertheless, well designed networks using the star configuration have proved to be very reliable.

Loops

Control is localized in a loop network just as it is in a star. However, a loop's controller does not make a direct connection to each terminal. (Remember, we are us-

Common Network Architectures

Topology	Control	Typical No. of Nodes	Services Available	Comments
star	localized	tens	data, voice	same principle as time-shared computers, but modern nets share mass storage rather than a CPU; if controller fails, so does the network.
loop	localized	tens	data	modern loops are often clusters of micro-computers; if the controller fails, another micro may be able to assume control.
ring	distributed with token-passing arbitration	tens to hundreds	data	messages are passed from node to node around the ring; distributed control prevents catastrophic failure of the system.
baseband bus	distributed with contention or token-passing arbitration	tens to hundreds per cable segment	mainly data; voice still experimental	intelligent nodes take turns transmitting over a common coax cable link; network expands easily.
broadband bus	distributed; individual channels can exploit different forms of control	tens to hundreds per channel	data, voice, and video	expensive, but this approach allows many simultaneous transmissions to take place on a single coax cable; similar in principle to cable TV

Table 4-1. Characteristics of some common network architectures.

ing "terminal" here to represent a variety of equipment.) Instead, the controller and terminals are linked together in a chain, the ends of which are joined. Messages are routed from node to node until they reach the proper destination. If the loop controller fails, the entire system becomes inoperative. Modern loops consisting of clusters of microcomputers may be able to shift control from one micro to another, so that if the loop controller fails, its duties can be assumed by another microcomputer.

Rings

At first glance, the topology of a ring (see Fig. 4-2) looks almost identical to that of a loop. There is one important difference, however. Whereas control is localized in a loop, it is distributed in a ring. The process of network arbitration, which determines which node has the right to transmit at any instant of time, is fairly complex in a ring and usually involves token-passing. A token is a digital word that confers the right to transmit on its holder. A single token is circulated around the ring, and only the node that possesses the token can transmit. Once a transmission has been completed, or once a prescribed amount of time has elapsed, the node holding the token relinquishes it to the next node in the ring. If a node is unable to finish a transmission before the token has to be given up, it waits until the token comes around again before completing the message. (In other words, all transmissions are time-division multiplexed.) Usually, a token is passed in clockwise or counterclockwise order around the ring. Data transmissions and tokens are sent only to the next node in the ring. A node that receives a token, but does not need it, immediately passes it on. Likewise, data received by a node is accepted if it has been addressed to the node; otherwise, the data is simply passed on to the next node. Eventually, the message will reach its destination.

If the node that originates a message later receives it back, either no one wanted the message, or the designated receiver was inactive. If a message does not come back to its sender, either the intended recipient has received it, or the ring has been broken; it is impossible to tell what has happened unless the sender requests an acknowledgement from the recipient. Token-passing is a fairly complex procedure, but since there is no central controller, a token-passing ring is not likely to fail catastrophically. There is always the possibility, however, that the token will be lost because of equipment failure or a break in the ring. Special measures must be taken by a manufacturer to guard against this, since once the token has been lost, all network activity ceases.

Baseband Buses

The stations in a baseband-bus network take turns transmitting over a common length of twisted-pair wire or coaxial cable. A baseband bus carries ordinary digital data; this stands in contrast to a broadband bus, which requires that data be impressed on a radio-frequency carrier before transmission (more on this later). Network control is distributed, and arbitration is handled either by contention or by token-passing. Under a contention protocol, stations compete for the privilege of transmitting on the bus. There are two popular forms of contention: carrier-sense multiple access with collision detection (CSMA/CD), and carrier-sense multiple access with acknowledgement (CSMA).

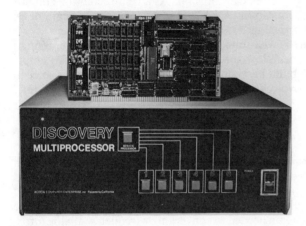

Fig. 4-3. One approach to networking is that taken by Action Computer Enterprise with its Discovery Multiprocessor™. The single-board computer shown perched above the chassis is just one of up to 16 such user-dedicated processors that normally reside within the unit. (Courtesy of Action Computer Enterprise Inc., Pasadena, CA)

Under CSMA/CD, any node can transmit to any other node or group of nodes as long as the bus is not already in use. A node wishing to transmit must first "listen" to make sure that the bus is free. If it is, the node proceeds to transmit a digital packet consisting of the identification code of the sender, the digital address of the recipient, and up to a thousand bytes or so of data. All of this is broadcast over the bus in serial fashion. It is possible for two nodes to listen, find the bus clear, and begin transmitting at the same time. The result is a digital collision. Once a collision has been detected under CSMA/CD, all nodes are alerted by a jamming signal. After the jamming signal stops, each would-be sender waits a random amount of time (usually on the order of tens of microseconds) before listening and attempting to transmit again. Since delays are chosen at random, the chances of a second collision are remote.

In the absence of collision detection, a contention protocol must use acknowledgement to make sure that messages get through. The procedure is quite similar to what was described for CSMA/CD: nodes listen first, and transmit only when the bus is free. However, if two nodes start to transmit at the same time, each remains oblivious of the other and continues until its transmission has been completed. It then waits for an acknowledgement from the message's recipient. Since the signal on the bus was garbled nonsense, no acknowledgement will be forthcoming, and each of the senders will once again listen and attempt to transmit. Simple CSMA with acknowledgement is less costly to implement than CSMA/CD, but network efficiency suffers because colliding transmissions run to completion before being repeated.

Bus arbitration can be handled by token-passing instead of contention. On a bus, the order in which a token is passed around is not the same as the physical order of stations along the bus (except by coincidence). This stands in contrast to a ring, where a token can only be passed clockwise or counterclockwise. Data and the token are broadcast from one node to all nodes on the bus. However, data are accepted only by the node (or nodes) to which they have been addressed, and the token is accepted only by the node next in line to transmit. The token and data transmitted by a node need not be destined for the same recipient. As in a ring, only the station possessing the token can transmit. As a result, collisions do not occur under token-passing arbitration. A node that sends a message cannot be sure of that message's safe arrival unless it requests an acknowledgement.

Baseband-bus architecture is well suited to high-speed data exchange, though manufacturers offer economical, low-speed baseband systems as well. Attempts are currently being made to build baseband-bus networks that can carry voice in addition to digital data, but voice capability will not be available for some time.

Broadband Buses

Devices linked by a broadband bus take turns sending messages over a common length of coaxial cable; in that respect, broadband and baseband buses are similar. However, before being transmitted on a broadband bus, digital data are impressed on a radio-frequency (RF) carrier with the aid of an RF modem. When a message is received, an RF modem is again needed to convert high-frequency analog information back into digital form. The great advantage of using RF modems is that many messages can be transmitted simultaneously over a coaxial cable; the entire system is reminiscent of cable TV. Both the sender of a message and its intended recipient must be operating in the same frequency band, or channel. Current broadband-bus networks offer as many as 100 separate information channels. For communication to take place in a given channel, two or more devices must be connected to the coaxial cable through RF modems tuned to the same channel. Signals in one channel do not interfere with signals in another, since different carrier frequencies are used. Hence, as long as messages occupy different channels, they may be broadcast concurrently over the same piece of coax. The process of separating information into different channels is known as frequency-division multiplexing (FDM). Unlike time-division multiplexing, which only provides the illusion of simultaneity, frequency-division multiplexing really does allow several messages to travel over a single cable at the same time.

Ordinarily, many devices share a single channel, so some form of arbitration must be available. Control is generally distributed in a broadband-bus network, and contention or some other protocol is used to decide who transmits on a channel at any given instant. This, of course, is time-division multiplexing. CSMA with acknowledgement of delivery is probably the most common form of channel arbitration in broadband-bus networks. CSMA/CD could be used, but collision detection requires complex equipment; therefore, simple CSMA is more prevalent at the present time. Other arbitration schemes can be used as well.

The large capacity of broadband-bus networks makes them attractive when a great number of devices must be linked together. In addition to data, a broadband system can carry voice and video information (just like cable TV). The need for video is probably not widespread at the moment; however, a network with video capability might prove to be useful for building security, hospital-patient monitoring, or education. The biggest disadvantage of a broadband-bus network is its high cost; RF modems and channel-switching equipment are expensive items.

WHICH NETWORK IS BEST?

Picking the right network is no easy matter; cost, network capacity, and speed are just a few of the factors that must be considered when weighing one network against another. Broadband buses can handle very large numbers of users, and they offer the fringe benefits of voice and video capability. However, the startup cost of a broadband network is very high. As a result, broadband buses are economical only if the initial number of users is large. Proponents of baseband networks, such as the Ethernet system developed by Xerox, claim that the video capability of broadband systems is not universally needed, and that data transmission is the main thing. They also claim that voice, which is now handled adequately by an office PABX, will soon be available on baseband networks. PABX manufacturers have jumped into the fray as well, saying that the new digital PABX systems can carry voice and data with equal facility. Furthermore, they point out that the cost per node of a digital PABX is less than that of a broadband or baseband network.

Most users are not equipped to make heads or tails of the conflicting claims of network manufacturers. When shopping for a network, it is certainly wise to consult with a reputable systems integrator first. His analysis and recommendations are likely to be more accurate than your own. Some manufacturers of dedicated word processors and general-purpose computers offer proprietary networks for use with their own equipment. In many cases, using a proprietary network may be the easiest solution to the problem of which network to buy. Still, it makes sense to get the opinion of an impartial consultant first, just to be sure that the network you buy is really the one you need, and not the one the manufacturer would like you to have.

SECTION II
WORD PROCESSING

CHAPTER FIVE
Printers

The most important piece of peripheral equipment in any word-processing system is the printer, since it alone is responsible for the quality of the final copy produced. Choosing the right printer is not easy, nor is it likely to get easier as new printing technologies proliferate. Nevertheless, the task of narrowing down the field is far from hopeless; it just requires careful analysis beforehand. With that in mind, we can proceed to examine the relative merits, from the standpoint of word processing, of the major printer technologies available today.

The first point to consider when buying a printer is print quality: Does the output of the machine look like a page from a book or like a cash-register tape from the supermarket? Certainly, the latter would be unsuitable for business correspondence, but for interoffice memos or technical reports it might be entirely adequate. When comparisons of print quality are made, most printers fall readily into one of three categories. The first of these, known as letter-quality, comprises those printers that produce well defined, easily readable characters suitable for correspondence—where conveying the best possible impression is usually important. By and large, letter-quality printers generate fully formed characters that look as though they had been typewritten.

At the other extreme are those printers categorized as being of draft quality. These units sacrifice print quality in favor of speed and usually generate characters on a dot-by-dot basis. Documents produced on these machines have an unmistakable "computer look," which probably accounts for a great deal of the aversion to using dot-matrix printers for business correspondence. It is interesting to note that a similar objection was raised when typewriters were first introduced: typewritten text was considered too mechanical and impersonal for correspondence.

Aside from the purely aesthetic objections to dot-matrix printing, there are certain practical problems with it. Since the dots are generally of uneven blackness, particularly after an ink ribbon has been in use for some time, text printed on a draft-quality machine does not reproduce well in a photocopier or facsimile machine. Likewise, optical character recognition equipment will not read it. And human eyes prefer solid characters, too. So, while dot-matrix draft-quality printers hold sway in the world of data processing, letter-quality printers that produce typewriter-like text are the favorites in word-processing applications.

The third category of printer is a relatively new one that straddles the fence between the two previously discussed extremes: it is known as NLQ or near-letter-quality. Machines of this type generate letters as combinations of dots, but the dots are very closely spaced—often overlapped—so that letters appear solid to the casual viewer. However, a closer look will reveal the deception. NLQ printers give the user the best of both worlds: high speed for data processing and very good text for correspondence.

Another important consideration when shopping for a printer is speed. In most instances, letter-quality text is produced at a slower rate than draft-quality. Printer specifications will often cite speed in units of cps, or characters per second. Another method for rating printer speed uses words per minute (wpm). To convert characters per second to words per minute, just multiply by 12. (This assumes an average word length of five letters.) For the sake of simplicity, this book uses cps for most speed ratings.

However, there are certain printers that operate so rapidly that another measure of speed is needed—hence, lpm or lines per minute. Fast devices of this sort are commonly known as line printers, since they operate on an entire line of text at one time. Machines that print one character at a time are properly referred to as serial printers to distinguish them from the line printers; in most instances, however, the "serial" adjective is omitted, and printers are assumed to be serial unless specifically referred to as line printers. In the sections that follow, both serial and line printers will be examined, though the reader should bear in mind that, for purposes of word processing, serial printers are adequate in the majority of applications.

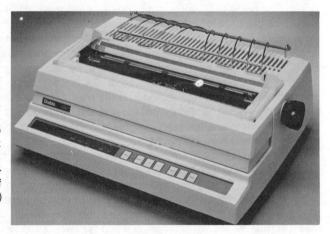

Fig. 5-1. The Diablo Model 630 letter-quality printer uses interchangeable metalized or plastic daisy wheels and prints at a top speed of 40 cps. (Courtesy of Diablo Systems Inc., a Xerox company. Diablo® and Xerox® are registered trademarks of Xerox Corp.)

SERIAL PRINTERS

Serial printers come in two types: impact and non-impact. The impact printers depend on small print hammers or wires that wallop the paper through a ribbon and thereby stamp a character's image on the page. Various kinds of impact printers can be distinguished on the basis of the mechanism that does the impacting. Thus, the prospective buyer must choose between daisy-wheel, dot-matrix, and converted-typewriter models. Non-impact printers are based on ink-jet, electrosensitive, or thermal technologies. In contrast with the impact printers, non-impact machines are much more quiet in operation, but they cannot print multi-part forms (i.e., carbon copies) the way an impact printer can.

Daisy-Wheel Printers

First introduced to the business world in 1972 by the Diablo Division of Xerox Corp., these machines have come to dominate the word-processing market. As illustrated in Fig. 5-2, the printing element in these units resembles a daisy, the petals of which bear embossed characters at their tips. Printing is accomplished by having the printhead traverse a line horizontally and stop when it reaches the spot where a character is to be printed. The daisy wheel rotates until the desired letter is in position, and an electronically driven hammer then smacks the embossed letter against an inked ribbon, which, in turn, hits the paper. Once an entire line has been printed in this manner, the paper is advanced by a transport mechanism so that the next line of text may be printed. The entire process is reminiscent of what happens in a typewriter, and, in fact, the resulting copy is indistinguishable from that produced by a fine typewriter.

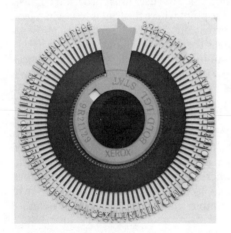

Fig. 5-2. A typical daisy printwheel with "petals" that bear embossed characters. (Courtesy of Diablo Systems Inc., Hayward, CA)

Nevertheless, there are important differences between a daisy-wheel printer and a typewriter. Whereas the paper carriage moves past a stationary printing mechanism in a typewriter, here a lightweight printhead flies in front of an immobile sheet of paper. With less inertia to overcome, this arrangement prints much faster than a conventional typewriter. Typical speeds for daisy-wheel printers and their variants range from 30-55 cps—about 3-5 times faster than a conventional electric typewriter operating at full speed. Recently introduced daisy-wheel printers from Brother and Smith-Corona operate at lower speeds but cost less. Top-of-the-line daisy printers cost $2,000-$4,000, while the budget units are priced in the vicinity of $1,000-$1,500.

Speed is not the only difference between daisy-wheel printers and typewriters. For example, most of these units are capable of producing proportionally spaced text, like that which appears in this book. Proportional printing allocates space to a letter on the basis of that letter's width. Thus, an "i" takes up less space than an "X" does. The copy that results is denser and looks a little better than the fixed-space printing of a typewriter. In order to generate proportional spacing, daisy-wheel printers utilize an internal microprocessor programmed to control horizontal character placement in increments of 1/120th of an inch. The vertical placement of characters is also precisely controlled in 1/48th-inch increments.

Precise character placement makes possible another daisy feature: shadow printing. This is a technique to produce boldface text without changing print wheels. When bold printing is desired, word processing software will first transmit a character to the printer. Once the character has been printed, a subsequent command from the computer causes the printhead to backspace to within 1/120th of an inch of its previous position and print the character again. Since the overprinting is very slightly misaligned with the original letter, the result is a "fat" character, which the eye perceives as being darker than the rest of the text.

Fonts (type styles, that is) are easily changed on a daisy-wheel printer simply by taking out the old wheel and putting in a new one. Dozens of styles are available from the manufacturers, including foreign-language fonts and special character sets for mathematical and scientific work. Unfortunately, these fonts cannot generally be changed under software control. Instead, the user must program a pause in the printing of the document just before the point where the font is to be changed. (Most word-processing software makes provisions for the insertion of pauses.) After the printer stops, the operator changes the printwheel and touches a designated key on the computer console to resume printing. A very few daisy-wheel printers, like the Qume TwinTrack, do allow the changing of fonts under software control without operator intervention. However, these machines have two separate printhead assemblies, each bearing a different font; as a result, they are bulky and expensive.

Daisy printwheels are available in metal or plastic. The metalized wheels are much more expensive than the plastic ones, but they last longer and provide better print quality. They also print at a slower pace than the plastic wheels. Some printers accept wheels of only one type; others, like the Diablo 630, can use either metalized or plastic print wheels. Still others, like the NEC Spinwriter, do not use a conventional daisy wheel at all, but a thimble-shaped print element instead.

Dot-Matrix Printers

Figure 5-3a shows a magnified view of what a dot-matrix character looks like. If the character is formed with many more dots that overlap each other, as in Fig. 5-3b, the result is said to be of near-letter-quality as explained earlier. In either case, the mechanism responsible for laying down the dots on paper is similar to what has been diagrammed in Fig. 5-4. The printhead contains a vertical column of tungsten-carbide wires, each housed within its own tube or channel and controlled by a separate solenoid inside the printhead.

In operation, a precision stepper motor moves the printhead horizontally across the paper in a series of tiny, discrete steps. At each print position, electronic circuitry within the printer selects a combination of print needles that define one vertical column of dots appropriate to the letter being printed. Upon selection, the print wires are fired, which causes them to shoot out and poke the paper through an inked ribbon. (The wires do not puncture the ribbon; their ends are blunt.)

A minimum of five horizontal steps is necessary for the printhead to complete the printing of one character. For near-letter-quality printing, more steps are required. Printheads generally have at least seven needles, but in order to print lowercase letters with true descenders (tails, as on "j"), at least nine needles are required. Some of the very cheapest dot-matrix printers are capable of printing only uppercase letters; however, the majority of the printers currently on the market will print lowercase letters as well. Dot-matrix printers are, as a rule, speedier than their daisy-wheel counterparts. The typical range of speeds is 80-200 cps, though some units are capable of attaining 600 cps.

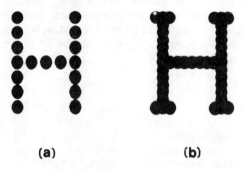

(a)   **(b)**

Fig. 5-3. Dot-matrix characters: Draft-quality output (a) consists of a sparse matrix with spaces between the dots, while NLQ printing (b) is distinguished by a greater number of dots overlapped to produce a solid image.

Every dot-matrix printer contains somewhere in its innards a chip known as a character generator. This integrated circuit is nothing more than a ROM that contains the dot patterns for all the characters that can be printed. Each ASCII code that the printer receives from the computer is translated by the character generator into a sequence of print-needle firings. Most manufacturers program their character generators with more than one character set; hitting a switch on the printer or feeding it some specified control code will choose a different character set. This is a very nice feature, one that cannot be duplicated on a daisy-wheel printer. Generally, these alternate character sets contain letters of similar shape but varying width. Character height is determined by the number of wires in the printhead and their spacing, so this dimension is not readily changed. Nevertheless, just having characters of various widths to work with allows the user considerable creative latitude.

Some manufacturers carry the matter one step further and provide alternate character sets not only of different widths but of different styles as well. Thus, with such machines one can switch from Helvetica to Times Roman or italics just by sending a few control codes to the printer. The number of dot-matrix printers offering software-selectable fonts is small; generally, these machines are in the near-letter-quality class, since considerable dot resolution is necessary to do a decent job of generating different fonts. The Malibu 200 and Sanders Media 12/7 are a pair of expensive dot-matrix printers that offer alternate fonts, but even the low-cost Epson MX-80 offers italics as an option.

Dot-matrix printers produce near-letter-quality output in a variety of different ways. Epson uses a multiple-pass technique: After printing a line of characters, the printer moves the paper by a small increment vertically and/or horizontally, then reprints the line. The resulting characters consist of two to four times as many dots as a normally printed character and look very good. Mannesmann Tally also employs a multiple-pass technique in its MT-1800 series of printers, but instead of shifting the paper on successive passes, the printer uses a printhead that pivots to stagger the dots on the second pass. Another method of producing NLQ output requires a printhead with densely packed needles arranged in two staggered rows. A head of this type can produce characters formed of overlapped dots in a single pass, and can be found on the IDS-460 and Prism printers from Integral Data Systems. Regardless of the technique employed, near-letter-quality printing proceeds at a slower pace than draft-quality printing. Most NLQ machines operate in two modes: one to produce drafts at high speed, the other to produce correspondence at a slower speed.

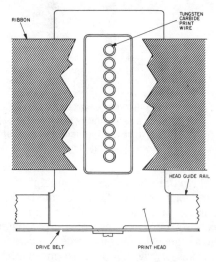

Fig. 5-4. A dot-matrix printhead as seen from the vantage point of a sheet of paper. Individual print wires are actuated by separate solenoids within the printhead, which slides laterally along a guide rail.

When comparing dot-matrix printers, the prospective buyer should pay heed to matrix-size specifications. A 5x7-dot matrix—five dots wide, seven dots high—handles uppercase letters well, but produces very crude lowercase letters without descenders. A 7x7 matrix is a little better, but descenders on lowercase letters are still impossible. Nine-wire printheads can produce 7x9 and 9x9 matrices, which permit descenders on lowercase letters, but the results are still of draft quality. Near-letter-quality printers produce denser matrices—for example, 18x9, 24x9, or 40x18—which are probably desirable in most word-processing applications. Another point to consider along with matrix size is the appearance of the font produced by the machine. By all means obtain a print sample from the manufacturer and judge it critically before buying any printer. Only a very few machines will allow the user to substitute other fonts later on, and even when this can be done, the necessary character-generator ROMs are not cheap.

Dot-matrix printers vary widely in cost; generally, for a higher price the buyer obtains a more rugged machine with more built-in intelligence and advanced features. Most machines on the market fall into the $500-$1,000 bracket, with those at the upper end of the scale offering the most advanced features. In the $1,000-$2,000 range the buyer will find the more rugged printers designed to take all the abuse a business's data-processing department can give. A very few dot-matrix printers can be found in the over-$2,000 range; these machines offer special features like interchangeable fonts and proportional printing.

Converted Typewriters

A number of firms offer either circuit boards that will convert an electric office typewriter into a printer or complete machines with the necessary conversion circuits already installed. In either case, these units are capable of producing excellent letter-quality text, but the printing speed is very slow—10-15 cps usually. Olivetti and IBM typewriters seem to be the favorites of the converter manufacturers. Some conversions produce a receive-only (RO) printer, while others enable the typewriter keyboard to communicate data to the computer. The latter types thus convert the typewriter into a terminal and are classified as KSR, keyboard send/receive, conversions.

Although conversions of this sort have the undeniable advantages of economy and excellent print quality, these must be weighed against the fact that typewriters were never designed for continuous service. If the typewriter is to be used only intermittently as a computer-output device, the buyer should have no reservations about making the conversion. However, if heavy and continuous use is anticipated, it makes more sense to invest in a daisy-wheel printer from the outset, instead of spending the money later on repairs and maintenance.

Typewriter-conversion kits cost from $300 to $600 and are available for a wide variety of office electric and electronic typewriters. The majority of these conversion kits interface electrically with the typewriter, though one manufacturer does offer a solenoid actuator that mechanically punches the typewriter keyboard. The interface with a computer is usually through a standard RS-232C serial port. These kits are truly economical only for the person who already owns the necessary typewriter. If the typewriter must also be purchased (another $1,000) it makes more sense to invest the money in a daisy-wheel printer. Converted typewriters can still be used in normal typewriter fashion when necessary.

Thermal Printers

In concept, these devices are very similar to the dot-matrix impact printers; however, the wires in a thermal printhead do not move and do not strike the paper. Instead, they are heated—on command—by individual heating elements. When heated, the special paper used in these printers turns black; thus, the horizontally traveling printhead leaves in its wake a trail of black dots. Because there is no ribbon to be struck, thermal printers run very quietly, which makes them attractive to computer and terminal manufacturers. Tektronix and Hewlett-Packard incorporaste thermal printers into many of their computers, and Texas Instruments uses thermal printers in its Silent 700 series of portable terminals.

Printing speeds range from 30 to 120 cps in current thermal printers. Some units print only in uppercase, but many are capable of lowercase printing as well. The major drawbacks of thermal printing are poor print quality and the need for special paper. One type of paper has dispersed within it microscopic bubbles of ink. When heated, these ink-filled bubbles rupture and stain the page. Another type of paper is coated with a waxy substance that chars readily when heated. Both kinds of thermal paper are relatively expensive and inferior in appearance to good-quality bond paper.

In light of this, it should be apparent that thermal printers are not serious contenders in the word-processing market. However, in other applications where light weight and silent operation are of paramount importance, thermal printers fill the bill very well. Another virtue of these machines is their low cost; an 80-column unit can be had for as little as $350. There are also 20- and 40- column models, the main applications of which are found in point-of-sale displays and electronic cash registers.

Electrosensitive Printers

Printers of this type rely on a matrix head made up of spark electrodes. The printhead works in conjunction with a special metallic-coated paper, which it scans in a manner similar to that described for impact matrix printheads. In this case, however, characters are formed by selectively igniting the electrodes. This burns off the paper's metallic coating in spots and lets its black base layer show through. Electrosensitive printers operate quickly (225 cps) and quietly, but the resulting silver-and-black copy is hardly of word-processing quality. Consequently, these printers see use mainly by programmers and computer hobbyists, who appreciate their low cost.

Ink-Jet Printers

Of the non-impact printers, ink-jet units are the only ones of significance to word processing. These units literally spray ink onto the page, thereby eliminating the need for ribbons or special paper. What is more, they are able to produce consistently dark and precise characters as long as their ink reservoirs remain full. Resolution is better than that which can be attained on an NLQ dot-matrix printer; in fact, some ink-jet printers can produce copy equal to that of a typewriter. Speeds greater than 200 cps are possible, though letter-quality output is usually produced at 30-50 cps.

There are many different approaches to the construction of an ink-jet printer; Fig. 5-5 illustrates the mechanism adopted by IBM for its Model 6640 printer. A pressurized, electrically conductive ink is ejected from a drop generator at a rate of 117,000 droplets per second. A piezoelectric transducer affixed to the drop generator converts electrical oscillations into mechanical vibrations, which expel ink droplets through an orifice. As it leaves the drop generator, each droplet is impressed with an electrostatic charge by the charge electrode. The magnitude of the applied charge will determine how far the droplet is deflected vertically as it passes through a constant electrical field maintained between two deflection plates. The more negative the droplet's acquired charge, the farther upwards it will be deflected as it flies between the plates. A character-generator ROM within the system controls the exact amount of charge induced on each droplet; this, in turn, determines the pattern deposited on paper by a succession of droplets.

Characters are literally painted one vertical column at a time. Once a column is complete, the entire printing mechanism is shifted laterally to a new position, where the next column of the character is squirted onto the page. Droplets not necessary to the formation of a character are given no charge. As a result, they are not deflected, but instead fly straight into a gutter, which prevents them from reaching the paper. As a matter of fact, fully 98 percent of the ink droplets end up in the gutter; from there they are recirculated through various pumps and filters back to the drop generator. This might appear to be an inefficient arrangement, but according to IBM it offers the most precise control of dot placement and the best print quality.

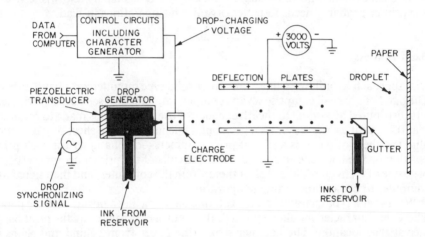

Fig. 5-5. One form of ink-jet printing depends on the vertical deflection of charged ink droplets to print characters one column at a time. By varying the charge on a drop of ink, the control circuits determine the trajectory of the drop and, as a result, the composite image produced by a succession of drops.

Other approaches to ink-jet printing use a printhead with seven, twelve or more nozzles arranged in a vertical column. Operation is very similar to that of a dot-matrix impact printer, except that the print wires have been replaced by ink jets. Siemens and Silonics both utilize systems of this sort in their ink-jet printers. In contrast with the IBM 6640, however, the Siemens PT-80 and Silonics Quietype feature a drop-on-demand system that ejects ink only when it is needed instead of continuously. This method is less complex and less expensive than that adopted by IBM, but the print quality is not quite as good. Multiple-nozzle ink-jet mechanisms can be adapted to color printing; PrintaColor offers machines that print with three inks and produce eight colors by overlapping various combinations of the primary colors.

As with all non-impact printers, ink-jet devices are relatively quiet, which lets them fit unobtrusively into the office environment. Moreover, ink-jet mechanisms adapt readily to the printing of characters in a variety of fonts and the production of color graphics (more on this later). For all of their advantages, however, ink-jet printers are not yet available for the masses. IBM's 6640 costs in the vicinity of $27,000, and even the least expensive ink-jet printers cost $3,000-$6,000. As ink-jet technology matures, prices may drop to more generally affordable levels.

LINE PRINTERS

Line printers are so named because they deal with text on a line-by-line basis. Speed is their forte, and while character quality can be quite good, it usually is not up to the standards of letter-quality serial printers. Line printers find their most frequent application in systems that handle a lot of output on a daily basis. The small businessman who finds himself backlogged occasionally and wishes for a line printer probably needs to better organize his operations instead.

Band Printers

One approach to building a line printer uses solid type mounted on a band or belt. The band of type will comprise several complete alphabetical sets, usually with letters distributed according to their frequency of use. The band is made to rotate so that the type it carries traverses a horizontal line in front of a sheet of paper. Behind the sheet of paper is a row of print hammers—one hammer for each print position on the line. The electronic control circuits of the printer accept one complete line of characters (80 or 132 of them) from the computer, and then signal the computer to cease transmitting temporarily.

Whenever a type character on the rotating band reaches a position on the paper where that character should be printed, the control electronics fire the print hammer at that location. The hammer strikes the paper from behind and slams it against the embossed typeface. Since a ribbon is interposed between the paper and the piece of type, this action transfers the image of the typeface to the paper. Many print hammers may be actuated simultaneously, but hardly ever does the entire line get printed at one time in these machines. The band continues rotating until every character in the line has been printed. At that point, the paper is advanced upward one line, the control electronics accept one more line of text from the computer, and the entire process repeats itself.

There is another type of line printer, known as a chain printer, that operates in much the same manner as the band printer but has a chain that carries the type around. Generally, band printers provide better character registration than chain printers. Typical speeds for both of these machines range from 400 to 2,000 lines per minute. In the past, line printers were also built with a rotating drum to carry the type, but these units have declined in popularity in recent years. Prices for the band printer and its relatives range from $5,000 to $10,000 typically.

Newer Technologies

The traditional line printer has seen competition of late from other technologies. In particular, several of the techniques used in serial printing have been applied with success to line printing. Dot-matrix methods can be used in line printers; all that is needed is a dot-matrix printhead that spans an entire line. Thus, if characters five dots wide are to be formed on a line 132 characters long, a printhead with 660 needles is required. In operation, the printer would accept a line of text from the computer, then print the top row of dots for all the characters simultaneously. The paper would then be advanced a small increment so that the second row of dots could be printed. This process would continue until all the rows of dots in this line of text had been printed, at which point a new line of characters would be requested from the computer.

Ink-jets have also been applied to line printing. The technique here is exactly parallel to what was discussed above, except that ink nozzles are substituted for print needles. Such machines have been built primarily for mass mailing and other high-volume applications where speed is essential.

Fig. 5-6. The Datasouth DS-180 dot-matrix impact printer features a nine-wire printhead and a top speed of 180 cps. Printing format commands, which can be programmed from the front panel, are retained in non-volatile memory after turn-off. (Courtesy of Datasouth Computer Corp., Charlotte, NC)

Ultra-High-Speed Equipment

Currently, the fastest printer in existence is the laser printer. With this type of machine, speeds of 20,000 lines per minute are possible. Under electronic control, the light from a low-powered laser "writes" on sensitized photographic paper or burns the coating off of a special printing paper. In either case, the speed of the operation is limited primarily by how fast the paper can be dragged through the machine.

Another speedster is the xerographic printer, which functions very much like a xerographic photocopier. In this instance, however, the image of the page to be printed is flashed on the screen of a CRT. The image is picked up by the xerographic apparatus and transferred to paper using heat and a dry powdered ink. Xerographic and laser machines are not line printers; their performance warrants classification as page printers, though this is not common practice. Equipment in this elite category carries a $50,000-$100,000 price tag.

GENERAL PRINTER FEATURES

Paper-Feed Mechanisms

The prospective buyer of a printer should be familiar with the features likely to be found on current equipment. One point worth considering is the type of mechanism used to feed paper through the printer. Basically, there are three paper-feed systems: friction, pin, and tractor. Friction feed should be familiar, since it is the method used in typewriters. A rotating rubber platen and metal roller pinch the paper and pull it into the machine. Friction feed works very well with single sheets of paper and is easy to use. It causes problems, however, when continuous multipart forms are being printed at high speed. What happens is that the forms slip out of registration, so printing is lop-sided and misaligned on the carbon copies.

Pin feed remedies this. Numerous pins stud the circumference of the right and left ends of a cylindrical roller and mesh with similarly spaced holes in specially punched paper. As the cylinder rotates, the paper is kept from slipping by the pins. The only disadvantage to pin feed is that it does not readily adapt to paper of differing widths.

Tractor-feed systems get around this limitation. Each tractor consists of a rotating belt studded with pins. To accommodate different sizes of paper, tractors can be positioned a variable distance apart and then locked into place. Rotating in unison, the two tractor belts pull the paper into the printer—hence, the name "tractor." Some systems are undirectional, pulling the paper one way, while others are bidirectional, capable of advancing or retracting the paper. Most daisy-wheel printers come with friction feed but offer tractors as an option. Dot-matrix and other high-speed printers offer pin or tractor feed. A very few printers, like the MPI 99G, provide both friction and tractor feed as standard items.

Paper

Computer paper comes in a variety of styles to suit the application and the feed system. For draft-quality printing, roll paper is convenient to use and inexpensive. The paper consists of one continuous sheet and must be cut or torn off after printing. Another paper style is known as fanfold and consists of one long, continuous strip of paper, perforated at regular intervals and folded fan-style into a stack. Depending on the paper weight, fanfold may be suitable for draft or correspondence printing. After leaving the printer, fanfold stock is torn apart at the perforations to yield single sheets. On some styles of fanfold paper the tractor-feed sprocket holes may even be detached. The final paper style is the single sheet, generally of high-quality bond, and suitable for letter-quality printing in a friction-feed daisy-wheel machine.

Paper is available in assorted widths and weights to handle just about any job. Widths range from 8½ to 14 7/8 inches for standard printers, and up to 25 inches for certain very wide printers used in data processing. For draft-quality printing, tissue-thin 13-lb. stock is available, while weights up to 20 lb. are better suited for correspondence. Letterheads are usually available as single-sheets, though it is possible to have them printed on fanfold stock. Another option is the use of tipped paper, which consists of high-quality bond sheets joined to cheap fanfold paper with a light adhesive. This allows a tractor-feed printer to print on single sheets, which can be separated from their carrier after printing.

Equipment Interfaces

Printers are generally designed to interface with a computer or dedicated word processor through a standard RS-232C serial port or a parallel port. The serial port has the advantage of being standardized, so set up is just a matter of plug-it-in-and-print. Parallel ports are capable of transmitting data at a faster rate than serial ports, but they lack industry-wide standardization with regard to signal polarities and socket-pin assignments. However, a de facto standard has been established in the Centronics parallel port. So many manufacturers have adopted the Centronics convention now that parallel interfacing has become almost as simple as serial.

Since two types of interface exist, this raises the question of which is better in a given situation. As mentioned above, the parallel port is capable of faster data transfers than the serial port. However, the vast majority of printers used in word processing operate at speeds below 120 cps, and since practically all serial ports can operate at 1200 baud (the equivalent of 120 cps), the issue of speed becomes irrelevant. With line printers and other high-speed equipment, however, the fast parallel port may have the advantage.

Serial ports are essential if data is to be transmitted to the printer by telephone. In this instance, the computer and the printer would each have to interface serially with a modem; the modems would then converse with one another over the phone lines. Serial ports are also capable of direct transmission over longer distances than parallel ports, because the many signal lines of a parallel port tend to interfere electrically with one another if cables are long.

Currently, manufacturers may offer both interfaces installed in the printer, or leave one or the other as an option. In most cases, the question of which interface to use will be decided by what ports are available on the computer or word processor.

Bidirectional Printing

The conventional typewriter prints a line from left to right, then advances the paper and returns to the left margin to begin printing the next line. Many printers operate in this way, too. However, in order to make printing faster and more efficient, a number of machines now employ bidirectional printing. On such equipment, successive lines are printed alternately left-to-right and right-to-left—a process which not only reduces wear on the printhead transport mechanism, but also eliminates the time wasted in bringing the printhead back to the left margin.

In order to support bidirectional printing, there must be a memory buffer within the machine to hold the contents of at least one line of text, and usually more. When a line is printed in reverse, printer control circuits simply output the contents of the buffer in reverse order. As long as the printer is dealing with full lines, the direction of printing alternates on successive passes. Should a line terminate in mid-page, however, the control circuits must decide whether to print the next line left-to-right or right-to-left. If this decision is made by an internal program that seeks to minimize the distance the printhead must travel, the printer is said to possess a logic-seeking capability. Logic seeking and bidirectional printing are very worthwhile features, especially in a printer that will see regular heavy use.

Some manufacturers have labeled serial printers capable of printing bidirectionally as line printers. Although these machines do logically analyze text by the line, they do not print more than one character at a time, and thus are not true line printers. With due regard for such semantic distinctions, the buyer should consider bidirectional printing as a highly desirable feature.

Fig. 5-7. The dual-mode MT-1800 dot-matrix impact printer from Mannesmann Tally uses a 9x7-dot format for draft-quality printing at 200 cps, and a 40x18-dot format for near-letter-quality printing at 50 cps. (Courtesy of Mannesmann Tally Corp., Kent, WA)

RO *vs.* KSR

Printers with an integral keyboard that can transmit data back to the computer are known as keyboard send/receive or KSR units. Besides being used to communicate with the computer, the keyboard is usually capable of controlling the printer directly, allowing operation akin to that of a typewriter. Printers without keyboards are known as receive-only or RO devices. Since the KSR option duplicates the function of a CRT terminal, it may not be required in many installations.

Internal Diagnostics

A number of printers feature built-in test facilities that monitor the condition of their internal circuits. In particular, such diagnostics include memory tests and a routine that exercises the printhead, causing a repetitive pattern of characters to be printed on command. Features of this sort are very desirable, if for no other reason than to assure the operator that the printer is not at fault when an error occurs. However, diagnostics do not make it possible for the user to repair the machine should something go wrong. In such an instance, the machine must still go back to the manufacturer or service center for repairs.

Fig. 5-8. A built-in keyboard allows the NEC Spinwriter 5520 to function as both a terminal and a printer. Letter-quality copy is produced at 55 cps using a thimble-shaped print element. (Courtesy of NEC Information Systems Inc., Lexington, MA)

Graphics

As noted earlier in the discussion of dot-matrix impact printers, ASCII-encoded data transmitted to a printer are translated by a character generator into a sequence of print-needle firings. It is possible on some printers to circumvent the character generator and, by so doing, to fire arbitrary patterns of needles under program control. This allows a computer equipped with suitable software to create dot-pattern images; graphs, drawings, even simulated halftone pictures, can all be produced without the need for additional expensive hardware. The typical dot resolution is close to 100 dots per inch, horizontally and vertically, which means that detailed images are possible.

Not only dot-matrix printers, but ink-jet, thermal, and xerographic types as well are capable of producing good to excellent graphics. When driven by the appropriate software, even daisy-wheel machines can print pictures; however, the resolution is limited because plotting is done with periods (.) and other characters. Moreover, daisy-wheel plotting is comparatively slow.

Operating Controls

Printers generally offer various controls and indicators to assist the user. Power switches are necessary, of course, as are baud-rate switches in printers equipped with serial ports. These should be set to match the transmission rate of the computer, which will probably also be variable. If the transmission rate is set too low, the printer will not be able to print at top speed. So, if a machine is capable of printing at 100 cps, a transmission rate of 1200 baud (120 cps) would be appropriate. Rates much less than this will slow the printer down unnecessarily.

There should also be a switch to put the printer on line or take it off. When on-line, the printer is capable of receiving data from the computer; when off, it ignores all incoming data. A printer is taken off line in order for adjustments to be made or to allow paper to be replenished. Normal printing resumes when the switch is returned to its on-line position.

Other common controls include switches to advance or retract the paper, both in tiny increments and by the line or page. On many machines there is a manual paper advance as well. A knob should be available to compensate for forms thickness; usually this is a micrometer adjustment that varies the distance between the printhead and the paper. When thick multi-part forms are being printed, the head clearance must be greater than that which would be used with single-ply paper. Printers incapable of printing multi-part forms—and this includes all non-impact printers—will of course not have this adjustment.

Top-of-form controls are also likely to be found. These inform the printer that its printhead's current position is to be considered as the top of the page. By counting linefeeds, the printer will then be able to determine when the bottom margin of a page has been reached; at that point it will eject the page and start printing at the top of a new sheet. Top-of-form adjustments are irrelevant when continuous roll paper is being used.

Printer Control Codes

A great many printer functions can be invoked or modified under software control. To accomplish this, the computer must transmit a control code—that is, an ASCII code between 0 and 31—which the printer recognizes as being not text but some type of command. There is no standardization with regard to control codes; one printer's commands will very likely be gibberish to another printer of different manufacture.

Control codes may be used to change character size or fonts, enable graphics operation, position the printhead laterally on the page, advance or retract the paper, and perform numerous other housekeeping functions. The more advanced the printer is in terms of internal intelligence, the larger its control-code repertoire will be.

Ribbons

Two principal types of printer ribbon are available: cloth and carbon film. Cloth ribbons are the least expensive, but yield comparatively rough output. When the finest print quality is desired—say, when preparing camera-ready copy—the more expensive film ribbons are used. These may be of either the single- or multi-strike type. In either case, the number of characters that can be printed with a film ribbon is considerably less than that which can be obtained with cloth; however, the characters formed are of higher quality. Film ribbons are used exclusively with daisy-wheel printers, since dot-matrix output does not warrant the extra expense.

CONCLUSIONS

The vast majority of word-processing systems will be served well by a serial printer, whether it be dot-matrix, daisy-wheel, converted-typewriter, or ink-jet. Line printers and the high-speed laser and xerographic types should be reserved for the few applications that generate overwhelming amounts of text—for example, mass mailing on a national scale.

Choosing the right printer is often a matter of compromise among the generally conflicting factors of speed, print quality, and cost. A dot-matrix printer offers high speed and economy along with draft-quality output. And as long as one is not offended by dots, there is no reason why a dot-matrix printer cannot be used for word processing. In scientific and technical work, for example, word processing with a dot-matrix printer is a sensible way to alleviate the drudgery of report writing at minimal cost.

Near-letter-quality matrix printers offer very good print quality that can often fool the naive observer. At the same time, the cost of an NLQ machine need not be excessive—witness the Epson MX-80. Machines in the NLQ category are attractive when the purchaser plans to use the same equipment for data and word processing. If such is the case, day-to-day financial records can be generated at high speed using the printer's draft-quality mode, while good-looking reports and correspondence can be printed at one-half or one-quarter the draft speed in the NLQ mode.

If the purchaser demands the very best print quality, a daisy-wheel printer is the clear choice. The only drawback of such a machine is its relatively slow speed when compared to a dot-matrix printer. Compared to a typewriter, though, a daisy-wheel printer is three to five times faster. On average, the cost of a daisy-wheel printer is relatively high, but it should be noted that there are certain dot-matrix printers of advanced design that cost more than a daisy-wheel machine. Today, most business correspondence and report writing is done on daisy-wheel printers, and this state of affairs is likely to remain unchanged for many years to come.

Ink-jet printers have been heralded as the wave of the future for several years now, but ink-jet printing has yet to become a major force in word processing. The very high cost of ink-jet printers capable of producing letter-quality text has doubtless been the reason. Assuming that the price of these machines can be reduced to a competitive level in the near future, however, this will be the technology to watch. Meanwhile, ink-jet printers of moderate cost and dot resolution offer a very quiet means of generating NLQ text and color graphics (more on this in Chapter Ten).

Finally, for the person who already owns an electric or electronic typewriter, a conversion kit can be used to adapt the typewriter to computer output. Provided that the application is such that the typewriter will not be driven beyond its limits, this is a good way to produce text of excellent quality. Unfortunately, the printing speed can only be described as leisurely, and the absence of tractors rules out printing on fanfold paper. If the user can abide hand feeding single sheets of paper and waiting several minutes for each page to print, this is the most economical way to obtain letter-quality output.

CHAPTER SIX
Special Word-Processing
Hardware

Getting started in word processing requires no more than software, a computer or dedicated word processor, and a printer. Many users will be satisfied with just these basic items; others, however, may need additional accessories that perform special functions, like phototypesetters, or that make operation more convenient, like automatic cut-sheet feeders. Even if no immediate need for such special equipment exists, it is conceivable that hardware enhancements may become necessary in the future. So, what follows is a brief introduction to some of the accessories that make a word-processing system more powerful and productive.

OPTICAL CHARACTER-RECOGNITION EQUIPMENT

Usually referred to by its initials, OCR, this type of equipment can convert type-written text into machine-readable digital data. Optical character readers scan text on a line-by-line basis much as a human reader does, but with limited cognitive powers. As a result, only special fonts can be recognized and read in this manner. OCR-compatible type elements are available for a variety of office typewriters and daisy-wheel printers.

OCR machines are essential in any business where original copy is produced on typewriters, but where the final output is produced by word processor. For example, consider the operation of a large national tabloid with contributing reporters scattered throughout the country. When one of these individuals files a report, OCR equipment might be used to enter the text into a word processor, where it would be edited and merged with other stories. At scan rates on the order of ten lines a second, OCR machines read text faster than an author's frenzied imagination can produce it.

Depending on the quality of the typewritten text submitted, scanners can enter 50,000-100,000 characters an hour—an improvement by almost an order of magnitude over keyboard entry by a person. OCR machines range in price from $10,000 on upward and adapt well to a wide range of applications.

COMPUTER-OUTPUT-ON-MICROFILM UNITS

Several hundred billion pages of computer output are generated annually in the United States alone. Even if only a small portion of this avalanche of paper were deemed important enough to save for reference, business would soon be buried in its own records. So, in order to store large amounts of data compactly but in an easily readable form, computer-output-on-microfilm (COM) equipment is used.

Microfilm storage is off-line, which is to say that it cannot be accessed by computer. This, in fact, is its particular advantage, since simple magnifying and projecting equipment suffices to enable a person to read microfilm records; there is no need for a computer, as when data are stored on magnetic disk or tape. Furthermore, the film itself is inexpensive enough so that old records can be discarded and new ones produced whenever an update is needed.

The most common form of microfilm is microfiche, a 5x7-inch sheet of film containing the equivalent of several hundred pages of text. Getting the information onto the film is accomplished in various ways, one of them being to actually write on the film with a laser beam, as in the Kodak Komstar microimage processor. Equipment of this sort has a high initial price, but the cost of the film is low enough to make this an attractive means of storing large amounts of text in a minimum of space.

PHOTOTYPESETTING UNITS

Machines of this sort are capable of producing camera-ready copy in a vast array of fonts and character sizes. Such equipment is used primarily in the newspaper and printing trades, where it has taken over much of the work that previously was done by linotype. Optical mechanisms including lasers are used to generate everything from headlines to fine print on photographic film or paper. The price of phototypsetters is high, but their speed, coupled with their ability to accept data from a word processor, makes them indispensable in high-volume printing.

FORMS PROCESSORS

Machinery in this category performs a variety of operations on the paper turned out by a word processor. Machines are available to detach and decollate fanfold computer forms. Decollation is the separation of a multi-part form into its component parts, that is, the original and one to five carbon copies. After decollation, continuous forms may be separated into individual sheets by a detacher that splits the paper apart along its perforations. Detaching and decollating machines that fit comfortably on a desktop cost in the vicinity of $1,000 apiece. If a word processor produces only a small volume of output, however, fanfold paper can be detached and decollated by hand.

Another helpful paper-handling accessory is the automatic cut-sheet feeder for printers with friction feed. Such a device holds several hundred sheets of paper, which it drops one at a time into a daisy-wheel printer. This arrangement eliminates the need for an operator to manually load and unload single sheets and speeds up the printing process. There is even equipment that feeds envelopes into a printer for addressing. Envelope and cut-sheet feeders may be necessities, not frills, in an office that generates large numbers of form letters.

PRINTER SILENCERS

Impact printers can be noisy beasts that fill an office with an unrelenting, mechanical roar. One effective, but not always practical, solution to this is banishing the printer to a room of its own. In cases where this is not possible, a special enclosure with sound-deadening walls is available to contain the printer and its noise. The sound-absorbing box is bulky, but the improvement in office ambience more than makes up for this. Some printers have built-in sound-absorbing material, and they may be quiet enough not to need the special silencing box. Also, printers that run intermittently are less likely to be annoying than those that labor under a heavy, continuous workload.

PRINT SPOOLERS

Printing an average page (2000 characters) on a daisy-wheel printer takes almost a minute. If a ten-page document is to be printed, nearly ten minutes of computer time will be spent transmitting short bursts of data to the printer, and waiting after each burst for the printer to catch up before sending out more data. In some applications, this delay makes no difference; in others, however, waiting for the printer is an intolerable waste of time.

To eliminate printing delays, some word-processing software is written to provide printing in background, a feature that allows the computer to divide its attention between the printer and the operator at the keyboard. There is one catch, however: computer response to keyboard commands may be sluggish, since the printer is competing for the computer's attention at periodic intervals.

A better solution to the problem can be found in a device known as a print spooler. This is nothing more than a large memory buffer controlled by a microprocessor and interposed between the computer and the printer. The computer transmits data to be printed to the spooler, which accepts the information as fast as the computer can send it. In just a short time, the computer will have unburdened itself of all text and will be free to edit or do anything else the operator desires. Meanwhile, the spooler patiently doles out text to the printer in periodic short bursts.

Transmission from computer to spooler and from spooler to printer can take place via serial or parallel pathways. If serial, the user should select the highest available transmission rate. Generally, this will be 9,600 baud, assuming that standard asynchronous serial ports are used. At 9,600 baud (or 960 cps), it takes approximately two seconds to transfer a 2,000-character page of text. A ten-page document can therefore be dumped in as little as 20 seconds. Compare this with the time it takes a daisy-wheel machine to print ten pages, about ten minutes, and the value of print spoolers should become apparent. If parallel ports are used, even faster data transfers are possible.

Print spoolers on the market now range in memory capacity from 16 to 60 kilo-bytes—the equivalent of eight to 30 pages of text. Prices seem to fall in the vicinity of $400 for stand-alone devices, and less for spoolers that fit into an on-board slot of the computer. The stand-alone devices are of course more versatile, since they can be used with any combination of computer and printer (provided the proper ports are available). Some units offer special features, such as driving more than one printer at a time or automatically numbering the pages. Even without such frills, however, a print spooler can be a worthwhile investment that will pay for itself in time saved.

SPEECH HARDWARE

Voice synthesis and recognition have intrigued researchers since the late 1940s. At RCA, Dr. Harry Olson and his co-workers were the first to produce a typewriter that recognized spoken letters and printed them out. Few secretaries lost sleep over it. Even today, electronic surrogates have caused hardly a ripple in most sec-retarial pools. The reason for this apathy is that voice-recognition equipment pre-sently handles something on the order of 100 words. Nevertheless, by 1985 one can expect recognizers with vocabularies of about 1,000 words, which should be sufficient to make voice control feasible in a great many applications.

As far as word processing is concerned, the voice entry of text is likely to remain just a tantalizing dream for decades. To understand why, consider the size of the English language: more than half a million words, some of which sound alike by nature (write/rite/wright/right), others of which we mangle into similarity (y'all/ yawl). To be sure, many words simply languish, forgotten by all except dictionary editors and professors. But even if these seldom used words are left uncounted, those that remain are still numerous and perverse enough to confuse voice-recognition equipment for many years to come.

As a result, the application of voice-recognition technology to word processing has been limited to the interpretation of commands. For instance, imagine a ter-minal operator speaking into a microphone and editing a line of text with simple two-word phrases:

RIGHT FIVE	(cursor moves right five spaces)
DOWN NINE	(cursor obliges by moving down nine rows)
DELETE WORD	(the word under the cursor vanishes)

This may seem far-fetched, but operation of this sort is entirely practicable today. Interstate Electronics has been experimenting with a voice-command terminal running a modified version of Micro Pro's WordStar software; the system is scheduled for introduction in 1982. No doubt some of the other manufacturers of voice-command terminals listed in the Directory have similarly interesting pro-jects under way.

Mention should also be made of the reverse side of the speech-technology coin: voice synthesis. The hardware to create lifelike computer speech has been around in affordable form for several years now. Generating speech is, in fact, much easier than recognizing it. Even now manufacturers are busy applying speech-syn-thesis hardware to a variety of consumer appliances and industrial equipment. In the context of word processing, system prompts and error messages are typical of the information that could be handled by computer speech. The only problem with speech output is that it might prove distracting in some office environments, especially if several pieces of equipment speak their minds at the same time.

In the final analysis, speech input and output are interesting technologies to watch. However, speech input will no doubt be relegated to interpreting simple commands for many years to come; great improvements in speech-recognition technology will have to be made before an executive can dictate his thoughts directly into a word-processing system. As for speech synthesis, the technology is much better developed, but is likely to have significance only in special situations —for example, word-processing terminals for blind workers.

GRAPHICS HARDWARE

There are several pieces of input hardware commonly used in graphics that can also be of service in word processing. Specifically, word-processing software can be written to allow the use of light pens and touch-sensitive screens in document editing. The light pen is similar in appearance to a conventional pen, and it is manipulated like one. However, a light pen writes not on paper, but on the face of a CRT.

It is possible to select characters just by pointing at them with the light pen. For instance, if an operator wants to delete a letter on a word processor with light-pen input, he points at the offending letter with the light pen, hits the "DELETE" key, and watches the letter disappear.

The role of the light pen is not particularly complicated: all it does is generate an electrical pulse whenever light strikes its tip. System software responds to this pulse by interrupting what it was doing and computing the location in memory of the character selected by the light pen. It may then modify that memory location, according to commands issued by the operator, and display the modification on the CRT screen.

Another useful input device is the touch-sensitive screen, which allows an operator to select information from a CRT display simply by touching it with his finger or a slim stylus. Touch-sensitive screens are available as integral components on some terminals; they may also be purchased as adapters that attach easily to a conventional CRT screen. It must be remembered, though, that word-processing software has to be written with a touch-sensitive screen in mind, or at least be modified to accommodate one, in order for such a device to be used. The same holds true for a light pen.

Light pens and touch-sensitive screens let the operator interact with the system in a natural way simply by pointing. Convenience of this sort adds to a system's cost, however, so these accessories are not widely used in word processing. Those systems that do incorporate them are likely to be dedicated word processors. Chapter Nine covers light pens and touch-sensitive screens in more detail within the context of graphics.

CHAPTER SEVEN
Editing A Document

One of the greatest advantages that a word processor confers on its user is the ability to edit text easily and quickly. In fact, editing a document becomes such a painless chore that the operator is likely to do the job not just faster, but better as well.

Editing is a broad topic. Text may have to be inserted, deleted, moved around, copied, and generally manipulated in just the same way as it is when pencil and paper are used. The big difference, of course, is that the writer has the assistance of some very sophisticated software, the workings of which constitute the focus of the present chapter.

GETTING ACQUAINTED WITH EDITORS

Screen-Oriented Editors

The editing functions of word-processing software have evolved from programs known as text editors, which were intended for editing of other computer programs rather than everyday text. The reason for mentioning this bit of software history is to point up a distinction between editing with a word processor and editing with a text editor. The latter forces the user to deal with text in terms of numbered lines, which is a convenient way of manipulating a program, but not the most natural way to edit ordinary text.

Consequently, most word-processing software offers a screen-oriented editor (also known as a cursor-oriented, two-dimensional, or full-screen editor). No matter what it is called, such an editor allows the user to manipulate a cursor in two directions, up/down or right/left, and move freely about the text on his CRT screen. This free access allows letters, words, sentences, paragraphs—in fact any parcel of text—to be singled out by the cursor and acted on by subsequent commands from the operator in a convenient, natural way.

Function Keys

The user of a dedicated word processor will discover a row of keys on his console unlike anything he may have seen on a conventional typewriter. These function keys invoke special features of the word processor. For example, there may be keys marked "DELETE" or "INSERT" or "INDENT"—perhaps two dozen different keys altogether. Pressing these keys at the right time is all that is needed to edit a document.

Word processing on a general-purpose computer is a little different. CRT terminals do not as a general rule offer specially labeled function keys. Instead, there will be a "CTRL" (control) key that can be used almost like a conventional shift key. When the control key is pressed at the same time as one of the alphabet or punctuation keys, a special code is generated. There are 32 of these special control codes having ASCII values between 0 and 31.

When a word-processing program receives one of these codes, it interprets the key press as a command rather than an item of text. Just what action a particular control key produces depends on who wrote the word-processing software; there are no conventions with regard to the use of control codes. Therefore, the user must memorize the functions performed by various control codes, and if he decides to use a different word-processing program, he will have to memorize a new set of control-code assignments.

Menu-Driven Software

In order to make editing easier for the user, word-processing software is often written to provide menus, that is, on-screen tables from which the operator can select an appropriate command, such as:

S = SCROLL UP	P = INDENT
D = SCROLL DOWN	K = KILL
I = INSERT	F = FORWARD SEARCH

Menus reduce the amount of information that the operator must commit to memory. Not only is this useful when control-code editing commands are used, it is also beneficial when function keys are available, since the menu guides the user to a suitable choice of command. Word-processing software will usually have a large command repertoire—more commands than there are function keys or control codes. Hence, multiple key presses must often be used to invoke a single command. In such instances, menus are especially welcome.

In the menu shown above, it will be noted that many commands are assigned mnemonically; frequently used commands should always be assigned in this way. However, since the number of commands is likely to be far in excess of 26, mnemonic assigments will not always be possible. Some conflicts can be resolved by cleverness—for example, the (K)ILL command is really a deletion, but since D had already been assigned, it could not be used. Of course, two-letter commands might also be used, but only as a last resort, since they are more cumbersome than single-key commands. It should also be noted that at some points in a word-processing program, commands require that the control key be pressed along with a letter, while at other times just a letter will do. The control key is used only when the program could interpret a key press as a letter instead of a command—that is, whenever text is in the process of being entered into the system.

In spite of the advantages cited above, menu-driven software does have some drawbacks. One is that the menus consume valuable space in program memory.

Another is that it takes time to put up the menu and remove it from the screen. And finally, menus consume space on the screen that could be occupied by text. None of these arguments is overwhelming, however, and menu-driven software continues to flourish, mainly because users like it. Programs without extensive menus, known as command-driven software, are also available and not really hard to use once the operator learns the commands. But even command-driven software is likely to use menus at some points.

Files

In computer parlance, a file is a set of related data that can be stored and retrieved together. Dedicated word processors often refer to files as "documents," a term more familiar and friendly to clerical workers. By whatever name they are called, files are the basic units of text storage. Files are assigned a name by the operator, who may then store them on disk and later retrieve them simply by using the proper file names.

One factor that the user must constantly keep in mind is the maximum file size, usually specified in bytes, or equivalently, in characters. The maximum file size is a function of computer memory (RAM) capacity and the amount of that memory consumed by the word-processing software. The memory space not occupied by software is available for text. If the user enters more text than the system can hold, the extra amount will overflow and be lost. Hence, the operator must pay constant attention to the size of his files. There will be some sort of command by which the user can determine the amount of text in memory and the amount of free space remaining. Before memory overflows, the text must be saved as a file on disk. A large document like a book will not fit into a single file, but sets of files can be linked together for printing later on.

To assist in the management of disk files, most word processors will display a directory of disk contents similar to the table of contents of a book. Information likely to be found in the directory includes file names, dates of creation and revision, authors' names, file sizes (in bytes, characters, words, lines, or pages), and even the amount of time spent working on each document. Dedicated word processors will have the most extensive directories, while word-processing software designed for microcomputers may have only rudimentary directory facilities, or none at all. In that case, to get a look at what files are on a particular disk, the operator must resort to using an operating system command to catalog the contents of the disk.

Speaking of operating systems, it would be well to note at this point that word-processing software written for general-purpose computers is usually designed to run on a specific operating system, since the software uses features of that operating system to manage its text files. Thus, software designed to run under CP/M will not work with Apple DOS, TRSDOS, Pascal, or any other popular operating system. (Pascal is a high-level computer language that happens to contain its own operating system.) Considerations of operating-system compatibility necessarily limit the range of word-processing software from which a microcomputer owner can choose; nevertheless, his options exceed those of the dedicated word processor user, who is restricted to software supplied by his machine's manufacturer.

BASIC EDITING FUNCTIONS

Cursor Movement

A well designed word-processing system will allow for quick and easy movement of the cursor on the CRT screen. Dedicated word processors customarily have special keys to move the cursor, while software for general-purpose computers relies on control-and-letter-key combinations. Left-right movement may be possible in units of a single space, a tab position, or a word—the latter being the distance between two blank spaces that enclose a contiguous group of characters. Up-down movement may take place in increments of a single line or paragraph. Holding down the terminal's repeat key when moving the cursor allows continuous motion without the need for pecking at the keyboard. Additional commands may allow the cursor to be moved to the top or bottom of the screen, or to the beginning or end of a particular line.

Scrolling

Most CRT terminals display no more than 25 lines of text, 80 characters to the line. Some dedicated word processors boast of full-page displays, 66 lines high and 95 character positions wide, but even these are inadequate to display the average document in its entirety. What is needed is a mechanism by which selected segments of a document can be positioned for viewing on the screen. Imagine for the moment that a document has been written out on a scroll, which may be unfurled to bring any desired section of text into view. This action can be duplicated electronically: Text may be scrolled upward so that each line jumps up an equal increment on the screen. At the top of the screen, the uppermost line vanishes, while at the bottom, a new line of text appears.

Scrolling continues as long as the appropriate key is held down. Its direction may also be reversed so that lines of text move down the screen instead of up. Other commands are available that produce an effect analogous to scrolling, but much more quickly. For instance, it may be possible to shift text up or down a full screen at a time. Another very useful set of commands allows the user to go to the top or bottom of the file, that is, to the beginning or end of the text. Still another variation enables the user to specify a line number and hit a key; the system responds by displaying the designated line mid-screen with logically connected text above and below it. For extra-wide documents, some systems will allow horizontal scrolling so that the full width of, say, a 132-column financial report can be examined in segments on the screen.

Tabbing

Tab stops are as useful on a word processor as they are on a typewriter. Eight or more individual horizontal tabs can be set; their locations are usually displayed as tick marks along the top of the CRT screen. When typing, the operator can send the cursor scurrying to the next available tab position by hitting a key designated for this purpose. The next character entered will appear on screen in the chosen column. Some systems even allow for vertical tabs. A related feature known as decimal tabbing can be found on the more sophisticated word processors. This automatically adjusts columns of mathematical data so that all decimal points line up vertically, regardless of the number of digits to the right or left of any decimal. Tables of financial data are thus very easy to construct.

Line Termination

There are three common methods for terminating a line of text on a word processor; a given system will offer one or two of the three. The first approach closely simulates the action of a standard typewriter. Once the desired line length has been defined, the user is alerted by a beep or buzz from the computer whenever a typed line extends past the right margin. It is up to the user to terminate lines manually with the carriage return key after hearing the beep. If the warning is ignored, the line will fill to the last column of the screen; text entered after this point will not be accepted by the system until a new line is started with the carriage return key. (Obviously, there is no typewriter-like carriage mechanism on a CRT terminal; what the carriage return key does is return the cursor to the left-hand margin and drop it down one line space.)

Terminating a line manually in this manner is sometimes necessary, but in most instances it is more convenient to have the computer terminate lines automatically. One of the favorite methods for doing this is known variously as wraparound or word wrap. With word wrap in effect, whenever a line of text exceeds the right margin defined by the user, the last word of the line is removed and inserted at the beginning of the next line (i.e., one line down). This means that a typist need never worry about hitting the carriage return at the end of a line. The only time that a carriage return is needed is when the operator wishes to denote the end of a paragraph.

The final method of line termination involves the use of a hot zone, that is, a special area just to the left of the right margin. Typically, the hot zone is seven spaces wide, though it can be adjusted to suit the line length. If a word terminates inside the hot zone, the next character entered will appear on screen at the beginning of the next line. If the last word of a line starts before the hot zone but extends beyond the right margin, the system usually requests that the operator hyphenate the word. Some of the more sophisticated dedicated word processors will even hyphenate automatically.

There is a subtle difference between word wrap and a hot zone. Word wrap relocates the last word when a line extends beyond the right margin with no regard for the length of that word. Hence, if a very long word is wrapped around, the line from which it came will be shorter than average. In contrast, a system using the hot-zone approach forces line termination within the hot zone. This limits the variation in line lengths to something less than the hot zone's width. However, the hot-zone user does have to hyphenate long words on occasion, and this makes text entry a bit slower than with word wrap. (Hyphenation can be used with word wrap, too, but it is not mandatory as it is with a hot zone.) In the final analysis, both word wrap and a hot zone make the entry of text easier for the typist. A given piece of word-processing software will feature one or the other of these automatic line-termination methods, but not both, so the prospective buyer should make certain of what he is getting beforehand.

Deletion

On paper, mistakes are erased away; on a CRT, they can be obliterated electronically. A good word processor will allow single characters, words, lines, and even entire blocks of text to be selectively deleted. Getting rid of a single character entails positioning the cursor over that character and striking the proper key. The character immediately disappears, and text to the right of the cursor moves one space to the left, thereby closing up the gap. Words are deleted in much the same way: the cursor is positioned over the leading character of the word, and the proper key for word deletion is struck. Simpler word processors may opt to omit the word-deletion feature, since repeated use of single-character deletion can obviously get rid of a word.

To delete an entire line, it is necessary to place the cursor over any character on the line. Hitting the line-delete key eliminates the line in question and shifts text below the cursor up one line space to close the gap.

Deleting a block of text requires that the beginning and end of that block first be identified. This is accomplished by moving the cursor to the start of the block and hitting a key. Then, the cursor is moved to the end of the block, and the same key is struck again. Markers will appear on screen to delimit the block of text selected, or the block may be highlighted (made brighter). In either case, the operator verifies that the block is indeed the one he wants to eliminate, and presses another key that performs the deletion. Text is then adjusted so that no gap remains.

Deletion is a powerful and necessary function, but it must be implemented carefully to prevent disastrous accidents. Well designed software will make it difficult for a wayward finger to destroy valuable text. Requiring multi-key command sequences for deletion is a common means of protection. Some systems even have an undelete feature that restores accidentally deleted text—very handy for the careless.

Insertion

Very often it is necessary to add a character, word, or sentence to text previously entered; a good editor makes insertions of this sort easy. To insert a single character, the cursor is first positioned over the spot where insertion is to occur. The user then strikes a key that puts the system into the insertion mode. Any subsequently typed character appears at the cursor position, and the cursor, together with all text to its right, is shifted one space to the right. Any number of characters can be entered while the character-insertion mode is in effect, provided that enough space exists between the end of the line and the right margin. When finished, the user resumes normal character entry by issuing the appropriate command.

Larger segments of text can be inserted by other commands. When invoked, these block-insertion commands generally clear the screen to the right of and below the current cursor position, thus leaving plenty of room for new text. (Words cleared from the screen are not erased from memory, however.) The operator then proceeds to type in as much text as necessary. When insertion is complete, the appropriate command returns the system to its regular character-entry mode, and a normal screen display is restored. Insertion may also take place as part of other editing operations, such as the two that immediately follow.

Block Moves

On occasion even the best writer finds that his words could benefit from rearrangement. With a word processor, moving blocks of text around is much easier and less frustrating than it is with pencil and paper. First the block of text to be moved is marked at beginning and end using the cursor and various command keys in a manner identical to that described for the deletion of blocks of text. After the block has been marked, the user typically issues a command that removes the block from its old position and sends it to a memory buffer temporarily. The cursor is then repositioned so that it lies where the first character of the moved block should appear. A subsequent command transfers the block of text from the buffer to its new location in the document. Block movement is thus a fairly complicated maneuver, entailing the transfer of a block to a buffer, the deletion of that block from its old position, and the insertion of the buffer's contents at a new point in the document.

Copying

This is an operation similar to the block moves discussed above. The only difference is that instead of deleting the block from its initial position, copying leaves the original where it was, while replicating the block at one or more points in the document.

Searching

In the course of preparing any form of written material, it frequently becomes necessary to compare or cross check various items scattered through the text. Word processors generally support such activity with a search function that locates the various occurrences of user-specified words in a document. After the search function has been called up, the system will request a search string, that is, a sequence of characters to be located. Once the operator has specified the search string, he may instruct the system to search either forward or backward from the current position of the cursor in the text. (Not all systems offer the backward search.) If the search string is found, it will be displayed in context on the screen, with the cursor resting on the first character of the string. After the text has been examined or modified, the search can be reactivated, and the system will hunt for the next occurrence of the string. If it fails to locate the designated string, the system stops searching and displays "String Not Found" or a similar message.

Computers are literal to a fault; if instructed to search for "printer," they will ignore "Printer" in most cases. Some word processors have search functions flexible enough to allow for capitalization of a word at the start of a sentence, or hyphenation at the end, but most word processors retrieve precisely what the operator specifies. Some software designers have the foresight to allow wild-card characters as part of a search string. For example, assuming that the question mark has been designated as a wild card, the search string "elect?" might dredge up "electronics," "electrode," or "electrical." Wild-card characters are particularly helpful when the user is searching for a range of related subjects derived from a common root word.

Searching makes no distinction as to word boundaries. If "bat" was specified as the search string, the system might locate "dingbat"—hardly the same thing. Fortunately, this sort of nuisance is easy to circumvent by including delimiting spaces in the search string. Thus, " bat " would ensure that only the desired three-letter word, and not a part of some other word, was retrieved.

Searching and Replacing

Quite often it is necessary not just to locate a word, but to replace it with another as well. For example, the writer of a technical manual might find it necessary to change part numbers in response to a design modification; all occurrences of "IC20" might need to be changed to "IC22." Revisions of this sort are tedious for a person, but computers take them in stride.

Search-and-replace works very much like a simple search, except that the user must specify both the search string and its replacement. There are several ways in which the search-and-replace function can be implemented; not all of them will be available on every system. One approach allows the operator to specify the direction of search (forward or backward relative to the current cursor position) and the number of times the action is to be repeated. The system then takes over and automatically performs the specified number of replacements.

Another option allows for the interactive replacement of words. As before, the user must first specify the search string and its replacement. Once the interactive search-and-replace function has been activated, the system searches out the first occurrence of the search string and pauses. The operator must then indicate whether or not replacement is to be performed in this particular instance. If his response is affirmative, the replacement is performed, and the system begins searching for the next occurrence of the designated string. A negative response from the operator resumes the search without performing the replacement. Interactive operation of this sort is valuable when only certain occurrences of a word need to be changed.

Searching and replacement can also be done in a global fashion, which is to say, throughout the document. Once activated, a global search-and-replace starts at the beginning of the file and works its way toward the end, replacing each occurrence of the search string that it comes upon with the specified replacement. Among its many uses, global search-and-replace enables the quick entry of frequently used words—for instance, legal terminology in a contract or technical jargon in a lab report. The user must first decide on distinctive but simple abbreviations for the words in question. These abbreviations are used when the document is initially entered into the system. Later, a global search-and-replace operation can be used to change the various abbreviations to full form. Some systems have a special glossary function that works in much the same way, except that the abbreviations and their replacements are permanently stored on disk. New abbreviations can be added to the glossary at any time, and old ones can be deleted.

Spelling Verification

To err may be human, but too many errors give a negative impression. Although using a word processor is no proof against mistakes, many systems are capable of spotting embarrassing errors in spelling before a document is printed.

With microcomputers, spelling verification is usually performed by a program separate from the word-processing software itself. These spelling checkers operate by comparing the contents of word-processor text files against a dictionary file containing from 15 to 45 thousand words. Dictionary entries are selected on the basis of their frequency of occurrence in everyday text. Most dictionaries are extensible, which is to say that the user may add new entries. Thus, a doctor would be able to add medical terminology to his system's dictionary, and so on.

Spelling checkers do not correct mistakes; they simply identify questionable words so that the operator can take appropriate corrective action if necessary. Words under suspicion may be displayed on the screen or listed on the printer in context; this is important, because context often determines the acceptability of a spelling. The user decides in each instance whether a word is correct or not and signals this to the program through the keyboard. A very few spelling checkers will correct text files directly; most just mark the misspelled word with an asterisk or other outstanding character. Later on, the operator uses the editing facilities of his word-processing software to correct all the marked entries in the text file. Naturally, he lets his system's search function find all the asterisk-marked mistakes. Dedicated word processors generally have more sophisticated dictionaries, or lexicons as they are sometimes called. The dictionary is often comprehensive enough to support the automatic hyphenation of words that overflow the hot zone at the end of a line. Automatic hyphenation is sometimes performed by means of an algorithm rather than by dictionary look-up; however, the results may not always be correct, since the English language is anything but consistent.

Spelling verification is far from fool-proof. Incorrectly spelled words may slip by unnoticed if the misspelling matches another correct spelling. For example, if "left" is spelled "lift," and the latter is in the dictionary, the mistake will not be caught. At the same time, perfectly good words may be flagged if they have not been included in the dictionary. In spite of such annoyances, however, spelling verification can be a useful time-saver, since it catches the glaring errors quickly. Those that remain can be detected by reviewing the file, if time permits.

CHAPTER EIGHT
Text Formatting and Printing

A word processor must do more than just edit and store text; it must allow a document to be printed in a format specified by the user. For instance, a business report might require double-spaced lines justified to yield straight right and left margins. With certain forms of correspondence, however, single-spaced lines and a ragged right margin might be preferable. Justifying a form letter, for example, would destroy the illusion of a hand-typed message. As we shall see, the operator of a word processor is free to tailor formatting to fit the needs of the document.

DEFAULTS

Well designed word-processing software will provide numerous formatting options. To save the user from having to specify a complete format for each and every document he prints, formatting functions are assigned default values. These are what the designer feels are the values likely to be used in the majority of situations. Unless overridden, defaults are always in effect; hence, the operator does not have to specify them explicitly each time. For example, the default setting for a left margin is usually equal to one inch (though it may be specified in character spaces rather than inches).

If a value other than the default is needed for a particular formatting command, it can be specified in various ways. In some cases, it may be desirable to permanently change a default setting. This operation is known as system generation or system installation, and it consists of a dialogue between man and machine in which the user is asked to input new default values. When this is done, the new defaults are permanently written onto the disk that contains the word-processing software. Defaults may be modified any number of times if necessary.

IMBEDDED COMMANDS

It is also possible to temporarily change formatting parameters using imbedded commands. These are typed into a document just like text; however, the software recognizes them as commands and does not print them out. Instead, the system responds to an imbedded command by altering the printing format of all subsequent text. Thus, margins can be pulled in for an inset paragraph, then expanded back to normal size. Likewise, it is possible to mix single-, double-, and triple-spaced lines in the same document.

Imbedded commands take a distinctive form that allows the word processor to differentiate them from text. One common method requires that all imbedded commands begin with a period (.) and be located at the start of a line containing no other characters. For example, ".LS 2" might signify a switch to double-spaced lines, while ".TM 7" might set the top margin seven lines down from the top of the page. The numbers in such commands are referred to as parameters; they override certain default values of the system until a new command is issued within the document.

Not all imbedded commands take parameters; some just act like switches that turn a function on or off. For instance, a title may be centered on the page with a ".CE" command, or underlining may be invoked with an imbedded ".UL" directive. Regardless of whether a command takes a parameter or not, it only has an effect on the text that follows, not that which went before.

COMMON FORMATTING COMMANDS

Line Spacing

The vertical separation between lines can usually be set for single spacing (6 lines per inch), double spacing (3 lines per inch), or triple spacing. Sophisticated systems may allow the specification of vertical spacing in 1/48th-inch increments so that invoices, checks, and other forms with irregularly spaced print positions can be handled. Taking advantage of such capability requires a daisy-wheel printer that can advance paper in 1/48th-inch steps.

Margins

Top, bottom, and left-hand margins can be explicitly specified; the right margin is determined by the position of the left margin and the length of the lines printed. Margins generally have default settings of about one inch, specified in terms of character or line spaces. The line length is likewise programmed in terms of character spaces, with a default in the neighborhood of 65. This yields a 6.5-inch line at a print density of 10 characters per inch. The maximum line allowed may consist of as many as 255 characters, but actually printing such a line requires a special extra-wide printer. Most printers used in word processing will print an 80- or 132-column line at 10 characters per inch, and proportionately more columns at 12 or 16 cpi.

Pagination

Once the user sets the number of lines per page—generally 66 for a single-spaced 11-inch sheet—his word-processor will divide documents into pages automatically and number those pages, too, if desired. At the same time, user-specified headers and footers can be printed on each page, again automatically. Typically, headers and footers contain information like the author's name or the chapter title; the header appears at the top of the page, the footer at the bottom. Either one can be suppressed.

Some systems can place page numbers in arbitrary positions on the page, while others restrict placement to one spot. Advanced software will even print page numbers alternately to the right side (on odd-numbered pages) and to the left (on even-numbered pages). This is desirable when system output is to be photographed and used in the production of a book or catalog with double-sided pages.

Sometimes it may be necessary to force printing to start at the top of a new sheet of paper. This is easily done with an imbedded page-break command. Another useful command is one that prevents a table or other block of text from starting on a page where there are not enough lines left to accommodate the entire block. By imbedding such a command before a table, the user protects the table from being split across page boundaries. When insufficient space exists, the entire table is shifted to the next page.

Reformatting

After editing operations like insertion or deletion, a page is frequently left in disarray; margins may no longer be straight, and hyphenated words may appear in lines where hyphenation is no longer required. It might seem logical to have the system clean up this mess automatically, but the process is too time-consuming to be done on a continuous basis. Instead, the user must issue a reformat command, which rearranges the on-screen text into the proper format, and even repaginates if necessary. The reformat command is an immediate, rather than imbedded, directive.

Justification

It is customary for the printing in books to be justified so that the left and right margins are both ruler straight; the present volume is a typical example. Linear perfection of this sort is achieved by padding lines with extra spaces until they extend from margin to margin. The simplest method is to add whole spaces between words. A number of word-processing packages for microcomputers use this technique; it works with any printer, but inter-word spacing is not uniform. Figure 8-1 illustrates the appearance of text justified by this method.

A better way to justify text is to pad it with microspaces, that is, tiny increments much smaller than a whole character space. This method requires a daisy-wheel or similar printer capable of horizontal positioning in increments of 1/120th of an inch. With such a printer and suitable software, the extra padded space is distributed evenly between all words on a line. Microspace-justified text is indistinguishable from professionally typeset material. Dedicated word processors can be expected to provide microspace justification, and a few of the better word-processing software packages for microcomputers also offer it, but most rely on the simpler technique of padding with whole spaces.

A document can also be printed in a style known as ragged right (or flushed left). In this case, the left margin is straight, but the right one meanders down the page. No attempt is made to pad spaces, and the resulting output looks as though it came out of a typewriter. The display in Fig. 8-2 has a ragged right margin. On occasion, it may be necessary to turn things around and make the right margin straight, the left one ragged. Ragged-left (or flushed right) printing sees relatively little use except in catalogs and advertising copy, where photos and blocks of text are intermingled.

Fig. 8-1. A screen photo showing the appearance of text that had been justified by padding lines with whole spaces. Compare this with Fig. 8-2.

Centering

Titles and headings must usually be centered on a page. A word processor can do this automatically if the proper command is imbedded before the text to be centered. Later when the document is printed out, the system counts the number of letters in the title, subtracts this from the maximum printable line length, divides by two, and adds this number of spaces before the first character of the title. Obviously, the operator could do this for himself, but the machine does it quickly and without complaint.

Subscripts and Superscripts

Imbedded commands to produce subscripts and superscripts on a daisy-wheel printer are available on most word processors. The system's CRT is not likely to show these features in true form, however, because displays based on character generators cannot shift characters up or down a half line space. Nevertheless, subscripts and superscripts will be printed correctly on paper.

Print Emphasis

There are a number of ways to make words stand out on a page. The simplest of these is underlining, a technique that works well on any daisy-wheel printer, but not on most dot-matrix machines. In order to underline, a word processor will transmit a character sequence to the printer that causes a letter to be printed, the printhead to be backed up, and an underline character (_) to be printed beneath the letter. This sequence of back-and-forth motion is repeated until all the letters of a word or phrase have been printed and underlined. Because dot-matrix printers are generally not capable of backspacing, they cannot underline in this way.

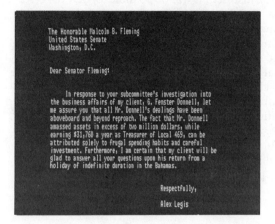

Fig. 8-2. Here is the same letter that appeared in Fig. 8-1, except that this time the right margin is ragged and the closing lines appear on the right. The letter did not have to be retyped; only a few formatting parameters were changed.

Bold characters are another way to emphasize a word. A daisy-wheel printer can print bold characters by overstriking or shadow printing; the two techniques are similar. In overstriking, a letter is printed, the printhead is backed up, and the letter is printed again. Letters may be overstruck several times in succession. If overstriking is performed in such a manner that the second strike is offset laterally from the first by 1/120th of an inch, the technique is called shadow printing, and its result is a fatter, bolder character. Dot-matrix printers cannot be made to overstrike or shadow print, but they are capable of printing wide characters when commanded to do so by the proper control code. It is up to the user to insert control codes as needed into his text to turn bold printing on and off.

Yet another way to produce emphasis is by switching to an alternate type font. With a daisy-wheel printer, an operator imbeds pause commands just before and after a word that he wants to print in an alternate font. These pauses enable him to change printwheels. After a change, printing is restarted by pressing some designated key. Advanced NLQ dot-matrix printers like those from Malibu and Sanders Technology can change fonts completely under software control; no operator intervention is necessary. All that is required is that the operator imbed printer control codes where necessary in the text.

ADVANCED FORMATTING FEATURES

Previewing

It is very desirable to be able to see exactly what the final formatted page will look like before actually printing it. Previewing of this sort will be found on dedicated word processors and a great many word-processing packages for general-purpose computers. If the document is to be justified, it will be possible to view the effect of justification on the CRT screen. The display will show lines padded with whole spaces, however, even if the printed output of the system is microspace justified.

Another limitation of previewing is that subscripts or superscripts, as has been mentioned, cannot be reproduced correctly on the screen in most instances. It is interesting to note, however, that on a system with a bit-mapped display—see Chapter Two for details—and no character generator, it is possible to write word-processing software that shows subscripts, superscripts, microspace justification, and any other feature requiring unrestricted character placement. Unfortunately, most readers are not likely to ever use a system of this sort for word processing.

On a personal computer with a 40-column display, accurate previewing is impossible. Even an 80-column display may sometimes prove inadequate when extra-wide documents are being prepared. If horizontal scrolling is available, however, it will allow a wide document to be viewed section by section.

Chaining Files

Small items like reports and letters will fit comfortably in a single disk file, but books, catalogs, and other substantial documents will occupy many files—often on more than one disk. Printing each one of these files individually is a nuisance. Fortunately, it is possible to join separate files together by imbedding a command at the end of each file that links it with another file to form a chain. Printing is initiated with the first file of the chain. Once the first file has been printed, the system loads the next file of the chain from disk and prints that also. This alternation of loading and printing proceeds, with no need for operator supervision, until the entire chain of files has been printed.

Passing Control Codes

As noted earlier in this chapter, and in Chapter Five as well, many functions of an intelligent printer can be invoked by sending the proper control codes to the printer. These printer commands are transmitted *via* the same serial or parallel pathway as textual data. The printer can easily distinguish commands from text, because all printable characters have ASCII values greater than or equal to 32, while all control codes have values less than 32.

Passing special control sequences to a printer requires that these codes be imbedded in text. Trouble arises, however, because these control characters are virtually certain to be recognized as valid editing or formatting commands by the word-processing system. Trying to insert control characters into text can be an exercise in futility unless the software makes some provision to allow it. Generally, the user will be required to preface each printer control code he inserts with some special character that tells the system, in effect, that the next character typed must be treated as text, though it looks like an editing or formatting command.

Not all word-processing software is capable of passing control codes in this way; so, if a printer with fancy software-controlled features is going to be used, look for word-processing software that can pass printer control codes. This applies mainly to word-processing on a general-purpose computer, because the software on a dedicated word processor is likely to be optimized so as to take advantage of all the special features of a particular daisy-wheel printer.

Form Letters

From a business standpoint, one of the most desirable features of a word processor is its ability to produce form letters. This is done by merging two separate files —one containing the text of a letter, the other personal data like customer names and addresses. The letter file has dispersed through it various marking codes. These designate spots where an individual's name, address, or other statistic will be inserted. The contents of the letter file are printed repetitively, using data relevant to a different person each time to replace the marking codes in the text. Only after all data in the personal-information file has been exhausted does the printing stop. If several personal-information files have been chained together, printing continues until the last file has been used up.

Boilerplate Documents

Contracts, medical reports, and many other documents often contain certain standardized paragraphs; in fact, they may have been written simply by combining the appropriate standard paragraphs with a small amount of original text. Combinations of this sort are easy to make on a word processor by merging selected entries from a file of standard, or boilerplate, paragraphs with particular information—such as names, dates, test results, and so forth—to produce a semi-custom document with a minimum of effort. The process is similar to the creation of a form letter, except that boilerplate documents are typically produced one at a time, and the information that they contain is customized for a particular client.

SOME COMMENTS ON BUYING SOFTWARE

The best way to buy software is with a demonstration. This is the only way to see what features the software has and how well they operate. Word processing software can vary considerably in the number of features available and the logic behind their operation. You may need a software package to perform relatively simple functions, such as the creation of business letters. In that case, some of the features discussed in the last two chapters will be superfluous. On the other hand, you may find that once you begin word processing the range of tasks that your program will be expected to peform will grow dramatically. You may then be glad that your word processing package has many undiscovered capabilities.

An excellent way to evaluate a word processing program is to compare it to one of the industry standards, such as MicroPro International's WordStar. WordStar contains virtually all of the features discussed above, and offers the options of integrated mailing list and spelling correction programs. You may not need all of WordStar's features, but through their logical formation and consistent operation you will see the manner in which an effective word processing program should be constructed.

SECTION III
BUSINESS GRAPHICS

CHAPTER NINE
Graphical Input Hardware

Graphical information is obviously quite different from text, so it should come as no surprise that special techniques and equipment have evolved to handle it. The standard alphanumeric keyboard, ideal for entering text, proves less than satisfactory with many types of graphical information. As a result, considerable research has been conducted over the last decade into ways of improving the efficiency of graphical input. In the course of that research, a variety of innovative, often exotic, devices has been developed.

Some of the more useful and readily available of these graphical input devices will be discussed in the pages ahead. This includes equipment like joysticks and tablets, which convert positional information into graphical coordinates, as well as bar-code-reading equipment. The latter are in fact very different from other graphical input devices because, instead of feeding spatial coordinates to a graphics program, they convert graphically encoded statistical data—stock numbers, for instance—into digital form. Thus, the primary application of bar-code readers is in data processing, not graphics. Nevertheless, bar-code readers are graphical devices, and their wide range of application is pertinent.

JOYSTICKS

Illustrated in Fig. 9-1 is one of the most common graphical input devices, the joystick. The large lever or stick that protrudes from the top of the case can be bent north, south, east, or west by the operator. As the stick is bent, two independent potentiometers (variable resistors) inside the device are made to rotate. One potentiometer responds only to north/south movement, while the other responds exclusively to movement east or west. Thus, each possible position of the joystick is represented by a unique combination of resistances in the potentiometers. By electronically sampling these resistance values at periodic intervals (say, every ten milliseconds), a graphics program can easily keep track of the angular position of the stick.

However, it is not the position of the stick that interests us, but rather that of a cursor that moves as the stick does. Each time that the program samples the joystick's resistances, it displays this cursor—often a cross or circle shape—on the screen at a point having coordinates proportional to the joystick reading. Thus, bending the stick this way and that produces X-Y motion of the cursor on the screen. Once the cursor has been positioned to the operator's satisfaction, hitting a switch next to the joystick or on the keyboard will produce some change in the display. For instance, depending on the software function evoked, the operator may draw a line, make a menu selection, or move a figure across the screen—all by just wiggling the stick.

It should be evident that the sole function of the joystick is to generate two independent electrical signals in a convenient way. The computer must be able to accept these signals, and the software must be written to make use of them. The joystick is not by nature a precision device, but visual feedback from the screen enables an operator to accurately position a cursor with a minimum of effort. Chapter Eleven provides information on some of the things that can be accomplished with a joystick or similar input device when the proper software is used.

Fig. 9-1. For users of the Apple II computer, The Keyboard Company's Joystick II enables easy man/machine interaction in a variety of graphics applications. (Courtesy of The Keyboard Company, Garden Grove, CA)

DIGITIZING TABLETS

Suppose that an application requires that a drawing, map, or chart already on paper be entered into a computer system. One way to do this is to assign a pair of cartesian coordinates to each point in the diagram, and then type these coordinates into the system so that a graphics program, working with the raw data, can reconstruct the diagram on a CRT screen. If this seems tedious in theory, it is even more so in practice.

A better approach to the problem is to use a digitizing tablet. With such a device, all the operator has to do is move a stylus or cursor (not to be confused with the one on the screen) over the surface of the diagram, which rests on the tablet. At each point whose spatial coordinates are to be entered, pressing a button will send the current X and Y coordinates of the stylus to the computer. The operator's only function here is to select the proper points on the diagram and accurately position the stylus or cursor over these points. Figure 9-2 illustrates a typical digitizing tablet with its movable cursor. The display in the background, which is available as an option, provides a continuous readout of the coordinates of the cursor.

It is easy to get the impression from looking at Fig. 9-2 that the chart resting on the tablet is somehow going to be copied into the system all at once. This is not true. As stated above, each point must be entered individually, and all that is entered is the position of the point—not its color or brightness. As a result, the digitizing tablet is best suited to the entry of line drawings rather than continuous-tone images. (The latter require a different device which will be covered further on.) Thoughtful readers are probably wondering now about the solid areas of color in the bar chart shown in Fig. 9-2. With the appropriate software, each rectangular bar can be entered by specifying the locations of its four corners; the program should then be able to generate an on-screen rectangle and fill it with color.

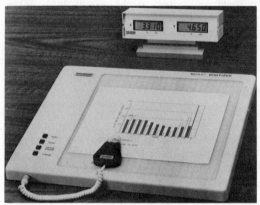

Fig. 9-2. Converting graphical information to digital form for computer input is easy with a digitizing tablet like this HIPAD™ unit from Houston Instrument. The X and Y coordinates of any point selected by the cursor are transmitted to the computer either singly or in a continuous stream. (Courtesy of Houston Instrument, Austin, TX)

Another unique feature of the digitizing tablet is that it makes possible the direct entry of drawings, rather than just the copying of pre-existing material. Assuming that the proper software is in use, straight lines are easily drawn by specifying endpoints with the tablet's stylus, and then letting the software draw a connecting line through corresponding points on the CRT screen. Curves of arbitrary shape can be drawn by switching to the continuous-stream mode, in which coordinate pairs are generated automatically by the tablet at a rate of about 100 per second. As the stylus is moved over the sensitive surface of the tablet, the coordinates of all points along the path of the stylus are fed to the computer. If the stylus lingers at a point, the software ignores all repeat entries of the same coordinate pair; this prevents the memory of the computer from filling with redundant data. In the hands of a competent graphic artist, a tablet operated in the stream mode is capable of generating exceptional images, which can be processed and transformed by system software in ways impossible with pencil and paper.

There are many ways to build a digitizing tablet. One of the more popular of these uses a sheet of magnetostrictive material, which has the property of delaying the propagation of an electrical pulse. This pulse is first sent through the magnetostrictive sheet horizontally, then vertically. The stylus is equipped to pick up pulses and signal their arrival to the internal electronics of the tablet. By measuring the time necessary for horizontally and vertically propagated pulses to reach the stylus, it is possible to determine the position of the stylus on the tablet to a high degree of precision—typically, to within 0.005 inch.

Other approaches to tablet construction make use of a buried gridwork of several thousand horizontal and vertical wires, each carrying a specially encoded signal that the stylus can pick up. Or the tablet may consist of a sheet of resistive material, to which horizontal and vertical voltage gradients are alternately applied. The stylus measures voltage, which, by Ohm's Law, must be proportional to position on the resistive sheet. Another method employs strategically placed microphones and a spark-generating stylus. The microphones pick up the sound of the spark, and by comparing the sound's time of arrival at the various microphones, the electronics of the system are able to extrapolate the position of the stylus relative to the microphones. This technique has even been extended to the construction of a three-dimensional digitizing tablet.

Depending on the application, the prospective buyer of a digitizing tablet can choose from models with a drawing space that ranges from 11x11 inches to 48x60 inches. For general-purpose use in the office or lab, the smallest models are usually adequate; they can be purchased for about $700. Larger tablets find application in engineering work for the most part.

TOUCH-SENSITIVE SCREENS

One of the easiest and most natural ways for a person to make a selection is by pointing at it. Realizing this, designers have come up with a variety of ways to make the screen of a CRT terminal touch-sensitive. Most of these devices are available both as kits that may be fitted to existing terminals, and as component parts of complete terminals. The circuitry associated with a touch-sensitive screen does nothing more than provide the computer system with the X and Y coordinates of the point on the screen that was touched. It is up to the software to correlate this information with the image or text displayed at that point and make a suitable response.

The value of a touch-sensitive screen stems not just from its ease of use, but from its flexibility as well. For example, industrial process control is one area in which touch-sensitive screens have been put to good use. On the CRT of the process-control terminal, the essential elements of the process can be displayed diagrammatically. In a chemical plant, for instance, the display would consist of tanks, pipes, and valves. The operator could control the flow of various chemicals just by touching the appropriate valves on the screen. In addition, by pressing some designated area, it might be possible to call up displays of several different processes, though it is likely that certain critical processes would have displays all to themselves. The screen not only enables the operator to control the system, it also provides him with a graphic display of the system's current status. For example, the level of fluid in a tank is something that could easily be displayed on the screen, as could the path of that fluid through a network of pipes. From the foregoing, it is safe to conclude that the possible applications of touch-sensitive screens are practically limitless.

At the present time, touch-sensitive screens are based on four competitive technologies: conductive-membrane, capacitive-plate, acoustic-wave, and infrared-beam. Of these, the latter two are the most elaborate and the most costly. However, no technique can be considered superior to the rest; each has its own advantages.

A conductive-membrane screen consists of two parts: a clear membrane with a conductive inner surface, and a glass CRT screen coated with a transparent layer of resistive material (i.e., a substance that resists the flow of electrical current). Pressing the screen forces the conductive membrane into contact with the resistive sheet at one point. A voltage is applied across the resistive sheet—first horizontally, then vertically—and the potential at the point of contact is measured. By Ohm's Law, one voltage is proportional to the horizontal position of the point of contact, the other to its vertical position. The circuitry scales these measured values and converts them to a pair of digital coordinates that may be read by the computer.

The capacitive approach uses a glass plate, on one side of which a number of isolated pads of transparent metallic film have been deposited. This clear plate is fastened in front of a CRT screen with the pads facing outward. Touching one of these pads with a finger or conductive stylus produces a change in capacitance (i.e., a change in the electrical charge that the plate can store), and this is detected electronically. The pad touched is identified by a digital code that can be read by the computer.

Acoustic-wave technology operates on the same principle as radar or sonar. Piezoelectric sensors oriented horizontally and vertically along the CRT screen send out acoustic waves that travel in alternate horizontal and vertical paths across the face of the CRT. These waves bounce off a finger or stylus and return to the transducers that emitted them. Measuring how long it takes for an echo to return determines the location of the reflecting object. Again, a pair of digital coordinates is made available to the computer.

The final method uses horizontal and vertical rows of tiny, infrared-emitting LEDs and, on opposing sides of the screen, horizontal and vertical rows of infrared detectors (phototransistors). Electronic circuits pulse the LEDs on and off and measure the response from the detectors. When a finger touches the screen, its position can be determined from the beams that it interrupts. Special compensating techniques prevent ambient light from affecting circuit performance.

Resolution may be an important factor to consider in some instances. Of the four systems discussed, capacitive screens currently offer the least resolution, with about 30 sensing pads on a 12-inch screen. This is fine for making selections from a menu, but not enough to be useful with a complicated graphic display. In such an application, one of the other technologies would be a better choice. Conductive-membrane screens can resolve position to within 0.05 inch or so, while acoustic-wave systems can, at least in theory, resolve to within 0.01 inch. To take advantage of such extremely fine resolution, however, the user must resort to touching the screen with a slim stylus. This means that the convenience of fingertip actuation must be sacrificed for the sake of increased resolution. For the user unwilling to make such a sacrifice, it is encouraging to note that the 0.25- to 0.50-inch resolution obtained with a fingertip is likely to be adequate in most cases.

LIGHT PENS

The light pen is, in concept, the simplest of the commonly used graphical input devices. It consists of a photodetector, an amplifier, and a lens to focus light on the photocell; all of this is packaged in a slim, pen-style case like that shown in Fig. 9-3a. In operation, the pen is first positioned over some feature on the screen that the user wishes to modify. Pressing a small switch on the pen then turns the device on, causing it to emit a pulse when light from the display strikes its sensitive tip. The important point to remember here is that CRT displays are continuously refreshed; thus, any given pixel of an on-screen image is not always illuminated, although it will appear so if the refresh rate is high enough. Since the display is being refreshed with the contents of a specific block of memory, it follows that the refreshing of a given spot on the screen must always be correlated with the reading of some specific location in memory.

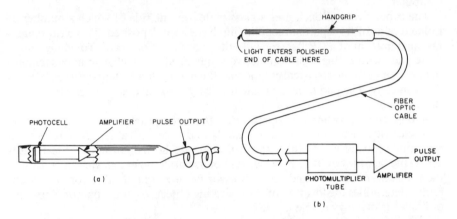

Fig. 9-3. Two varieties of light pen: (a) a conventional model with a solid-state photocell, and (b) high-speed type based on a photomultiplier tube, which receives light through a fiber-optic cable.

When the light pen detects the flash of light produced as a pixel is refreshed within its field of view, it sends an electrical pulse to a flip-flop, or one-bit storage register, in the computer. This causes the machine to interrupt its activities for the moment and determine the memory location whose contents were being displayed at the instant of interruption. Based on this information, the computer can then perform some user-designated task. For example, the selected pixel, or group of pixels, might be modified by writing new data into the appropriate area of memory. Or, it may be that the light pen is being used with a menu, in which case the computer will take one of several alternative courses of action in response to the pen's selection. In all cases, the nature of the action initiated by use of the light pen is determined by the software running at the moment.

Light pens based on solid-state photodetectors are useful in a great many applications; however, with certain high-resolution (and therefore high-speed) displays, solid-state photocells are not able to respond fast enough to keep up with the refreshing of the display. In such cases, light pens may be constructed using a photomultiplier tube, a vacuum-tube device that offers extremely quick response to flashes of light. An apparatus of this kind is illustrated in Fig. 9-3b. Note that the photomultiplier tube must be fed light pulses through a fiber-optic cable, since the tube itself is too bulky to be conveniently held in the hand. A shutter in the handgrip controls the passage of light and thus enables or disables the light pen.

Because the basic light pen requires for its operation some image to detect, it would seem that the pen would be useless on a blank expanse of screen. This limitation can be overcome, however, by the use of a software-generated tracking pattern. Suppose, for instance, that a light pen is to be used to trace a freehand sketch on a blank screen. Around the designated starting point the software causes a small raster or spiral pattern to be drawn. As the pen is moved, it will intersect some portion of this pattern and, in so doing, provide the computer with a fix on its new location. The machine responds by erasing the old pattern and drawing a new one around this second point. The next time that the pen is moved, a similar process occurs, and the tracking pattern follows the pen across the screen by leaps and bounds. Since our intention was to draw on the screen, the computer must also plot points that define the pen's trajectory. Tracking works well as long as the pen is not moved too rapidly. If this happens, the pen escapes the bounds of its tracking pattern, and the user has to start over.

Because they allow such convenient interaction with a CRT screen, light pens are very popular graphical input devices. With the proper software, they permit the user to make menu selections, draw lines, erase them, and move figures around on the screen. Pens often come as standard equipment on graphics-oriented computer systems, and they are also available as accessories for general-purpose computers. Resolution may be as fine as one pixel, which makes the light pen potentially more precise than a touch-sensitive screen. However, steady hands and keen eyes are needed to take advantage of this capability.

THE MOUSE

Like the joystick, the mouse is a small, hand-sized device for manipulating an on-screen cursor. On the underside of the mouse are a pair of wheels mounted at right angles to each other. These wheels spin as the user rubs the mouse around on a desktop. Circuits associated with the mouse convert wheel rotation into digital signals that the computer can use to position the cursor. The rotation of one wheel controls vertical cursor motion, while that of the other controls horizontal motion. If the mouse is lifted from the surface of the table and placed in a new spot, the cursor remains stationary, since the wheels have not turned. Switches located on the top of the mouse allow for the convenient control of various operations as the mouse is being used. Credit for spawning this electromechanical rodent goes to the Stanford Research Institute, but the Xerox Corporation is probably its most active proponent. Xerox computers rely on the mouse not only in graphical applications, but also in word processing, where it is used to make menu selections and edit text.

VIDEO DIGITIZERS

One of the most sophisticated approaches to the problem of graphical-data entry makes use of a video digitizer, a device that decodes the signal from a video camera and stores it in computer memory. There the data can be manipulated and transformed according to the whims of the user. Unlike the digitizing tablet, which requires that an operator manually locate points to be entered, the video digitizer takes in an entire scene automatically in just 1/30 second (or, if the video is non-interlaced, 1/60 second). What is more, the video digitizer is equally at home with either continuous-tone images or line diagrams. In fact, anything that can be photographed by a TV camera is fair game for the video digitizer.

The things that an ambitious user can do today with a microcomputer and a video digitizer were strictly within the domain of the university or military research lab a decade ago. In the realm of artificial intelligence, video digitizers enable computers to be used for pattern recognition, the machine analog of vision. Industrial research in this field has as one of its primary goals the development of assembly robots capable of handling non-standardized parts. Currently, a robot is programmed to do just one job, and if a part or a workpiece is not dimensioned or positioned exactly as the robot expects it to be, something will jam or break. Pattern recognition promises to produce robots that can sense the size, shape, and placement of parts; as a result, these machines will be more flexible and productive than present-day equipment.

Image-processing is another field where video digitizers are important. The contrast of a digitized scene can be enhanced by software to bring out obscure details, and special techniques can be employed to eradicate noise (i.e., fuzziness or "snow") from a picture of poor quality. Another possibility is the application of pseudocolors to a gray-scale or color image; this allows a digitized picture to be colored or recolored electronically in just a matter of minutes. The operator can carry the whole process one step further and combine computer-generated images or text with the digitized image in memory. When the desired effect has at last been achieved, pictures can be saved on videotape or film (see the next chapter for more details). Clearly, the implications of this technology for the graphic and video arts are staggering.

Top-of-the-line video digitizers consist of three separate subsystems: an analog-to-digital converter, a large block of image memory, and a video output generator. The converter accepts a standard video signal from a TV camera and converts it to digital form. It should be mentioned here that the vidicon tube inside a television camera operates very much like a CRT in reverse. The lens of the camera focuses an image on the vidicon's sensitive screen, which is scanned in a raster pattern by circuits in the camera. The signal produced by this process consists of video information, describing the brightness of each scanned point in the scene, and synchronizing information, which keeps a monitor's scan locked in step with that of the camera. The analog-to-digital converter must be precisely controlled so that it picks out and digitizes the proper information in the composite video signal supplied by the camera. In addition, this conversion must take place very quickly so that no video information is lost.

The second subsystem, image memory, must be large enough to contain all the video information extracted by the analog-to-digital converter. Suppose, for example, that we desire a picture 512 pixels wide and an equal number high. (This is a relatively common size; 512 is the ninth power of two, and thus a convenient number in digital systems.) If the display is bit-mapped so that each pixel corresponds to one bit of memory, a total of 32,768 bytes of RAM will be needed. With this much memory, however, each pixel can only be on or off (white or black). In order to display gray pixels, the amount of memory available must be substantially increased. Assigning eight bits of memory to each pixel will permit the display of 256 (two to the eighth power) levels of gray, which is enough for high-quality monochrome video. At the same time, this means that eight times as much memory, or more than 262 kilobytes, will be needed to store an image.

Since the total amount of image memory needed is far in excess of the 65,536 bytes that can be directly addressed by an eight-bit computer, it is clear that the computer's own memory capacity is inadequate for image storage. Even had we settled for an image of lesser quality, an inordinate amount of computer memory would still have been gobbled up in an attempt to store a picture there. As a result, high-quality video digitizers incorporate their own image memory, and allow the host computer to gain access to this block of memory through a "window" in the host's memory address space. This window is merely a set of addresses where data can be stored or retrieved; the principle is exactly the same as for memory-mapped I/O, which was discussed in Chapter Two. All the computer has to do in order to read or modify the contents of image memory is communicate with the few memory addresses that lie in the window. Circuits in the digitizer are responsible for shuttling data in image memory back and forth through the window when the computer requests it.

Color is a common option on video digitizers. The hypothetical system discussed above, with eight bits of memory per pixel, could just as easily display 256 colors as 256 shades of gray, provided that the proper video generator and monitor were used. At first glance, 256 colors would seem to be sufficient to handle just about any situation. However, included in this figure are all the possible intensities of any given color. There are some applications, such as the accurate shading of the surface of a solid object, that demand as many as 64 intensities of the same hue. At that rate, a 256-color palette would be filled with only four distinct hues. It would appear, then, that more bits per pixel must be used in order to obtain adequate color rendition. This can be done, of course, and the current decline in the cost of memory makes it all the more feasible. However, the versatility of the present system can be extended by means of a color map at very little additional cost. (Color maps were covered in Chapter Two.) An eight-bit-input, 24-bit-output map would allow any 256 colors, out of a possible 16.7 million, to be used at the same time. A map can be redefined by software to provide a set of colors suitable for the application at hand.

The final component of a video digitizer is the video output generator. This provides the signals needed to drive a raster-scan video monitor. The image on the monitor will coincide with what currently resides in image memory. The better digitizers provide several simultaneous video outputs, including composite monochrome, composite color, and RGB color with separate sync. These outputs may drive not only a monitor, but also a videotape recorder or any of the CRT hardcopy devices discussed in Chapter Ten.

Digitizers are usually designed to work with a particular computer bus, such as the ever-popular S-100 bus, the Multibus, or the DEC Q-bus. A high-quality video digitizer of the type discussed here costs from $2,000 to $8,000, depending on how much memory is provided. Most are expandable, so that a user may start out with a minimal monochrome configuration and later upgrade to color by adding more memory and the appropriate video generator. The cost of the television camera is extra, and can range from $300 to $10,000 (for a broadcast-quality unit). The more expensive models offer better image linearity and less variation in sensitivity across the field of view. A monitor will also be needed. Monochrome units can be purchased for less than $300, while a high-quality RGB color monitor can be expected to cost over $1,000. Clearly, this is expensive hardware. There are cheaper units of limited capability designed to mate with certain personal computers —most notably, the Apple II. These devices use the computer's internal memory to store images, and its video generator to display them. Although such simple digitizers are not in the same league as higher-priced equipment, their low cost (about $350 without the camera) does make them attractive.

BAR-CODE READERS

As noted earlier, bar-code readers are quite different from the rest of the equipment covered in this chapter. The bar-code reader converts graphically encoded statistical data into digital form, whereas each of the other devices converts, in its own unique way, spatial information into digital form. The graphical aspect of bar-code reading is only incidental to its primary function, which is to allow the fast and accurate entry of stock numbers and similar data into a computer. Having made that distinction, we can proceed to examine the three principal types of bar-code scanner.

Fig. 9-4. The ABT Bar-Wand is a hand-held bar-code reader compatible with the Apple II and Apple *III* computers. (Courtesy of Advanced Business Technology Inc., Saratoga, CA)

The simplest bar-code reader is the hand-held wand, illustrated in Fig. 9-4. Contained within the wand are an infrared-emitting LED, an infrared-sensitive detector, and a precision optical system. As the wand is passed over a bar code, white spaces reflect radiation back into the wand, while black bars simply absorb it. The sequence of reflections and absorptions is converted by the infrared detector into an electrical signal that is passed on to the computer, where software (sometimes with the aid of special hardware) decodes it.

Another way to read a bar code makes use of a fixed-beam scanner. In essence, the situation here is the reverse of that which obtains with the bar wand: the bar code must be moved across the field of view of the code reader, which remains stationary. Fixed-beam scanners are common at supermarket checkout counters and on conveyor systems; in the latter case, the scanner reads the codes on containers as they roll past.

The final type of bar-code reader is known as a moving-beam scanner. Like the fixed-beam scanner, it remains stationary, but its beam scans an arc several hundred times a second. A bar code must still be moved in front of the moving-beam scanner in order to be read; however, positioning is not as critical as it is with the fixed-beam scanner. The code can traverse any part of the scan area and still be read. Moving-beam scanners are useful on assembly lines and anyplace else where moving, coded items must be read.

There are more than twenty different kinds of bar code in use today. Figure 9-5 shows examples of four of the more common types, while Table 9-1 summarizes some of the important characteristics of each system. Numeric codes like UPC and 2-of-5 encode only ten distinct characters, the numbers 0-9. This is typical of the majority of bar-code systems. The few systems that do encode letters provide an alphabet limited to upper-case letters and punctuation symbols.

The fourth row of Table 9-1 merits further explanation. Some codes store all information in the dark bars. For example, in 2-of-5 a narrow bar represents a zero, while a wide bar stands for a one. In contrast, some codes store information in the spaces as well as the bars. An example of this is UPC, in which a blank space represents a zero, and a black bar equals a one. Codes of either type begin with a specific start pattern, follow that with a sequence of bars and spaces that represent data, and end with a stop pattern.

Fig. 9-5. Examples of some common types of bar code. Such codes are in everyday use in retail establishments. Information is encoded in the width and placement of the bars.

Each of the codes listed in Table 9-1 is self-checking, which means that the coding method is such that it provides some inherent statistical means by which data can be checked for validity. Checking is done by the software that decodes the data, and if a bad scan occurs, an error signal of some kind is generated. Some codes are bidirectional and can be scanned in either direction; the rest require a scan in one specific direction.

The final row of Table 9-1 shows some typical applications of the bar codes listed. UPC (or Universal Product Code) was adopted for supermarkets in the United States in 1973. Under this system, each manufacturer is assigned a unique

Characteristics of Some Common Bar Codes

Name of code	UPC	2-of-5	Code 39	Codabar
No. of characters in alphabet	10	10	43	18
Type of code	numeric	numeric	alphanumeric	numeric & symbol
Information in spaces as well as bars?	yes	no	yes	yes
No. of bar widths	4	2	2	2
Self-checking?	yes	yes	yes	yes
Bidirectional?	no	yes	yes	yes
No. of characters per block of code	6-11	fixed	variable	variable
Applications	supermarket point-of-sale	inventory control	library & industrial stock control	medical & point-of-sale

Table 9-1. Characteristics of some common bar codes.

code for his products. Stores use this code to keep track of inventory and sales for each particular product. The 2-of-5 system is popular for industrial inventory control and has numerous variants. The ability of Code 39 to handle letters as well as numbers makes it attractive for libraries and any business that wants to keep track of things by name or title. The last entry, Codabar, sees use in medical and general point-of-sale applications.

Several options exist with regard to the printing of bar-code labels. If the quantity needed is sufficiently large, labels may be custom printed by a professional printer. Another possibility would be to buy one of the special printers made expressly for bar-code printing. However, if a business already owns a dot-matrix or daisy-wheel printer, and only a moderate quantity of labels is needed, the office printer may be able to do the job. A few firms sell software for this purpose, and the user may even be able to write his own (see the article by Anderson for details).

CHAPTER TEN
Graphical Output Hardware

An essential requirement in any graphical application is that the user be able to see the fruits of his labors. This need can be satisfied in one of two ways: either by using an electronic display or by producing hard copy (that is, an image on paper). Electronic displays are most important during the design phase, since they provide a chance for the operator to appraise his work as it progresses. Later, when the work is finished, hard copy is the most convenient way to show results to colleagues or submit them for publication.

The predominant electronic display for graphics is the CRT, though there are other useful display devices as well. Some applications require only a monochrome display, while others benefit greatly from the use of color. The CRT in its various forms can handle both types of display admirably, even though the device is a throwback to the prehistory of electronics. Solid-state flat-panel displays may one day supplant the venerable CRT, but that time is not yet at hand.

Hard copy can be produced on photographic film or paper in a variety of ways, ranging from the robot-like digital plotter, which literally draws an image with pen and ink, to the new direct-to-film machines, which produce a photographic slide or print from a video signal. Here again, the user has the option of color or monochrome images. Since hard-copy equipment is available in a wide range of styles and prices, the buyer must balance cost against performance before making a purchase.

ELECTRONIC DISPLAYS

Right from the start it is important to make a distinction between two types of electronic display: line-drawing and point-plotting. Line-drawing displays, which may also be called calligraphic or stroke-writing, are so named because the images they produce contain smooth, straight lines. Curves consist of numerous, connected, straight-line segments, and even letters may be fashioned from short straight lines. In contrast, a point-plotting display builds all images from collections of points; thus, lines both straight and of arbitrary curvature are drawn as sequences of closely spaced points. Letters, too, are formed with dots.

Line-drawing and point-plotting displays differ in more than just appearance. Line-drawing displays are incapable of representing solid objects and surfaces; their forte is the image that contains only lines and, by extension, a few isolated

129

points. In this instance, points may be considered as lines no longer than they are wide. The need for occasional points notwithstanding, line-drawing displays are most efficient when used to draw lines. By comparison, the point-plotting display is much more versatile: it can display any image—solid surface, straight line, curved line, or isolated point—as an ensemble of dots. Another important advantage of the point-plotting display is that both color and monochrome models are available. In contrast, the line-drawing display is almost always monochromatic, with green or white lines on a dark background.

A decade ago, most of the displays used in graphics were of the line-drawing type. Today, the market share of each class of display is more evenly balanced, but the point-plotting display is gaining fast in popularity. Soon, it will dominate the field of graphics. The boom in user acceptance of the point-plotting display is as much a matter of economics as it is of performance. The declining cost of semiconductor memory, for which the point-plotting display has a voracious appetite, has bolstered the popularity of the point-plotting display. One of the few places where the line-drawing display still has the technical edge is in high-precision engineering drafting and design. Here, the high resolution and stability of the line-drawing display make it the favorite. Since engineering work consists predominantly of line drawings, the inability of the line-drawing display to portray solid surfaces causes few problems.

The most important point-plotting display is the raster-scan CRT, which was covered earlier in Chapter Two. Certain flat-panel displays of the plasma and liquid-crystal types serve well when portability, rather than performance, is of the utmost importance. Line-drawing displays are primarily of two types: random-scan CRT and storage tube. The former differs from the familiar raster-scan CRT mainly in the way that information is fed to the tube; physically, random- and raster-scan devices operate on the same principles.

The Raster-Scan CRT Revisited

The construction and operation of the raster-scan CRT have already been discussed in Chapter Two, so what follows is part expansion and part repetition of the previous material. Two facets of raster-scan operation deserve special emphasis: the raster pattern and display refreshing. The raster is the screen-filling pattern that the electron beam traces out on the face of the CRT. This pattern must be refreshed by repeated tracing—30 times a second if interlaced, 60 times a second if not—to keep the on-screen image from fading. Every point on the screen is scanned as part of the raster, with no regard for which points actually convey information relevant to the image. In order to display a solitary white dot at the bottom of the screen, it is necessary to scan hundreds of thousands of pixels with the beam turned off, and then to turn it on for a brief instant when the desired position is reached. Clearly, time is being wasted in this case. So is memory, because each pixel in a bit-mapped display requires at least one bit of memory to store its status, which is to say, its luminous intensity. If gray levels or colors are being displayed, many more bits of memory must be devoted to each pixel.

If every single pixel on the screen of a CRT conveys information useful to the formation of an image, the raster-scan process is operating at 100 percent efficiency. The fewer information-bearing pixels there are in a display, the less efficient the raster-scan process becomes in terms of the utilization of time and memory. It stands to reason that for drawings of relatively low complexity—simple line drawings, in particular—the raster-scan process is not the ideal one to use from the standpoint of efficiency. In such instances, the random-scan CRT provides faster response and smoother interaction between man and machine. This is important, because people get annoyed waiting for a machine to respond.

It would be a mistake, however, to judge the raster-scan CRT solely on the basis of speed or memory requirements. In the majority of applications, the raster-scan CRT is adequately fast. As for memory, current advances in large-scale integration are packing more bits on a chip, and doing it at less cost per bit. We can afford to be extravagant with memory. This was not the case in the sixties and seventies. Memory was expensive, so line-drawing displays with modest memory requirements dominated graphics. Today, high-resolution raster-scan displays one thousand pixels wide and an equal number high are practical, if not common. As the cost of memory continues to decline, displays of even higher resolution will become affordable. This will allow smoother-looking lines and curves to be drawn, since the individual pixels will be harder to discern. It should also be noted that the only practical way to display solid areas of gray is with the raster-scan CRT. Likewise, displaying surfaces or solids in color requires a three-gun raster-scan tube, the shadow-mask CRT. On balance, then, the advantages of the raster-scan CRT outweigh its shortcomings, and the increased application of this device in computer graphics may safely be anticipated.

Flat-Panel Displays

There are a number of flat-panel point-plotting display devices competing for a share of the graphics market. In terms of resolution, they are all inferior to the raster-scan CRT. Even more discouraging is the inability of most of these devices to display gray levels or color. Nevertheless, flat-panel displays do have some saving graces, chief among them being light weight, low power consumption, rugged construction, and a space-saving flat exterior.

One of the better known flat displays is the plasma panel. This device operates by selectively ionizing cells of a neon-based gas trapped between two sheets of glass. Any cell of the flat grid can be turned on, after which it remains lit until being turned off again electronically. Refreshing of the display is therefore unnecessary, since it possesses an inherent memory. Images are displayed by igniting various patterns of cells, which then glow with an orange color. The best resolution currently attainable is about 60 cells/inch—only half of what can be achieved on a raster-scan CRT. The writing speed is relatively slow, so changing a complete display may take a second or so. The biggest advantage of this technology is its portability. The military appreciates this and consumes about one-third of all the plasma-panel displays manufactured. Because of the expense involved, consumer products rarely make use of plasma displays.

Another interesting flat-panel, point-plotting display is the liquid-crystal dot matrix. Since this technology relies on reflected ambient light, rather than self-illumination, to produce a display, its power requirements are practically infinitesimal. In appearance, the display consists of crisp, black dots on a white background. The resolution of an LCD display is still inferior to that of a raster-scan

CRT, and the overall size of the few LCD graphic displays that have appeared is relatively small. Still, this is a technology that bears watching. As time goes on, larger displays with better resolution will undoubtedly be produced.

The Random-Scan CRT

The only difference between the raster- and random-scan CRT is that the latter is a line-drawing device, whereas the former plots points. As far as the physical construction of the tube is concerned, there is no difference between the two types. Whether the display plots points or draws lines is determined entirely by the support circuits that feed information to the tube.

Fig. 10-1. On a random-scan CRT, the electron beam traverses a path that includes only the significant lines of an image. For instance, the rectangle above is first drawn in 1-2-3-4-1 vertex order. The beam is then turned off and deflected to the vertex 5 of the triangle.

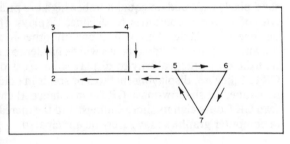

The best way to explain the distinction between random and raster scanning is with an example. Suppose the rectangle and triangle in Fig. 10-1 are to be displayed on a random-scan CRT. Starting at vertex 1, the electron beam is turned on, and the deflection circuits begin sweeping the beam to the left on the CRT screen. The vertices of the rectangle are traversed in 1-2-3-4-1 order by the beam, which remains on all the time. The resulting image consists of smooth, straight lines (white or green) on a black field. To trace out the triangle, the beam is turned off and deflected to vertex 5 of the triangle. No line appears between vertices 1 and 5. Next, the beam intensity is returned to full strength, and the deflection circuits make the electron beam traverse the triangle in 5-6-7-5 vertex order. Finally, the beam is turned off again and returned to its starting point, vertex 1, by the deflection circuits. Naturally, the CRT image must be continuously refreshed to keep it from fading away, so the whole process outlined here is repeated again and again.

In contrast to the raster-scan process discussed above and in Chapter Two, random-scanning wastes no time with void areas of the screen; only points relevant to the image are addressed by the beam-deflection circuits. All figures are drawn as collections of smooth, straight lines; this applies to curves as well. The display can be updated quickly, which makes realistic animation possible. But figures must consist only of lines, since solid areas cannot be efficiently represented. Consequently, the user must resort to using wire-frame diagrams to display solid objects. (Wire-frame diagrams look like a "skeleton" of wires. They define only the surface contours of an object, and allow the viewer to see right through the lattice.) Only a limited range of beam intensities is employed on random-scan CRTs: full on, off, and maybe an intermediate value. Thus, it may be possible to highlight certain lines, but not to display a wide range of gray levels. Theoretically, the shadow-mask CRT could be scanned in random fashion to yield a color display, but the relatively limited resolution and low light output of the shadow-mask tube have discouraged its use in random-scan applications. Random scanning's formerly important characteristic, that of demanding less memory than raster scanning, means less and less as the cost of semiconductor memory continues to plummet. Interactive terminals intended for engineering design work are the natural habitat of the random-scan CRT.

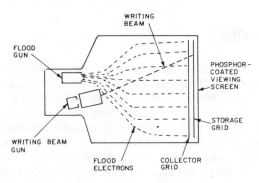

Fig. 10-2. The direct-view storage tube.

The Direct-View Storage Tube

Like the plasma panel, the direct-view storage tube (DVST) possesses an inherent image memory, which makes continuous refreshing of this line-drawing display unnecessary. This was important at the time the DVST was introduced (1968), because the memory consumed by a refresh display was expensive. Today, this advantage has lost much of its earlier significance, but the stability and resolution of displays produced on the DVST remain excellent.

Figure 10-2 illustrates the construction of the storage tube. The writing-beam gun, which is very much like the electron gun in a CRT, emits a focused beam that can be deflected horizontally and vertically—again, just as in a CRT. The important difference here is that, instead of writing on a phosphor-coated screen, the beam deposits a pattern of positive charge on a dielectric-coated wire mesh, the storage grid. A separate electron gun, known as a flood gun, bombards the storage grid with a broad shower of electrons. Regions of positive charge on the storage grid attract these electrons, which then pass right through the grid to hit the phosphor screen. There they produce a luminous image. Most flood electrons ricochet off negative regions of the grid and, consequently, never reach the screen. The collector grid located before the storage grid serves mainly to smooth out the flow of flood electrons. An image drawn on the screen of the DVST will remain visible for up to an hour. Getting rid of the image sooner than that requires the application of a positive voltage to the storage grid for a second or more. This produces a bright green flash on the screen and obliterates the old image.

An image appears on the DVST line by line. New lines can be added to an image by the operator, but it is impossible to selectively erase any particular line from the display. Instead, the entire screen must be erased, after which the image is redrawn minus one or more lines. Because of this, the storage tube is not conducive to interactive work. Not only is the green flash that accompanies each erasure annoying, it precludes any attempt at producing smooth animation. Another potential limitation is that the only color available is green, and that in only one intensity. In light of these shortcomings, the use of the DVST is primarily limited to engineering work, where the stability and high resolution of its displays are of overriding importance.

HARD-COPY DEVICES

Hard copy generally refers to an image on paper, though it can also mean a color slide or mylar transparency. There are many ways to convert an image from digital form into tangible copy, and new ones are continually being developed. This is especially true with regard to color reproduction, where considerable activity has taken place of late. It is safe to assume that the emergence of low-cost computers with color-graphic capability has provided much of the impetus behind the development of color hard-copy equipment. Unfortunately, it is entirely possible for color-copy equipment to cost more than the computer that drives it. If black-and-white reproduction or low-resolution color will suffice, however, hard copy can be had at a more agreeable price.

Color Ink-Jet Printers

Several firms have adapted ink-jet printing mechanisms of the type discussed in Chapter Five to the printing of color graphics. To print color these machines use three inks—yellow, cyan, and magenta—which can be applied in combination to yield a spectrum of colors. By overlapping the available inks in pairs, it is possible to produce red, green, and blue. If all three inks are overlapped, the result is black. And by applying no ink at all to an area, white is produced by default. Thus, a total of eight distinct colors can be rendered: three by applying inks singly, four by applying inks in combination, and one (white) by applying no ink at all.

Some readers may be wondering why it is that a broader range of colors cannot be printed. After all, the three subtractive primary colors—cyan, magenta, and yellow—are theoretically capable of producing almost the entire color spectrum. The restricted eight-color palette of these ink-jet printers is an artifact of the method by which the three inks are applied. They are not mixed in the way that an artist would mix his paint; instead, they are simply overprinted, one dot above another. Since the inks (actually dyes) are translucent, incident light is able to penetrate them and be reflected from the white paper below. If two dots have been overlapped, each dye subtracts a separate component of the light that passes through it. As a result, the light reflected to the viewer's eye has a color that depends on which wavelengths have been subtracted and how completely each has been removed. If a given pair of primary colors can be mixed in varying proportions, a range of colors will be produced. But simply overlapping a pair of dyes in layers of fixed thickness produces just one color per set of dyes—the reason, of course, being that whether dye A overlaps dye B or vice versa, the same components are subtracted in the same ratio each time. Since ink-jet printers cannot mix dyes in various ratios before spraying them on paper, but are instead limited to overlapping dyes in layers of fixed thickness, the range of colors produced is necessarily limited.

There are ways around this limitation, however. On some machines, color dithering—which is to say, intermingling—can be used to increase the apparent number of colors available. If dots of two distinct colors can be interspersed in such a way that the eye is unable to resolve individual dots, the result is perceived as a new color. This technique works well, but it requires a printer of high resolution for best results. Otherwise, the individual dots will be apparent. Producing dithered color requires that each pixel of a CRT image be rendered as a matrix of dots on paper; 2x4, 4x4, and larger matrices can be used. New colors are produced by filling these matrices with various combinations of yellow, cyan, and magenta dots.

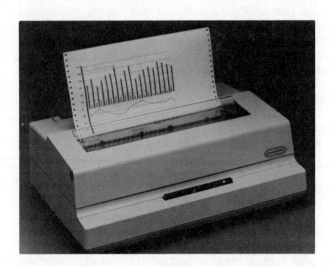

Fig. 10-3. The Printa-Color IS-8001 ink-jet printer is well suited to producing hard copy of graphics, like the bar chart shown above, as well as text. The machine prints in eight colors. (Courtesy of PrintaColor Corp., Norcross, GA)

Color ink-jet printers come in two styles: those that dispense a drop on demand, and those that selectively deflect drops out of a continuous stream (see Chapter Five for further details). Drop-on-demand printers like those from PrintaColor (Fig. 10-3) and Advanced Color Technology offer resolution on the order of 100 dots per inch, horizontally and vertically, at moderate cost. Text can be printed as well as graphics, but the blacks produced by some printers may be less than satisfactory. It is difficult to formulate three primary dyes that can be overlapped to produce both a deep, dark black for text and true red, green, and blue colors for graphics. Drop-on-demand printers typically use multiple nozzles for each of the three primary inks. In contrast, continuous ink-jet printers, like those from Applicon, require just one nozzle for each color. Continuous-jet printers are more expensive than the drop-on-demand types, but they offer very high resolution (500 dots per inch) comparable to that of a photographic print. Color dithering is therefore very effective with continuous-jet machines.

Both types of color ink-jet printer offer quiet, reliable operation and clean, vibrant colors. The higher resolution of the continuous-jet machines makes them well suited to the most demanding applications, such as computer axial tomography (CAT scanning) and satellite image processing. The drop-on-demand units have lower resolution, but for the charts and graphs that constitute the bulk of business graphics, they are ideal. In addition, these units can handle continuous forms, while continuous-jet color printers are currently limited to single sheets. Both types of printer are reasonably fast. Drop-on-demand printers can be had for less than $6,000, while the continuous-jet models can be expected to cost considerably more.

Impact Dot-Matrix Printers

Probably the least expensive way to obtain graphical hard copy is by means of a dot-matrix printer with graphics capability. In such a device, some provision is made to bypass the character generator and give the user full control over the firing of individual print needles. Typically, seven needles are used to print graphics, even if a printer has a nine-wire printhead. In this way, standard seven-bit ASCII codes can be fed to the printer to specify dot patterns. For instance, suppose that the top print wire is controlled by the least significant bit of an ASCII code, the next lower wire is controlled by the next more significant bit, and so on. Suppose also that the firing of a particular needle can be specified by setting its corresponding bit to one. In this case, to fire the top and bottom wires simultaneously, a program would have to transmit a binary 65 (1000001) to the printer. This happens to be the standard ASCII code for the letter "A." In order for the desired graphic pattern to be printed instead of "A," it is necessary to first send the printer a control code that sets up the graphics mode.

A recent development in the world of dot-matrix printing has been the introduction of color printers. These generally use four-color ribbons having lengthwise bands of cyan, yellow, magenta and black; the latter is for text printing. Although the colors are the same as those used in ink-jet printing, there are severe restrictions on how these colors can be combined. To be specific, colors cannot be freely overlapped, because the inks contain opaque pigments instead of translucent dyes. Dyes have a tendency to migrate when placed side by side on a ribbon, and this produces color contamination. To keep the bands of color well defined, pigments suspended in a mineral-oil vehicle are used instead of dyes. This solves the migration problem, but the opacity of the pigments limits the value of overlapping as a color-generation technique. (If a truly opaque ink is printed over another ink, all that a viewer will see is the color of the ink on top.) Some overlapping combinations work, but the results depend strongly on the order in which the inks are applied. As a result, it is necessary to resort to dithering and intermingling to obtain a sufficiently broad spectrum of colors.

There are other limitations to dot-matrix color-printing. For one, multi-color ribbons have shorter useful lives than single-color ribbons of the same size. Another potential problem, especially when large solid areas of color are being printed, is overheating of the printhead. The effect of this can be lessened by using a low-density dot pattern instead of solid color to fill in large areas. Still another nuisance is the tendency of color bands to become contaminated with other pigments, which may be picked up when colors are overprinted. For this reason, some printers absolutely forbid the overlapping of colors, while others place restrictions on the order in which overprinting can occur: light colors first, dark colors last.

When price is an important consideration, it is hard to beat the value of dot-matrix graphics. For the user who needs only black-and-white images, a graphics-equipped dot-matrix printer can be purchased for $500-$1,000. At this price, the buyer gets resolution of 100-200 dots per inch, plus the ability to use the same equipment for printing text. If color graphics are desired, a machine like the Prism printer from Integral Data Systems can provide them at approximately one-fourth the cost of a color ink-jet printer (about $1,600). True, there are limitations to dot-matrix color printing, but in many applications, the low price may well be the deciding factor.

Fig. 10-4. When equipped with its optional multi-pen changer, the Houston Instrument DMP-7 digital plotter can produce 11x17-inch charts and drawings in eight colors. An internal microprocessor shoulders much of the plotting burden, so programming is relatively quick and easy. (Courtesy of Houston Instrument, Austin, TX)

Digital Plotters

The dot-matrix and ink-jet printers discussed above behave very much like the raster-scan CRT: they scan every inch of a page on a line-by-line basis, laying down ink in the spots that need it, and skipping over the spots that do not. In contrast, the digital plotter is more like the random-scan CRT: it draws lines where they are needed and pays no regard to areas of the page that will remain blank. In construction, the digital plotter consists of little more than a robot arm, as Fig. 10-4 illustrates. This is a flat-bed plotter: the pen is mounted in an arm that can move up, down, right, or left over the surface of a stationary sheet of paper. In another type of plotter, known as a drum plotter, the arm moves left or right, while the paper moves up or down. With either style of plotter, the pen can be raised or lowered under control of the computer, which communicates with the plotter through a standard serial or parallel port. The pen is lowered to draw a line and raised when the arm moves to the beginning of a new line. The model illustrated in Fig. 10-4 is equipped with eight pens, which the arm can pluck one at a time from the rack on the left side of the plotter. First one color is plotted, then another, until all lines of the diagram or chart have been drawn.

Given the appropriate commands, plotters are also capable of lettering a diagram automatically. This means that a user does not need to send specific plotting instructions each time a letter is drawn. Instead, it is only necessary for the user's program to position the pen to the desired point on the page and invoke the lettering function. The plotter then takes over and draws the letters whose ASCII codes the program sends it, using letter-shape data stored in ROM. Letters can be drawn in several sizes, upright or sidewise, on most plotters.

Naturally, plotters can draw on paper, but they can also lay down an image on vellum or mylar. Vellum is used when engineering diagrams and other kinds of camera-ready line art are being prepared, while transparent mylar is needed to produce transparencies for overhead projection. Depending on the size of the plotter, sheet sizes from 8.5x11 to 48x60 inches can be used. The larger sizes are fine for engineering and architectural work, but for general-purpose office use, like preparing graphs and flowcharts, the smallest sizes are usually quite adequate. A resolution of 100, 200, or 400 increments per inch is common; the higher the resolution, the smoother the lines will appear. (Horizontal and vertical lines always appear smooth; it is the slanted or curved line that shows tiny stairsteps. In this regard, the plotter is unlike the random-scan CRT, which always draws smooth straight lines, regardless of their slope.) Maximum pen speeds are on the order of several inches per second—not blindingly fast, but since the pen wastes no time scanning the whole page, diagrams are produced in short order. Even though the plotter is basically a line-drawing instrument, it can be used to produce solid areas of color as well. To do this, it is only necessary to draw a series of contiguous, parallel lines within the region to be colored.

Small plotters suitable for general-purpose office work can be purchased for $1,000-$2,000, depending on the size of the drawing surface and the amount of native intelligence in the instrument. Having a built-in microprocessor that controls some of the plotting functions makes the plotter easier to program. Consideration should also be given to whether the manufacturer of the plotter can provide plotting software, or whether the user will be required to prepare the bulk of it himself. If an application is specialized, the user has no choice but to prepare his own software or have someone else do it for him. However, plotting the charts and graphs that constitute the bulk of business graphics is a fairly standardized affair, and plotter manufacturers often sell software for this purpose.

Direct-to-Film Equipment

At present, the most faithful means of reproducing a CRT screen, whether it be in color or gray levels, is with one of the direct-to-film recording devices that convert a video signal into a slide or print (see Fig. 10-5). In terms of the ability to render a broad range of colors and gray levels accurately, these units are unsurpassed. Furthermore, compared to the common practice of directly photographing a CRT with a camera, using a film recorder yields an image with less linear distortion. There are two principal sources of distortion that plague the efforts of those who would photograph a CRT screen: The first of these is the screen itself, which is virtually guaranteed to show some bowing of peripheral straight lines, especially if the screen is large. The other source of distortion is the camera—or, to be more precise, the person who sets it up. Using an expensive lens is no proof against distortion if the lens is not centered and its axis is not perpendicular to the screen. Not only does a film recorder eliminate distortion of this sort, it also obviates the need for dimming the room lights to get rid of screen reflections.

Film recorders can accommodate a wide range of film speeds, types, and sizes. It is possible to produce color slides or prints, black-and-white prints, and Polaroid instant photos using film sizes from 35 mm to 4x5 inches. After being exposed, all of these films, with the exception of the Polaroid materials, require photographic processing. This is the chief disadvantage of the film recorder compared to other hard-copy devices.

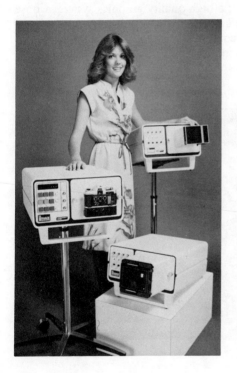

Fig. 10-5. Videoprint™ units from Image Resource convert a standard raster-scan video signal into photographic hard copy. Depending on the configuration chosen, the user can produce slides or prints in various sizes using color, black-and-white, or Polaroid film. Direct-to-film equipment such as this provides the most faithful reproduction of a CRT image. This method results in less distortion than a simple photograph of the CRT display. (Courtesy of Image Resource Corp., Westlake Village, CA)

A standard raster-scan video signal is needed as input to the film recorder. This may be a composite black-and-white or color signal, or it may consist of separate RGB color and sync signals. In any case, once the video signal is decoded, its contents are displayed on a small CRT, the screen of which is optically coupled to a photographic film. If a color print is desired from a color signal, a set of three exposures is made on the same film through red, green, and blue (or cyan, yellow, and magenta) filters. The output of the CRT is always black-and-white—hence, the need for three separate exposures through filters. Although the three-exposure approach might seem like a drawback, in fact it is an advantage, because it allows the user greater precision in the specification of color.

Three-filter exposure also permits color copy to be produced from black-and-white video signals. To accomplish this, the final image must be planned in several layers, each defined by a separate black-and-white image. For instance, in order to produce a simple color slide consisting of an orange triangle and a tan rectangle, it would be necessary to define two images—one of a triangle, the other of a rectangle—on a black-and-white computer system. First the triangle would be displayed on the system monitor, and the signal driving the monitor would be fed to the recorder, where a set of three exposures would be made. These exposures would be timed to yield the color desired—in this case, orange. Next, the second image would be displayed, and another set of three exposures would be used to put a tan rectangle on the same slide as the orange triangle. Pseudocolor manipulations of this sort make the film recorder a very versatile tool.

Film recorders are most practical with a high-quality graphics system, whose complex, high-resolution CRT images warrant low-distortion color or gray-level reproduction. Prices for film-recording equipment currently fall in the vicinity of $5,000-$10,000; simpler, stripped-down models could conceivably be made available at a lower price if the demand becomes great enough.

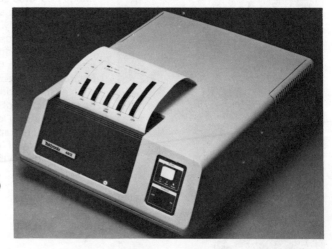

Fig. 10-6. The Tektronix 4612 Video Hard Copy Unit relies on an electrostatic process to produce economical, strictly black-and-white copy (no grays) from any raster-scan video source. (Courtesy of Tektronix Inc., Beaverton, OR)

CRT Copiers

A number of different technologies have been harnessed to the task of providing hard copy from a video signal. Unlike film recorders, the equipment under consideration here produces finished copy on paper in a matter of seconds with no need for further processing or enlargement. (Of course, a film recorder with Polaroid film produces immediate copy, but the size of such a print is relatively small.) Illustrated in Fig. 10-6 is an electrostatic CRT copier, the Model 4612 from Tektronix. Inside this unit, small belt-driven stainless-steel electrodes deposit a pattern of electrical charge on paper. This pattern, or latent image, is identical to the CRT image being copied. To make the pattern of charge visible, the paper is passed over a reservoir of dry toner, the fine particles of which are attracted by charged regions of the paper. Next, the toner, which consists of powdered carbon and wax, is fused to the paper by an electrical heating element. Momentary heating melts the wax, which later cools and bonds the carbon particles to the paper. The resulting image is permanent and ready for use in 24 seconds. Images are strictly black-and-white with no gray levels. The 4612 works with any standard raster-scan video signal, while a companion unit, the 4611, is designed to provide hard copy for storage-tube terminals.

Applications in which gray levels must be reproduced necessitate a different approach to screen copying. The Tektronix 4634 illustrated in Fig. 10-7 forms images on a dry silver photographic paper capable of rendering 12 levels of gray. The paper is exposed by sliding it past a special elongated CRT that displays just one vertical line of an image at a time. Each time the paper is advanced a small step, a new slice of the image is flashed on the CRT. Stepping and exposure alternate until the entire image has been exposed. Optical coupling between the paper and the elongated CRT is furnished by a fiber-optic faceplate, which transfers light efficiently and with no distortion. After 8.5 seconds the entire image will have been transferred to the paper. which must then be developed by applying heat. The total time from start of exposure to end of thermal development is just 26 seconds.

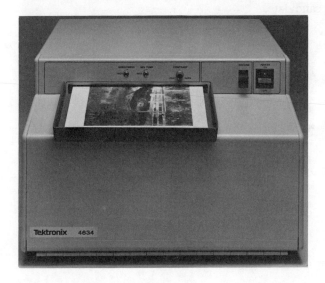

Fig. 10-7. Using a standard raster-scan video signal as input, the Tektronix 4634 Imaging Hard Copy Unit produces a con-tinuous-tone black-and-white print with 12 levels of gray in a matter of seconds. (Courtesy of Tek-tronix Inc. Beaver-ton, OR)

CRT copiers of the type described above fall into approximately the same price category as color ink-jet printers and film recorders. The chief advantages of a CRT copier are the ease with which it interfaces with a computer and the speed at which it produces finished copy. Any computer with one of the standard video outputs will work with a CRT copier; there is no need to tie up communications ports and no need for screen-dump software (that is, programs to transfer the contents of screen memory to a hard-copy device).

Conclusions

In the world of graphical hard-copy equipment, there is something for just about everyone. If cost is of major concern, a dot-matrix printer with graphics capability should be given serious consideration. Not only will the machine turn out good-looking graphics for less than a thousand dollars, it can also print text. If color is needed, there are dot-matrix printers with that capability, too, and they can be had for much less than any other color hard-copy device. For the person who produces a large number of line drawings, graphs, and charts, a digital plotter may be the best option. Plotters are capable of turning out drawings in a variety of sizes and in color. Their ability to draw on paper, vellum, or mylar makes them especially versatile. The drop-on-demand ink-jet printers offer clean, good-looking colors and images of moderate resolution. If higher resolution is needed, a continuous ink-jet printer can provide sharply detailed images that rival those produced photographically. And, if a print, slide, or negative is what the situation demands, a film recorder is the clear choice. Its video interface makes it especially easy to connect to any computer or graphics terminal that provides one of the standard video outputs. Finally, for those who want fast, full-size, black-and-white copy with a minimum of fuss, an electrostatic or fiber-optic CRT copier with video interface is a very good candidate.

CHAPTER ELEVEN
General Features of a Graphics System

Thus far we have concentrated our attention on the various pieces of special equipment used in graphics; naturally, this is only half of the story, because software is needed, as always, to make the computer do what we want. Compared to word-processing software—which has but one objective, the production of text—graphics software finds a broader range of application. For instance, graphics systems can be used to simulate airplane or rocket flight for pilot training, to model the molecular configuration of proteins and other compounds in chemistry, to design mechanical and electronic components in engineering, to provide detailed building plans and landscape layouts for an architect, or to produce animated film and special effects for the movies. In spite of the many uses to which graphics software can be put, there are certain features shared by all graphics systems. Drawing a straight line between two points, for example, is a typical function that the user can expect to find in virtually every graphics program. In the pages ahead, we will examine some of the important features and functions common to graphics software.

FUNCTION KEYS AND MENUS

Function keys of the type discussed earlier in connection with word processing can also be found on graphics terminals and computers. The only difference between graphical function keys and those used on a dedicated word processor lies in the nature of the operations performed. Typical graphical function keys might cause line segments to be drawn or erased, or they might initiate a "filling" operation that paints the interior of a closed polygon with color. If a graphics program is being run on a general-purpose computer without function keys, standard alphanumeric or control characters will be used to input commands, just as they are when word processing is done on the same computer.

The user of graphics software can also expect to see menus of the sort used in word processing, though he may make selections with a light pen or mouse instead of with the keyboard. Because of their complexity, most interactive graphics programs are menu-driven rather than command-driven. One interesting point about the menus employed is that very often they will consist of icons, or small pictographic symbols, rather than words. For instance, on a system used in electronic circuit design, a menu might be organized as a table of tiny logic gates and components, from which the designer can choose a circuit element just by pointing at the appropriate icon with a light pen. Not only do icons take up less space than text, they may even be easier to use, since pictures can be recognized more quickly than words.

DRAWING LINES

One of the most common features to be found in graphics software is a provision for the drawing of straight lines. There are several ways in which this can be accomplished; Fig. 11-1 illustrates one method. First, the cursor is positioned by means of a tablet, joystick, or other input device so that it rests at one of the endpoints of the intended line segment (Fig. 11-1a). A key is then pressed to mark the spot, and the cursor is moved to the opposite end of the line segment (Fig. 11-1b). Finally, another key is pressed, which causes a line to be automatically drawn between the two marked points, as Fig. 11-1c demonstrates.

Fig. 11-1. A common method of line drawing requires that one end of the desired line segment first be mark- ·ed by positioning the cursor (a) and striking the appropriate key. Next, the cursor is moved to the other end of the line (b), and a second key is struck.

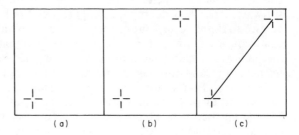

(a)   (b)   (c)

To erase this line, the user could always redraw it using the color of the background; in other words, a white line on a black field would have to be redrawn in black to be erased. Advanced systems may incorporate a special erase function for deleting a line segment or figure. In that case, the part of the display to be erased would have to be identified, usually by moving the cursor until it rests on the undesired line segment or figure. Hitting the proper key would then eliminate part of the image from the screen. Selective erasure of this sort will work only on a CRT display; storage tubes require that the entire screen be erased and redrawn—minus the unwanted line segment or group of lines.

Another means of drawing straight lines on a refresh display is the so-called rubber-band method; see Fig. 11-2. To draw a rubber-band line, the cursor is first placed at the point where the line is to originate (Fig. 11-2a). A designated key is then struck, and the cursor is moved toward the other endpoint of the line. As the cursor is moved by the operator, the system automatically draws a connecting line between the cursor and the point of origin (Figs. 11-2b and 11-2c). This connecting line is redrawn five or more times a second; hence, the line appears to be elastic, stretching between the moving cursor and the point of origin. Rubber-band line-drawing techniques are useful when a line must be placed relative to some other feature on the display. This allows the lie of the line to be continually adjusted by the operator until things are just right. At that point, hitting the appropriate key freezes the line into its final position. Rubber-band lines are easiest to implement on a random-scan CRT, where images can be updated very quickly. They are impossible on a storage-tube display, which cannot be updated at all without erasing the entire screen.

As noted in previous chapters, lines drawn on a random-scan CRT or storage tube will be smooth and straight, while those drawn on a raster-scan CRT will, on close inspection, be seen as aggregates of numerous, tiny dots. Figure 11-3 illustrates the appearance of three lines as they might be rendered on a point-plotting display. Only the vertical and horizontal lines can be considered truly straight; any other line will have a stairstep configuration. As Fig. 11-3 makes clear, a sloping line is generated from dots that lie as close as possible to the ideal straight line; however, since dots must always fall on the intersections of an imaginary grid, and not in between, they seldom lie exactly on the line they represent. The higher the resolution of the display, the smaller the stairsteps become, and the more realistic our approximation to a straight line appears. By the same token, curves will also appear more realistic on a display of high resolution.

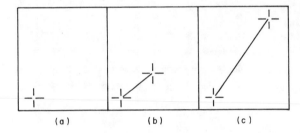

(a)   (b)   (c)

Fig. 11-2. The rubber-band method of drawing lines requires that one endpoint be defined by positioning the cursor and striking the proper key (a). Next, the operator moves the cursor toward the other end of the desired line. As he does this, the system draws a line that connects the current position of the cursor with its point of origin.

GRAPHICAL CONSTRAINTS

No matter what method is used to draw a line, it is often advantageous to restrict the placement of the line in some way. For example, suppose the operator wishes to draw a horizontal line using a joystick or a tablet as an input device. Once one endpoint has been fixed, it would be convenient if the software could be made to ignore all vertical coordinate information supplied by the input device. In this way, the second endpoint could be easily specified with no concern for accurate vertical positioning. After all, the line is supposed to be horizontal, so why bother specifying the vertical coordinate of the second endpoint, when it has to be identical to that of the first?

By ignoring either horizontal or vertical coordinate information in this way, the system is applying a directional constraint to the process at hand. The value of the directional constraint is that, by rejecting irrelevant information, it makes the operator's job a little easier. Directional constraints can be handled in software, in which case they may be enabled or disabled by touching some key designated for this purpose. They may also be an artifact of the hardware used, as when two separate potentiometers, or paddles, provide X-Y input information that might otherwise be furnished by a joystick. In this instance, leaving one paddle stationary as the other is adjusted constitutes an effective directional constraint. There are other types of constraint as well. A modular constraint limits the placement of points and lines to positions defined on a coordinate grid. This is useful in the design of printed circuitry, for example, where mounting all components in accordance with a standard grid makes automated assembly techniques possible. Under a modular constraint, any figure defined by the operator is automatically adjusted by the system so that some or all points of the figure lie on the grid, which may not be visible on the screen.

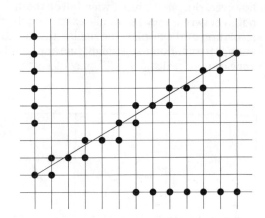

Fig. 11-3. On a raster-scan display, only vertical and horizontal lines are truly straight. Any line that slopes will consist of numerous stairsteps, as the diagonal line above illustrates. The higher the resolution of the display, the less apparent the stairstep effect will be.

COORDINATE POSITION DISPLAY

Another feature of use in the drawing of lines, and for other purposes as well, is the coordinate position display. This is nothing more than a readout of the coordinates of the present position of the cursor:

$$X = 247, Y = 156$$

Usually, this appears in one corner of the screen, though it may be turned off if the operator desires. With the help of the coordinate position display, the user can position the cursor much more accurately than he could by eye. The range of each coordinate depends on the resolution of the display; 0-200 is typical of a low-resolution screen, while a range of 0-1,000 or more is common on a high-resolution display. Naturally, the unit of measurement in each case is the pixel. Position is specified relative to an origin (0,0), which may be located in either the upper or lower left-hand corner of the screen. The coordinate display is updated several times a second so that it always represents the present position of the cursor.

DRAWING CIRCLES AND ELLIPSES

On paper, the draftsman uses a compass to draw circles; on a graphics system, the action of the compass can be simulated in software. To draw a circle, the operator starts by positioning the cursor where the center of the circle ought to be. Next, he presses a key that registers this information with the system, and moves the cursor to any point on the circumference of the desired circle. Alternatively, he might enter the radius of the circle directly as a number. In either case, all that remains is for him to touch some designated key, which will initiate the plotting of a circle of the proper radius around the desired center point (see Fig. 11-4). Ellipses can be plotted in a similar way, except that two points (the foci of the ellipse) must be specified along with the desired eccentricity, or lopsidedness, of the figure. Sometimes, what was intended as a circle comes out looking like an ellipse. This can arise when the horizontal resolution of the display does not match the vertical. Well designed software will compensate for this, so that circles do in fact look round, rather than egg-shaped. Circle-drawing functions are typically capable of plotting arcs as well as full circles.

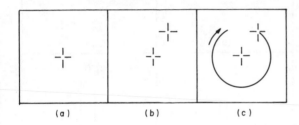

(a)   (b)   (c)

Fig. 11-4. To draw a circle, the center is first defined by positioning the cursor and touching the appropriate key (a). Next, the cursor is moved to any point on the circumference of the circle (b), and another key is struck. This causes the circle to be plotted point by point (c).

IMAGE TRANSFORMATIONS

There are three principal transformations that can be applied to any image on the screen of a graphics display; these are rotation, translation, and scaling. Transformations can be compounded, so that a figure can be rotated, moved, and scaled to a different size all at once, if necessary, rather than in a series of discrete steps. Any form of apparent movement of a figure can be produced by concatenating, or stringing together, some set of simple transformations. Figure 11-5 illustrates the effect of applying a sequence of simple transformations to a figure. The tiny rocket ship starts out in the upper left-hand corner of the display (11-5a), gets translated to the middle of the screen (11-5b), then rotated 90 degrees clockwise about its center (11-5c), and finally scaled to twice its former size (11-5d). Had we applied the same transformations in a different order, the resulting image would have been the same in this case, but this will not be true in general—especially when rotation occurs about some point other than the center of an object. Things get even more complicated in three dimensions, since rotation can take place around three axes instead of just one. In most instances, three-dimensional images are projected onto a two-dimensional screen, so some degree of imagination is necessary when interpreting the results (more on this later).

GRAPHICAL SYMBOLS

Certain drawings may be rightfully viewed as collections of symbols arranged and connected together in some meaningful way. For instance, the schematic diagrams used to depict electronic circuits consist of symbols for logic gates, transistors, resistors, and other components connected by lines that represent wires of the circuit. Similarly, the schematic of a chemical manufacturing process contains symbols for vats, pumps, valves, reaction vessels and other equipment linked by lines that represent pipes. Since the constituent elements of schematic diagrams of this kind are standardized, it stands to reason that a graphics system should generate them automatically, instead of requiring that the operator redraw each instance of a particular symbol.

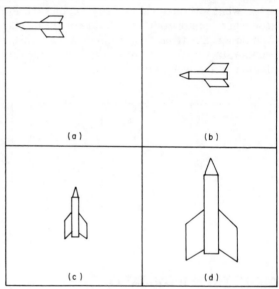

Fig. 11-5. Some examples of image transformation: A rocket ship, which starts out in the upper left-hand corner of the screen (a), is first translated to the screen's center (b). Next, the rocket is rotated clockwise 90 degrees (c). Finally, it is scaled to twice its original size (d). Rotation, scaling, and translation can be applied any number of times, and in any order.

For the sake of efficiency, then, design-oriented graphics systems customarily incorporate standard sets of symbols, from which an operator can choose specific elements as required. In addition to the pre-defined symbols, there will usually be some means by which the user can create and edit his own set of symbols. Once defined, a symbol table is stored permanently on magnetic disk, where it resides until needed by the system. The operator is free to choose the symbols he wants from a menu. Any symbol selected will appear on the screen, where it can be moved around by means of a joystick, light pen, or other input device. On some systems, the symbol appears to be dragged along by the cursor; on others, the cursor assumes the shape of the symbol. In either case, once the symbol has been positioned to the operator's satisfaction, touching the appropriate key freezes the symbol in place. Lines may later be added to the diagram to establish the necessary connections between symbols.

On a graphics system, the alphabet is treated like any other symbol set. Letters may be selected and dragged into position as described above, or they may simply be typed in starting at a point defined by the cursor and extending to the right of it. The operator can usually choose between several different fonts and character sizes, and he may even be able to design his own character sets. On a high-resolution display, even the most intricate fonts can be depicted very accurately.

INKING AND PAINTING

Although it is convenient to have lines drawn automatically by the computer, it may sometimes be more desirable to let the operator do his own drawing free-hand. This mode of operation is known as inking if the lines produced are only one pixel wide, painting if they are broader. Obviously, inking is just a special case of painting. The prime reason for making a distinction between the two is that line-drawing displays are capable only of inking. The more versatile point-plotting displays allow lines of any width to be drawn; hence, either painting or inking is possible.

The mechanism of either process is conceptually simple. Positional data from an input device like a tablet or joystick are sampled at periodic intervals. A series of dots or lines is plotted on the display at points corresponding to coordinates supplied by the input device. If a wide line is desired, not just one point but a cluster of them is plotted for each coordinate pair supplied by the input device. By varying the size of the cluster, it is possible to paint lines of different width on a raster-scan display. The on-screen line produced by painting or inking tracks the motion of the input device quite accurately. Problems arise only when the joystick or tablet stylus is moved too abruptly. In this case, the system may not respond quickly enough, and some coordinates may be lost. The result, a line with holes in it, can be avoided by moving the input device at a moderate speed.

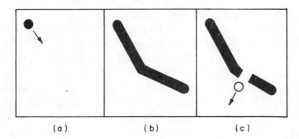

(a)   (b)   (c)

Fig. 11-6. The sequence above illustrates how a brush may be used to paint on an electronic display. If the brush is "up," it can be moved anywhere on the screen without making a mark. But if the brush is "down," it leaves a trail behind it.

Figure 11-6 shows successive glimpses of the painting process. The blob in the upper left-hand corner of the screen in Fig. 11-6a is known as a brush; it defines the width and color of the line drawn. (On a black-and-white display, the color of the brush is limited to black or white.) The brush moves around on the screen in response to the action of the input device. If the brush is "up," no plotting occurs. By pressing the proper key, however, the operator can put the brush "down" and begin painting. In Fig. 11-6b the brush has painted a broad swath across the screen. To erase a painted line, the color of the brush must be changed to match that of the background. In Fig. 11-6c a white brush has been used to erase a section of the previously painted dark line. Directional constraints of the type discussed earlier can be very helpful when horizontal or vertical lines must be drawn.

FILLING AN AREA WITH COLOR

One of the handiest features to be found on a graphics system is the ability to fill an open area with color. To do this, the operator first positions the cursor to lie somewhere within the bounds of the area to be colored. Next, he chooses a color and invokes the fill function. In response, the system floods every inch of the specified region with color, no matter how irregular the boundary of the region might be. Filling is not only a useful function, it is also one of the most dazzling, especially for a newcomer to graphics. In most cases, the user will want to make sure that the boundary of the region being colored has no holes; if it does, color will spill over into adjacent areas of the screen.

HALFTONING

The simplest and most economical way to construct a raster-scan display is with a one-to-one bit map: each pixel has assigned to it just one bit of storage. As a result, an individual pixel can be either on or off, white or black, with no levels of gray between the two extremes. For line drawings and similar applications this is entirely adequate, but what if the user needs to create a continuous-tone image? In that case, he may want to borrow a trick from the newspaper and printing trades— namely, halftoning. If a newspaper photograph is scrutinized under a magnifying glass, a pattern of ink dots of variable size will be apparent. All the dots are black; the illusion of gray levels is produced because the eye mixes the white of the paper with the black of the ink. The bigger the dots, the greater the ratio of black to white in a region, and the darker the gray appears to be.

On a CRT there is no easy way to change the size of a pixel, so halftoning is done in a somewhat modified form. The display is divided into cells of a convenient size, say, three or more pixels wide, and an equal number high. The apparent grayness of a cell is determined by the ratio of black pixels to white pixels in the cell. As a result, halftoning software can specify gray levels by turning on various patterns of pixels in a cell. Patterns must be chosen with care, since those that are too regular will produce a distracting "wallpaper" effect when spread over a large area of the screen. The declining cost of memory and the advent of low-cost color displays have made halftoning almost a forgotten art.

DITHERED COLOR

As noted in Chapter Two, one way that a manufacturer can provide a broad range of colors on a display with a limited amount of memory is by using a color map. But the number of simultaneous colors that can be displayed by a system is not increased when a color map is used. Instead, the map simply permits the user to change the colors in the display set to suit the application. Obtaining a broader range of simultaneous colors requires either the purchase of a new system with more display memory, or the use of dithered color. The latter approach is the more economical of the two and very easy to implement. Dithering is the intermingling on a CRT of pixels of various colors, which the eye fuses and interprets as a new color. For example, if blue and green pixels alternate in a region, that area will appear blue-green to an observer. Those skeptics who refuse to believe that something can be had for nothing will feel vindicated, no doubt, to learn that more colors are obtained at the expense of display resolution. Be that as it may, dithering is a very popular technique for extending the range of colors on a CRT.

THREE-DIMENSIONAL DISPLAYS

Trying to represent three-dimensional information accurately is always difficult, especially when it must be displayed on a flat screen. One common approach is the use of perspective projection, by which distant objects are made smaller than those up close, and parallel lines are made to converge as they recede into the distance. Perspective projection is not always unambiguous, but in most instances it works well. It should be noted that the job of generating the proper perspective in a scene is handled automatically by the computer, not by the operator.

Another useful, though less widely used, display technique is stereoscopic projection. This is not a new phenomenon at all, but one that first appeared in the nineteenth century. Since that time, its principal application has been as a form of entertainment. The essence of stereoscopic projection is that each eye is presented with a slightly different view of the same subject. This imparts the same sense of depth that a viewer with binocular vision gets from a true three-dimensional scene. The first stereoscopic images were captured by a camera with two lenses, which were separated by approximately the distance between a person's eyes. The pair of images captured would later be viewed with an apparatus that allowed each eye to see only one image. The viewer of a pair of carefully contrived stereoscopic images automatically fuses them to yield a scene with apparent depth.

Stereoscopic images can be projected on a CRT by alternately showing first one image, then the other. The viewer, equipped with special glasses, sees one image with the left eye, and one with the right. The glasses contain special lenses of PLZT (lead lanthanum zirconate titanate), a transparent ceramic that can be darkened by applying a voltage pulse to it. If the pulses are applied synchronously with the images flashed on the CRT, each eye will see only one of the two images. Ordinarily, each image occupies a separate field—that is, the even or odd scan lines—of a complete video frame.

Depth cues in a three-dimensional scene may also be handled by intensity modulation: near lines are made brighter than far lines. This is a fairly crude method that proves adequate only with simple scenes. On a random-scan CRT lines may actually be made brighter, while on a raster-scan CRT they will be made slightly wider. The effect is the same.

On occasion it may be possible to put the so-called kinetic depth effect to good use. If an object rotating about a horizontal or vertical axis is viewed on a flat screen, the brain receives a subtle depth cue from the relative velocity of different parts of the object. Specifically, parts of the object farther away from the viewer will be moving more slowly than parts close to the viewer, and they will be moving in the opposite direction. The effect is difficult to appreciate just by reading about it. As long as an object continues to spin, the observer has no trouble interpreting depth; once the spinning stops, however, the viewer loses his bearings and is left confused. This is particularly true of wire-frame diagrams, which are notoriously difficult to interpret.

A technique that can resolve the inherent ambiguities in a wire-frame diagram is hidden-line elimination. Figure 11-7a illustrates a wire-frame diagram of a house; Figs. 11-7b and 11-7c were derived from 11-7a by eliminating certain sets of lines. Fig. 11-7b is clearly a top view, while 11-7c is a view from the bottom. Now take a look at Fig. 11-7a and note how that diagram seems to vacillate between a top and a bottom view. Having software automatically eliminate hidden lines is an effective way to clarify a three-dimensional display. Unfortunately, hidden-line elimination is time-consuming unless special hardware is used.

On a raster-scan display, which is the only type capable of representing solid objects, three-dimensional images may require hidden-surface elimination in addition to hidden-line elimination. Obviously, the back side of an object should not be visible when that object is viewed from the front (fishbowls excepted). Although it is possible to forgo hidden-line elimination with wire-frame diagrams, hidden-surface elimination is an absolute necessity when solid objects are depicted on a 3-D graphics system. Hidden-surface elimination is a time-consuming process, especially for scenes of considerable complexity. As a result, special hardware is often used to speed up the process of hidden-surface removal on interactive systems, like flight simulators, where quick response is needed. Added realism can be imparted to solid objects by shading their surfaces so that they appear to be illuminated by a directional light source. Simple graphics software will usually avoid solid 3-D objects altogether because representing them accurately is such a complicated process.

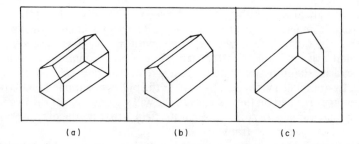

(a)   (b)   (c)

Fig. 11-7. Much of the ambiguity in a wire-frame diagram is removed when hidden lines are eliminated. In this case, figures (b) and (c) are obviously top and bottom views, respectively, of a house. Figure (a)—from which (b) and (c) were derived—is confusing because it can be interpreted as either a top or a bottom view.

In spite of the various tricks discussed above, flat-screen displays of three-dimensional objects are never completely convincing, though they are usually adequate. When something better is desired, however, and money is no object, there is equipment capable of projecting a true 3-D image. One system based on a vibrating mirror mechanism costs in the vicinity of $100,000. In the future, holographic displays may revolutionize the field of 3-D graphics, but for now, most users will have to be content with a flat-screen display.

CHAPTER TWELVE
Business Graphics Software

Having discussed the various features of graphics hardware and software, we are now ready to take a look at some of the useful things that a graphics system can do. In particular, the emphasis here will be on business graphics, which, for the sake of the present discussion, will be taken to include almost anything graphic, with the notable exception of games and engineering-design software. There may be some disagreement over this definition of business graphics. After all, there is probably some context in which games might be considered valid forms of business software with a serious purpose. And engineering-design software is certainly relevant to the business of engineering. Nevertheless, it does seem that the notion of games as business software is far-fetched at best, and that engineering design is far too complex and esoteric a discipline to be of interest here. Therefore, these two topics will not be considered further, though it would be well to point out that the information presented in previous chapters is as relevant to games and engineering design as it is to business graphics.

The field of business graphics is an exciting one that is just now coming into its own. Many new software products have been introduced in recent months, and even more can be expected as manufacturers compete for their share of a potentially lucrative market. From the standpoint of the consumer, this is good news because it means there will be a substantial array of products from which to choose. It also means that those persons unacquainted with graphics software may end up bewildered by it all. To help put the business-graphics market in better perspective, the remainder of this book is devoted to a survey of some of the types of software available now.

GRAPH AND CHART PLOTTERS

Without a doubt, one of the most useful examples of business software is the program that prepares charts and graphs automatically from data supplied by the user. The kinds of graphs that can be produced include pie charts, bar graphs, and line graphs. Some software will allow several sets of data to be plotted on the same graph, perhaps in different colors, so that comparisons can be made between, say, last year's sales and this year's. Figures 12-1 and 12-2 show some examples of the on-screen output of a typical graph-plotting program.

The important thing to note about graphing software is that it eliminates all the drudgery normally associated with graph plotting; this includes setting up the axcs, calculating scale factors, placing the labels, and plotting the data. All that the user has to do is enter the data in some prescribed format and select the type of graph he desires. In most instances, the operator can plot the same data set in several different ways. Thus, a line graph, a bar graph, and a pie chart could be produced in quick succession so that the effect of each presentation might be evaluated.

Certain types of data are best served by a particular type of graph. The pie chart does a good job of representing the whole as the sum of its parts. For example, most of us are familiar with government-published pie charts showing how a typical tax dollar has been spent. Each wedge of a pie chart depicts the relative contribution of a part to the whole in a way that is easier to comprehend than a table of statistics.

Fig. 12-1. A typical pie chart produced by an automatic graphing and plotting program. Pie charts are useful in depicting proportional relationships of data.

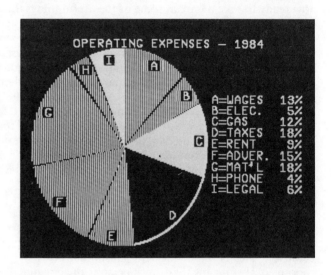

Data representing a time series can be handled effectively by means of a bar chart or a standard line graph. In both cases, time in months or years would be plotted along the X axis, while productivity or some other function would occupy the Y axis. In general, a functional relationship between two sets of data can be handled equally well by a bar chart or a line graph, though continuous functions or large data sets will usually be more at home on the line graph. Some graph plotters will work with mathematically defined functions as well as data sets. For example, a user might be curious to know what the following equation looks like:

$$Y = X\sin(1/X)$$

To find out, he would have to enter the function above along with the domain, or set of X values, that he was interested in. Not all graph plotters will accept mathematical equations; some just work with user-supplied sets of X and Y data values. As an added refinement, advanced graph-plotting software may perform various statistical analyses (standard deviation, etc.) in addition to plotting data.

Once a graph has been plotted, the user will probably want to produce hard copy. Some plotting programs are compatible with a specific brand of graphics-equipped dot-matrix printer. But if the program being used lacks this capability, or if the particular printer that it requires is not available, two options exist. One is to use a screen-dump program that transfers the contents of display memory to whatever hard-copy device is at hand. The other is to use a CRT copier with a video interface. As explained in Chapter Ten, a machine with a video interface can extract all the data it needs to reconstruct a display from the video signal that feeds the system's monitor. No screen-dump program is needed.

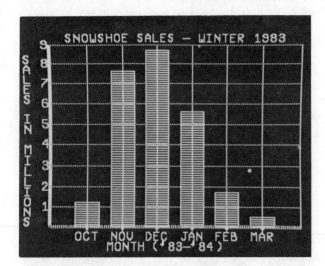

Fig. 12-2. Another useful type of diagram that can be produced by graph-plotting software is the bar graph. Labeling, axis scaling, and plotting are all handled automatically by the program.

TYPE-FONT GENERATORS

Some graphics programs allow for the easy design and printing of type fonts. During the design process, the program displays a grid of cells, each one of which represents a pixel of the character being designed. The operator indicates which cells should be white, and which black, for each letter of the alphabet. Any number of character sets can be defined in this way and stored on magnetic disk. Usually, a simple text editor will also be a part of the software. It allows the letters created to be typed, erased, and arranged into a document on the CRT screen. Getting the letters off the screen and onto paper requires some sort of screen-dump program and hard-copy device, or a CRT copier with video interface. The fancy copy created can be reproduced by photocopying or offset printing and incorporated into advertising, letterheads, and so forth. If the output of the printer or other hard-copy device is photoreduced, it will look very sharp—in some cases, indistinguishable from typeset text.

TWO-DIMENSIONAL AND THREE-DIMENSIONAL DRAWING PROGRAMS

A very useful and versatile type of graphics software is the program that allows diagrams to be composed electronically. Figure 12-3 illustrates a flowchart of a chemical process that was prepared on an Apple II using The Complete Graphics System, a very good drawing program from Penguin Software. Examination of Fig. 12-3 will reveal that the drawing is in fact composed of a limited number of unique picture elements: tanks, cylinders, valves (bow-tie shapes), and arrow heads. Since these primitive elements are repeated numerous times in the diagram, it made sense to define them as symbols. In this way, each element would have to be drawn only once.

Defining the symbol set took about 45 minutes, a good portion of which was devoted to learning how to use the system. An experienced operator should be able to define a simple figure in less than five minutes. In any event, once defined, a symbol set is saved on disk so that it may be called up whenever needed. Thus, if the operator is mainly interested in diagrams of a particular type, such as flow-charts or electronic schematics, he would define the necessary symbol set just once.

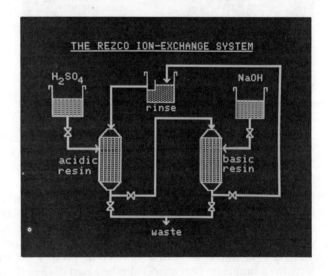

Fig. 12-3. A schematic diagram of a chemical process produced using a 2-D drawing program. Tanks, valves, arrowheads, and cylinders were treated as graphical symbols, which were first defined, then arranged on the screen. Connecting pipes were painted in.

Building the final diagram out of symbols proved to be a pleasure. After a symbol was called up, it was translated and rotated into position on the screen using the Apple's paddles, and then frozen into place. A coordinate display helped ensure that each symbol was positioned very accurately. Once everything was in place, the interconnecting pipes were painted in using a small brush controlled by paddles. (The terminology used here was introduced in the previous chapter.) Next, the tanks and cylinders were filled with various dithered colors, which showed up on a black-and-white monitor as dot patterns of interesting texture. These may be visible if the figure is examined closely. The final step in preparing the diagram was the addition of labels, which were easily typed in from the keyboard. The finished image was saved on disk and later photographed for this book. If hard copy had been desired, a screen-dump program would have been needed to extract the contents of display memory.

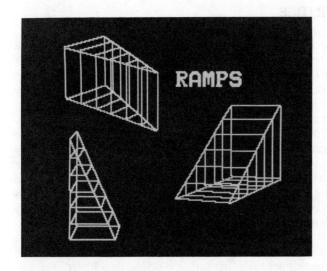

Fig. 12-4. A design created with the help of a 3-D drawing program. After a ramp had been defined mathematically, these images of the same ramp were generated. These were then rotated, scaled, and translated to produce three different views of the ramp.

The same software package was used to produce the three-dimensional design in Fig. 12-4. First, a ramp was defined as a set of 26 vertices and 29 lines. The numerical coordinates of each vertex were entered into the system, and the connecting lines were defined in terms of the vertices they joined. This was the hard part, and it took about ten minutes. Of course, a ramp could have been defined more compactly with just six vertices and nine lines, but a wire-frame diagram is sometimes easier to interpret when cross-sections of the figure have been drawn in.

The system was requested to draw the same ramp three times. In each instance, the image of the ramp was rotated, translated, and scaled until the desired effect had been obtained. Note that these manipulations were performed independently on each of the three ramps in Fig. 12-4, and that each ramp was derived from the same data set. Here is where the power of a true 3-D graphics program lies: once defined, an object can be viewed at any distance and from every conceivable angle. There is no need for the operator to draw front, back, and side views separately. After the three ramps had been arranged in the desired pattern, lettering was added and the picture was saved on disk. Later, the finished drawing was retrieved from disk and photographed.

Close inspection of Fig. 12-4 will reveal the stairstep nature of sloping lines, which gives away the fact that this diagram was prepared on a raster-scan system. On a high-resolution system, these stairsteps would not be apparent, though they would of course still be there. Solid 3-D objects are much more of a challenge than wire-frame diagrams, and powerful graphics-oriented computers, rather than personal computers, are needed to handle them. Even so, Figs. 12-3 and 12-4 bear witness to the variety of interesting things that can be done with a personal computer and the right software. Finally, let us note that the programs discussed in this section should not be confused with engineering-design software; they are instead just drafting programs. Computer-assisted engineering entails much more than the production of diagrams.

SCREEN-DUMP UTILITIES

It has been mentioned several times in the course of this chapter that there must be some way to transfer the contents of display memory to a hard-copy device if printed output is desired. A program that does this is known as a screen-dump utility, though the process might be more accurately termed a screen-memory dump. In any event, the important point to be made with regard to screen-dump programs is that they are machine-specific. In other words, a particular screen-dump utility works with one brand of computer and one type of hard-copy device.

A screen-dump program must not only extract the contents of certain memory locations, it must do this in the proper chronological order. For example, the printhead of a dot-matrix or ink-jet printer scans a sheet of paper from left to right, then returns to the left margin before making the next pass, which begins only after the paper has been advanced one line. In order to work, a screen-dump utility must read display memory in a similar way, starting with the memory location that corresponds to the upper left-hand corner of the screen and continuing to the right. Once the entire line has been dumped, the program begins anew with the memory location corresponding to the first position on the next lower line.

All of this seems easy in concept, but in practice it may prove to be more difficult. For example, if a typical dot-matrix printer is used, it will be necessary to divide the display screen into horizontal lines seven pixels wide. From the discussion of dot-matrix graphics in Chapter Ten, we know that the printing of the top row of pixels in a display line will be done by the upper needle in the dot-matrix printhead, and that the second row will be printed by the second needle, and so on for all seven rows of pixels in a line. Since the printing of up to seven dots takes place at one time, data must be transferred to the printer in groups of seven bits. If the display has been bit-mapped in one-to-one fashion, each pixel can be either on or off, as determined by a 1 or 0 stored in memory. If a pixel is on when the screen-dump program reads its status, the appropriate print needle will be fired—otherwise not.

Life would be simple if screen memory were arranged in such a way that a vertical column of seven pixels was represented by a single byte of memory (with one bit left over). This would allow all seven bits to be fetched at once. What is more likely, however, is that the seven bits we seek will be scattered hither and yon in memory. To make matters worse, the allocation of display storage is different in computers of different manufacture, so a screen-dump program designed for one machine will be useless on another.

The upshot of all this is that the large number of different computers in use prevents the manufacturer of a hard-copy device from supplying a general-purpose screen-dump utility with his machine. By the same token, makers of computers do not furnish screen-dump software because of the diverse requirements of different types of hard-copy equipment. As usual, the software void has been filled by independent software suppliers. Screen-dump routines for a particular combination of hard-copy device and computer generally sell for $30-$60, which may be more than some of them are worth. Nevertheless, the user unable to write his own software has no practical alternative.

INTERACTIVE COMPUTER/VIDEO

In recent years there has been considerable activity directed toward teaming up the computer with a standard video player, usually for purposes of computer-assisted instruction. The value of video in this context is that it can often represent things more clearly than a computer simulation. This is not meant to disparage computer graphics at all, but rather to point out that there are times when a video recording is simpler and cheaper to produce than computer animation. For example, consider what it would be like to simulate on a computer all that goes on during a complex medical operation, so that students could observe and learn. Not only would the job be slow, difficult, and expensive, it would also be a waste of computer resources, since better results could be obtained by recording a real operation.

Linking a computer and a video player together expands the horizons of computer graphics. The video player provides the images, while the computer allows a user to access the information he needs in the order that suits him best. Software is usually written to pose questions about the video material, record and grade the user's responses, back up and review material if needed, and search out specific material requested by the user. In the business world, these capabilities have been harnessed to the task of training employees with encouraging results. Another application has been in the creation of a video data base containing thousands of images indexed and accessible by computer. Systems of this nature have been used to store medical slides, satellite photos, and even text. The storage density of laser-optical discs is on a par with that of microfilm, which means that a lot of information can be stored in very little space. Furthermore, information stored on video disc or tape can be accessed directly by computer, whereas microfilm-encoded material cannot.

Currently it is the laser-optical video disc that is generating the most activity in interactive computer/video, but tape units can be used as well. As has been described earlier, a reflective laser disc has information encoded as tiny, non-reflective dots arranged in 54,000 circular tracks on its surface. Both sides of the disc can be used, so this brings the total number of tracks per disc to 108,000. Each track holds one complete frame or video image. The allocation of one frame per track makes it possible for a still image to be projected by reading the information on one track continuously.

Reading is done with a small, solid-state laser, the beam of which is reflected off the spinning disc and intercepted by a photodiode. Non-reflective information-bearing dots absorb the beam rather than reflecting it back to the sensor. The chopped beam that falls on the photodiode causes it to produce a series of electrical pulses. Electronic circuits in the machine decode these pulses and convert them to a standard video signal, which is fed to a monitor. The chief disadvantage of the laser-disc player is that it does not record. Discs must be prepared by firms that specialize in video-disc recording and manufacture.

Clearly then, the video-disc approach will be economical only if the user needs a large number of discs. If the requirements of the application are more modest, video-tape systems like those offered by Cavri Systems and others may be more economical, since tape units can record as well as play back. This means that taped material can be prepared in-house. No matter whether tape or disc is chosen, however, the ability to combine video with computer-generated text and graphics has great potential in employee training, advertising, and video data storage. Readers interested in learning more about interactive computer/video technology will find the article by Daynes informative (see the Bibliography).

SOME PARTING COMMENTS

Virtually every aspect of word processing and business graphics has been covered in this book. We have looked at the differences between dedicated word processors and microcomputers running word processing programs. Word processing software for microcomputers has been discussed, as has the peripheral hardware necessary for the storage and printout of information. The myriad forms of computer graphics have been touched upon, and we have looked at both common and exotic hardware and software for producing them. In the remaining pages of this book, the reader will find a comprehensive Glossary of word-processing and graphics terminology, a handy Bibliography, and, most important of all, an exhaustive Manufacturer's Directory containing up-to-the-minute data on suppliers of hardware and software. In all ways we have tried to make this a truly professional book. We hope it will play a major, integral role in the computer decisions and implementations that management personnel and individual users will inevitably face in the coming years.

APPENDIX

APPENDIX

BIBLIOGRAPHY

Anderson, John. "UPC Bar Codes With the Centronics 737," *Byte*. May, 1981, p. 228.

Anon. "Touch-sensitive CRT screens join computers and nonusers," *Electronic Design*. October 15, 1981, p. 61.

Benson, Terry. "Graphics Capabilities for the Small Business," *Interface Age*. February, 1982, p. 66.

Brown, Bruce E. and Stephen Levine. "The Future of Computer Graphics," *Byte*. November, 1980, p. 22.

Connolly, Ed. "Printers prepare for a colorful future," *Electronic Design*. May 27, 1982, p. 99

Daynes, Rod. "The Videodisc Interfacing Primer," *Byte*. June, 1982, p. 48.

Finseth, Craig A. "Managing Words: What Capabilities Should You Have with a Text Editor?," *Byte*. April, 1982, p. 302.

Glatzer, Hal. *Introduction to Word Processing*. Berkeley: Sybex, 1981.

Krause, Robert and Nathan Walker. "Solve data-entry productivity problems with bar codes," *Electronic Design*. October 15, 1981, p. 207.

Kuhn, Larry and Robert A. Myers. "Ink-Jet Printing," *Scientific American*. April, 1979, p. 162.

Manuel, Tom. "The Hard-Disk Explosion: High-Powered Mass Storage for Your Personal Computer," *Byte*. August, 1980, p. 58.

McLeod, Jonah. "Baseband, broadband or PABX? The local net debate rages on," *Electronic Design*. February 18, 1982, p. SS-50.

——————. "Optical disks loom as replacement for tape," *Electronic Design*. September 30, 1981, p. 97.

Newman, William M. and Robert F. Sproull. *Principles of Interactive Computer Graphics*. New York: McGraw-Hill, 1979.

Perry, Robert L. "Word processing: The A to Z of Software," *Personal Computing*. March, 1982, p. 72.

Sideris, George. "Data-storage technologies step up to new levels," *Electronic Design*. January 21, 1982, p. SS-13.

——————. "Network architectures offer performance variety," *Electronic*

Design. September 30, 1981, p. SS-9.

_____. "Network hardware is key element in connection costs," *Electronic Design.* September 30, 1981, p. SS-53.

Veit, Stanley S. "Everything You Wanted to Know About Printers," *Personal Computing.* March, 1981, p. 58.

Watson, Allen. "A Simplified Theory of Video Graphics—Part I," *Byte.* December, 1980, p. 142.

_____. "A Simplified Theory of Video Graphics—Part II," *Byte.* December 1980, p. 142.

White, Robert M. "Disk-Storage Technology," *Scientific American.* August, 1980, p. 138.

Williams, Thomas. "Digital Storage of Images," *Byte.* November, 1980, p. 220.

Yencharis, Len. "1982 Technology Forecast: Office Automation," *Electronic Design.* January 7, 1982, p. 239.

Zarrella, John. *Word Processing and Text Editing,* Microcomputer Applications. Suisun City, Calif., 1980

DIRECTORY
OF
MANUFACTURERS

CONTENTS

DIRECTORY
OF
MANUFACTURERS

1. BAR-CODE READERS

ABT Inc., 12333 Saratoga-Sunnyvale Rd., Saratoga, CA, 95070, (408) 446-2013

Control Module Inc., 380 Enfield St., Enfield, CT, 06082, (203) 745-2433

Creative Equipment, 50 N.W. 68th Ave., Miami, FL, 33126, (305) 261-7866

Hewlett-Packard, 3404 E. Harmony Rd., Fort Collins, CO, 80525, (303) 226-3800

Interface Mechanisms Inc., P.O. Box N, Lynwood, WA, 98036, (206) 743-7036

Metrologic Inst. Inc., 143 Harding Ave., Bellmawr, NJ, 08031, (609) 933-0100

Photobell Inc., 26 Just Rd., Fairfield, NJ 07006, (201) 227-3613

Scanco Inc., 4 Quincy St., Norwalk, CT, 06850, (203) 853-9882

Teknekron Controls Inc., 2121 Allston St., Berkeley, CA, 94704, (415) 843-8228

2. COMPUTER FORMS, STANDARD AND CUSTOM-PRINTED

Check-Mate, P.O. Box 103, Randolph, MA, 02368, (617) 963-7694

Checks-To-Go, 8384 Hercules St., La Mesa, CA, 92041, (800) 854-2750

Moore Computer Supplies, Box 20, Wheeling, IL, 60090, (312) 459-0270

NEBS Computer Forms, 78 Hollis St., Groton, MA, 01471, (800) 225-9550

TMI Computer Forms, 680 Bizzell Dr., Lexington, KY, 40504, (800) 354-9063

Trinity Forms Co., Carrollton, TX, 75006, (800) 527-0625

3. COMPUTERS, GENERAL-PURPOSE

ADDS Inc., 100 Marcus Blvd., Hauppauge, NY, 11787, (516) 231-5400

Apple Computer Inc., 10260 Bandley Dr., Cupertino, CA, 95014, (408)

996-1010

Archives Inc., 404 W. 35th St., Davenport, IA, 52806, (319) 386-7400

Artec Electronics, 605 Old Country Rd., San Carlos, CA, 94070, (415) 592-2740

BMC Computer Corp., 860 E. Walnut St., Carson, CA, 90746, (213) 323-2600

Columbia Data Prods. Inc., 8990 Route 108, Columbia, MD, 21045, (301) 992-3400

Commodore Int'l, 487 Devon Park Dr., Wayne, PA, 19087, (215) 687-9750

CompuPro/Godbout, Box 2355, Oakland Airport, CA, 94614, (415) 562-0636

Data General Corp., 15 Turnpike Rd., Westboro, MA, 01581, (617) 485-9100

Datapoint Corp., 9725 Datapoint Dr., San Antonio, TX, 78284, (512) 690-7151

Delta Prods., 15392 Assembly Ln., Huntington Beach, CA, 92649, (714) 898-1492

Digital Equipment Corp., 129 Parker St., Maynard, MA, 01754, (617) 897-5111

Dual Systems Corp., 720 Channing Way, Berkeley, CA, 94710, (415) 549-3854

Durango Systems Inc., 3003 N. First St., San Jose, CA, 95134, (408) 946-5000

Fortune Systems, 1501 Industrial Rd., San Carlos, CA, 94070, (415) 595-8444

Harris Corp., 1025 W. NASA Blvd., Melbourne, FL, 32919, (305) 727-9100

Heath Co., Benton Harbor, MI, 49022, (616) 982-3200

Hewlett-Packard, 19447 Pruneridge Ave., Cupertino, CA, 95014, (408) 725-8111

Honeywell Info. Systems, 200 Smith St., Waltham, MA, 02154, (617) 890-8400

IBM, 1133 Westchester Ave., White Plains, NY, 10604, (914) 696-1900

IMS International, 2800 Lockheed Way, Carson City, NV, 89701, (714) 978-6966

Intelligent Sys. Corp., 225 Technology Pk., Norcross, GA, 30092, (404) 449-5961

MicroDaSys, Box 36275, Los Angeles, CA, 90036, (213) 731-0876

Monroe Systems, Box 9000R, Morristown, NJ, 07960, (201) 540-7636

Morrow Designs, 5221 Central Ave., Richmond, CA, 94804, (415) 524-2101

North Star Comp., 14440 Catalina St., San Leandro, CA, 94577, (415) 357-8500

Ohio Scientific, 1333 S. Chillicothe Rd., Aurora, OH 44202, (800) 321-6850

Perkin-Elmer Data Sys., 106 Apple St., Tinton Falls, NJ, 07724, (201) 747-7300

Prime Computer, 145 Pennsylvania Ave., Framingham, MA, 01701, (617) 879-2960

Prodigy Systems Inc., 497 Lincoln Hwy., Iselin, NJ, 08830, (201) 283-2000

Sperry Univac, 2722 Michelson Dr., Irvine, CA, 92713, (714) 833-2400

Systems Group, 1601 Orangewood Dr., Orange, CA, 92668, (714) 633-4460

TeleVideo Systems Inc., 1170 Morse Ave., Sunnyvale, CA, 94086, (408) 745-7760

Texas Instruments, Box 1444, MS 784, Houston, TX, 77001, (713) 494-5115

Three Rivers Computer, 160 N. Craig St., Pittsburgh, PA, 15213, (412) 621-6250

Vector Graphic, 500 N. Ventu Pk. Blvd., Thousand Oaks, CA, 91320, (800) 235-3547

Wicat Systems, 1875 S. State St., Orem, UT, 84057, (801) 224-6400
Wintek Corp., 1801 South St., Lafayette, IN, 47904, (317) 742-8428
Zilog Comp. Sys., 10340 Bubb Rd., Cupertino, CA, 95014, (408) 446-4666

4. COMPUTERS, HIGH-RESOLUTION GRAPHIC

Aydin Controls, 414 Commerce Dr., Ft. Washington, PA, 19034, (215)
542-7800
California Comp. Prods., 2411 W. LaPalma, Anaheim, CA, 92801, (714)
821-2011
Chromatics Inc., 2558 Mountain Ind'l Blvd., Tucker, GA, 30084, (404)
493-7000
Evans & Sutherland, 580 Arapeen Dr., Salt Lake City, UT, 84108, (801)
582-5847
Grinnell Systems, 2159 Bering Dr., San Jose, CA, 95131, (408) 263-9920
Hewlett-Packard, 3404 E. Harmony Rd., Fort Collins, CO, 80525, (303)
226-3800
Tektronix Inc., P.O. Box 500, Beaverton, OR, 97077, (503) 644-0161
Terak Corp., 14151 N. 76th St., Scottsdale, AZ, 85260, (602) 998-4800

5. COM EQUIPMENT

Bell & Howell Co., 857 W. State St., Hartford, WI, 53027, (414) 673-3920
California Comp. Prods., 2411 W. LaPalma, Anaheim, CA, 92801, (714)
821-2011
CELCO, 70 Constantine Dr., Mahwah, NJ, 07430, (201) 327-1123
Coherent Inc., 3210 Porter Dr., Palo Alto, CA, 94304, (415) 493-2111
Datagraphix Inc., Box 82449, San Diego, CA, 92138, (714) 291-9960
Eastman Kodak Co., 343 State St., Rochester, NY, 14650, (716) 325-2000
Image Graphics Inc., 107 Ardmore St., Fairfield, CT, 06430, (203) 259-1394
Keyan Industries, 196 Plain St., Braintree, MA, 02184, (617) 848-7636
3M Co., 3M Center, St. Paul, MN, 55144, (612) 733-1110
Rhyins Optical Corp., Box 393, Ridgefield, CT, 06877, (203) 438-8535
Taylor Merchant Corp., 25 W. 45th St., New York, NY, 10036, (212) 757-7700
Western Reserve Elec., 2150 Highland Rd., Twinsburg, OH, 44087, (216)
425-4951

6. CRT COPIERS

Axiom Corp., 5932 San Fernando Rd., Glendale, CA, 91202, (213) 245-9244
Aydin Controls, 414 Commerce Dr., Ft. Washington, PA, 19034, (215)
542-7800
CELCO, 70 Constantine Dr., Mahwah, NJ, 07430, (201) 327-1123
Data General Corp., 15 Turnpike Rd., Westboro, MA, 01581, (617) 485-9100
Gould Instr. Div., 3631 Perkins Ave., Cleveland, OH, 44114, (216) 361-3315
Honeywell, Test Instr. Div., Box 5527, Denver, CO, 80217, (303) 773-4700
Houston Instrument, One Houston Square, Austin, TX, 78753, (512) 837-2820

Image Graphics Inc., 107 Ardmore St., Fairfield, CT, 06430, (203) 259-1394
Image Resource, 2260 Townsgate Rd., Westlake Village, CA, 91361, (805)
   496-3317
Perkin-Elmer Data Sys., 106 Apple St., Tinton Falls, NJ, 07724, (201)
   747-7300
Tektronix Inc., P.O. Box 500, Beaverton, OR, 97077, (503) 644-0161

7. DIGITIZERS, TABLET

Apple Computer Inc., 10260 Bandley Dr., Cupertino, CA, 95014, (408)
   996-1010
Broomall Comp. Graphics, 700 Abbott Dr., Broomall, PA, 19008, (215)
   328-1040
California Comp. Prods., 2411 W. LaPalma, Anaheim, CA, 92801, (714)
   821-2011
Computervision Corp., 201 Burlington Rd., Bedford, MA, 01730, (617)
   275-1800
Elographics Inc., 1976 Oak Ridge Tpke., Oak Ridge, TN, 37830, (615)
   482-4038
Excellon Automation, 23915 Garnier St., Torrance, CA, 90509, (213) 325-8000
Gerber Sci. Inst. Corp., P.O. Box 305, Hartford, CT, 06101, (203) 644-1551
Houston Instrument, One Houston Square, Austin, TX, 78753, (512) 837-2820
Kurta Corp., 206 S. River Dr., Tempe, AZ, 85281, (602) 968-8709
Nicolet Inst. Corp., 2450 Whitman Rd., Concord, CA, 94518, (415) 827-1020
Science Access. Corp., 970 Kings Hwy. W., Southport, CT, 06490, (203)
   255-1526
Summagraphics Corp., 35 Brentwood Ave., Fairfield, CT, 06430, (203)
   384-1344
Talos Sys. Inc., 7419 E. Helm Dr., Scottsdale, AZ, 85260, (602) 948-6540
Tektronix Inc., P.O. Box 500, Beaverton, OR, 97077, (503) 644-0161

8. DIGITIZERS, VIDEO

Carl Zeiss Inc., 444 Fifth Ave., New York, NY, 10018. (212) 730-4400
Colorado Video Inc., P.O. Box 928, Boulder, CO, 80306, (303) 444-3972
Computer Station, 11610 Page Svce. Dr., St. Louis, MO, 63141, (314)
   432-7019 [for the Apple II]
Digital Graphic Sys., 935 Industrial Ave., Palo Alto, CA, 94303, (415)
   856-2500 [for the S-100 bus]
Imaging Technology Inc., 61 N. Broadway, Salem, NH, 03079, (603) 893-6415
   [for the Multibus and DEC Q-bus]
Matrox Elec. Sys., 5800 Andover Ave., Montreal, Que., H4T 1H4, (514)
   735-1182 [compatible with S-100, LSI-11 and other buses.]
Octek Inc., 7 Corporate Plaza, Burlington, MA, 01803, (617) 273-0851
   [for the DEC Q-bus]
The Micro Works, P.O. Box 1110, Del Mar, CA, 92014, (714) 942-2400
   [for the Apple II]

9. DISK DRIVES, ADD-ON FLOPPY

Apparat Inc., 4401 S. Tamarac Pkwy., Denver, CO, 80237, (303) 741-1778
[Apple II and TRS-80]
Chrislin Inds., 31352 Via Colinas, Westlake Village, CA, 91362, (213) 991-2254
[LSI-11]
Lobo Drives Int'l, 935 Camino Del Sur, Goleta, CA, 93017, (805) 683-1576
[Apple II and S-100]
Matchless Systems, 18444 S. Broadway, Gardena, CA, 90248, (213) 327-1010
[Heath, Apple II, TRS-80, and S-100]
Micropolis Corp., 21329 Nordhoff St., Chatsworth, CA, 91311, (213) 709-3300
[S-100]
Micro-Sci Inc., 17742 Irvine Blvd., Tustin, CA, 92680, (714) 731-9461
[Apple II]
Percom Data Co., 11220 Pagemill Rd., Dallas, TX, 75243, (214) 340-7081
[TRS-80 and others]
PerSci Inc., 12210 Nebraska Ave., W. Los Angeles, CA, 90025, (213) 820-7613
[TRS-80 and others]
Trak Microcomputer, 1511 Ogden Ave., Downer's Grove, IL, 60515, (312)
968-1716 [Xerox, Heath, Apple II, IBM, and TRS-80]

10. DISK DRIVES, ADD-ON WINCHESTER

Adaptive Data & Energy, 2627 Pomona Blvd., Pomona, CA, 91768, (714)
594-5858 [S-100]
Advanced Elec. Design, 440 Potrero Ave., Sunnyvale, CA, 94086. (408)
733-3555 [LSI-11, PDP-11]
AMT, Route 30 W., Greengate Prof. Bldg., Greensburg, PA, 15601, (412)
837-7255 [S-100, Heath, TRS-80, Xerox, IBM P.C.]
Apparat Inc., 4401 S. Tamarac Pkwy., Denver, CO, 80237, (303) 741-1778
[Apple II and TRS-80]
CMC International, 11058 Main, Suite 125, Bellevue, WA, 98004, (206)
453-9777 [S-100, Heath, TRS-80]
Corona Data Sys., 21541 Nordhoff St., Chatsworth, CA, 91311, (213)
998-0505 [Apple II]
Corvus Systems, 2029 O'Toole Ave., San Jose, CA, 95131, (408) 946-7700
[Apple II and III]
Datamac Inc., 680 Almanor Ave., Sunnyvale, CA, 94086, (408) 735-0323
[IBM P.C.]
Data Peripherals, 965 Stewart Dr., Sunnyvale, CA, 94086, (408) 745-6500
[S-100; removable/fixed disk]
Data Systems Design, 2241 Lundy Ave., San Jose, CA, 95131, (408) 727-3163
[LSI-11; Winchester & floppy backup]
Executive Sys., 15300 Ventura Blvd., Sherman Oaks, CA, 91403, (213)
990-3457 [S-100; Winchester & cartridge tape backup]
Industrial Micro Systems, 628 N. Eckhoff, Orange, CA, 92668, (714) 978-6966
[S-100; Winchester w/removable hard-disk backup]
Lobo Drives Int'l, 935 Camino Del Sur, Goleta, CA, 93017, (805) 683-1576

[Apple II and S-100]
Micropolis Corp., 21329 Nordhoff St., Chatsworth, CA, 91311, (213) 709-3300
[S-100]
Morrow Designs, 5221 Central Ave., Richmond, CA, 94804, (415) 524-2101
[S-100]
Nestar Systems Inc., 430 Sherman Ave., Palo Alto, CA, 94306. (415) 327-0125
[Apple II]
Percom Data Co., 11220 Pagemill Rd., Dallas, TX, 75243, (214) 340-7081
[TRS-80 and others]
Quality Computer Services, 178 Main St., Metuchen, NJ, (201) 548-2135
[Apple II, Heath, S-100, IBM P.C.]
Zobex, 7343 J. Ronson Rd., San Diego, CA, 92111, (714) 571-6971
[S-100 and IBM P.C.]

11. INTERACTIVE COMPUTER/VIDEO SYSTEMS

Allen Communications, 3004 Arapahoe Ave., Boulder, CO, 80303, (303) 449-2971
Cavri Systems, 26 Trumbull St., New Haven, CT, 06511, (203) 562-4979
Coloney Prods., 1248 Blountstown Hwy., Tallahassee, FL, 32304, (904) 575-0691
New Media Graphics, 139 Main St., Cambridge, MA, 02142, (617) 547-4344
Ron Lane/Positron, 30 Lincoln Pl., Suite 3S, NY, NY, 10023, (212) 586-1666
Video Associates Labs, 2304 Hancock Dr., Austin, TX, 78756, (512) 459-5684
Wicat Systems, 1875 South State St., Orem, UT, 84057, (801) 224-6400

12. MODEMS

Anderson Jacobson Inc., 521 Charcot Ave., San Jose, CA, 95131, (408) 263-8520
Bizcomp, P.O. Box 7498, Menlo Park, CA, 94025, (415) 966-1545
ComData Corp., 7900 N. Nagle Ave., Morton Grove, IL, 60053, (312) 470-9600
General Atronics, 1200 E. Mermaid Ln., Philadelphia, PA, 19118, (215) 233-4100
General DataComm Industries, 1 Kennedy Dr., Danbury, CT, 06810, (203) 797-0711
Hayes Micro. Prods, 5835 Peachtree Crs. E, Norcross, GA, 30092, (404) 449-8791
MJF Enterprises, 921 Louisville Rd., Starkville, MS, 39759, (601) 323-5869
Novation Inc., 18664 Oxnard St., Tarzana, CA, 91356, (213) 996-5060
Omnitec Data, 2405 S. 20th St., Phoenix, AZ, 85034, (602) 258-8244
Penril Corp., 5520 Randolph Rd., Rockville, MD, 20852, (301) 881-8151
Prentice Corp., 266 Caspian Dr., Sunnyvale, CA, 94086, (408) 734-9810
Racal-Vadic Inc., 222 Caspian Dr., Sunnyvale, CA, 94086, (408) 744-0810
Universal Data Sys., 5000 Bradford Dr., Huntsville, AL, 35805, (205) 837-8100

13. NETWORK EQUIPMENT (INTEGRATED HARDWARE & SOFTWARE)

Action Computer Enterprise, 55 W. Del Mar, Pasadena, CA, 91105, (213)
 793-2440 ["Discovery" multiprocessor; up to 16 terminals; MP/M op. sys.]
3COM Corp., 1390 Shorebird Way, Mountain View, CA, 94043, (415)
 961-9602 ["Ethernet" equipment]
Corvus Systems Inc., 2029 O'Toole Ave., San Jose, CA, 95131, (408) 946-7700
 ["Omninet" links up to 64 personal computers of various kinds]
Datapoint Corp., 9725 Datapoint Dr., San Antonio, TX, 78284, (512)
 690-7151 ["ARC" joins proprietary computers and digital PABX]
Destek Group, 1923 Landings Dr., Mountain View, CA, 94043, (415) 968-4593
 ["DesNet" links even dissimilar processors together]
Intertec Data Sys., 2300 Broad River Rd., Columbia, SC, 29210, (803)
 798-9100 ["CompuStar" accommodates up to 255 terminals]
Lanier Business Prods, 1700 Chantilly Dr. NE, Atlanta, GA, 30324, (404)
 329-8000 [dedicated word processors can be clustered to share resources]
Modcon Div., Gould Inc., Box 83, Andover, MA, 01810, (617) 475-4700
 ["Modway" for industrial applications]
Nestar Sys. Inc., 2585 E. Bayshore Rd., Palo Alto, CA, 94303, (415) 493-2223
 ["Cluster/One" joins as many as 65 Apple IIs together]
Prime Computer, 145 Pennsylvania Ave., Framingham, MA, 01701, (617)
 879-2960 ["Primenet" for firm's minicomputers]
Proteon Associates, 24 Crescent St., Waltham, MA, 02154, (617) 894-1980
 ["Pronet"; ring; for LSI-11, PDP-11 and other equipment]
Rolm Corp., 4900 Old Ironsides Dr., Santa Clara, CA, 95050, (408) 988-2900
 [Digital PBX handles voice and data traffic]
Ungermann-Bass, 2560 Mission College, Santa Clara, CA, 95050, (408)
 496-0111 ["Net/One" can be set up for broadband or baseband use]
Wang Laboratories, 1 Industrial Ave., Lowell, MA, 01851, (617) 459-5000
 ["WangNet"; broadband voice/data/video]
Xerox Corp., 317 Main St. E., Rochester, NY, 14445, (716) 586-6335
 ["Ethernet" high-performance baseband system]
Zilog Inc., 10340 Bubb Rd., Cupertino, CA, 95014, (408) 446-4666
 ["Z-Net" general-purpose office network]

14. OPTICAL CHARACTER-RECOGNITION EQUIPMENT

Astronautics Corp. of America, Box 523, Milwaukee, WI, 53201, (414)
 671-5500
Burroughs Corp., OCR Sys., 9 Ray Ave., Burlington, MA, 01803, (617)
 273-2222
Dest Data Corp., 2380 Bering Dr., San Jose, CA, 95131, (408) 946-7100
Key Instr. Inc., 1520 W. Rosecrans Ave., Gardena, CA, 90249, (213) 324-1194
Lundy Elec. & Sys. Inc., 1 Robert Ln., Glen Head, NY, 11545, (516) 671-9000
Research Tech. Int'l, 4700 Chase Ave., Lincolnwood, IL, 60646, (312)
 677-3000
Scan-Optics Inc., 22 Prestige Park, E. Hartford, CT, 06108, (203) 289-6001

15. PLOTTERS

Broomall Computer Graphics, 700 Abbott Dr., Broomall, PA, 19008, (215) 328-1040

California Computer Prods, 2411 W. LaPalma, Anaheim, CA, 92801, (714) 821-2011

Gerber Scientific Instr. Co., Box 305, Hartford, CT, 06101, (203) 644-1551

Hewlett-Packard, 3404 E. Harmony Rd., Fort Collins, CO, 80525, (303) 226-3800

Houston Instrument, One Houston Square, Austin, TX, 78753, (512) 837-2820

Image Graphics Inc., 107 Ardmore St., Fairfield, CT, 06430, (203) 259-1394

Megatek Corp., 3931 Sorrento Valley Blvd., San Diego, CA, 92121, (714) 455-5590

Nicolet Instr. Corp., 2450 Whitman Rd., Concord, CA, 94518, (415) 827-1020

Numonics Corp., 418 Pierce St., Lansdale, PA, 19446, (215) 362-2766

Pedersen Instr., 2772 Camino Diablo, Walnut Creek, CA, 94596, (415) 937-3630

Printronix Inc., 17421 Derian Ave., Irvine, CA, 92713, (714) 549-7700

Radio Shack, 700 One Tandy Center, Fort Worth, TX, 76102, (817) 390-3011

Rapidata Inc., 20 New Dutch Lane, Fairfield, NJ, 07006, (201) 227-0035

Strobe Inc., 897 Independence Ave., Mountain View, CA, 94043, (415) 969-5130

Tektronix Inc., P.O. Box 500, Beaverton, OR, 97077, (503) 644-0161

Watanabe Instr. Corp., 3186 Airway, Costa Mesa, CA, 92626, (714) 546-5344

16. PRINTERS, CONVERTED-TYPEWRITER

Actek, 12225 S.W. 2nd St., Suite 200, Beaverton, OR, 97075 [Olivetti]

Bytewriter, 125 Northview Rd., Ithaca, NY, 14850, (607) 272-1132 [Olivetti]

Dataface Inc., 2372A Walsh Ave., Santa Clara, CA, 95050, (408) 727-6704 [Olympia ES or Remington 200]

Howard Industries, 2051 E. Cerritos Ave., Anaheim, CA, 92806, (714) 778-3443 [Olivetti]

Mediamix, P.O. Box 67B57, Los Angeles, CA, 90067, (213) 475-9949 [IBM Electronic]

Network Data Sys., 1500 NW 62 St., Ft. Lauderdale, FL, 33309, (305) 772-9320 [IBM Selectric]

Vista Computer Co., 1317 E. Edinger, Santa Ana, CA, 92705, (714) 953-0523 [IBM Electronic; card fits in Apple II slot]

Xymec, 17795 Skypark Circle, Suite G, Irivine, CA, 92714, (714) 557-8501 [Olivetti]

17. PRINTERS, DAISY-WHEEL

BDS Corp., 115 Independence Dr., Menlo Park, CA, 94025, (415) 326-2115

C. Itoh Electronics Inc., 666 Third Ave., New York, NY, 10017, (212) 682-0420

Datapoint Corp., 9725 Datapoint Dr., San Antonio, TX, 78284, (512) 690-7151

Dataproducts Corp., 6200 Canoga Ave., Woodland Hills, CA, 91365, (213) 887-8451

Diablo Systems, 24500 Industrial Blvd., Hayward, CA, 94545, (415) 786-5000

NEC Information Systems, 5 Militia Dr., Lexington, MA, 02173, (617) 862-3121

Olivetti Inc., 505 White Plains Rd., Tarrytown, NY, 10591, (914) 631-3000

Qume Inc., 2350 Qume Dr., San Jose, CA, 95131, (408) 942-4000

Radio Shack, 700 One Tandy Center, Ft. Worth, TX, 76102, (817) 390-3011

Smith-Corona Inc., 65 Locust Ave., New Canaan, CT, 06840, (203) 972-1471

SSI Inc., 2841 Cypress Creek Dr., Ft. Lauderdale, FL, 33309, (305) 979-1000

Wang Laboratories, 1 Industrial Ave., Lowell, MA, 01851, (617) 459-5000

Xerox Corp., Xerox Square, Rochester, NY, 14644, (716) 423-3411

18. PRINTERS, DOT-MATRIX

Amperex Inc., 230 Duffy Ave., Hicksville, NY, 11802, (516) 931-6200

Anacom General Corp., 1116 E. Valencia Dr., Fullerton, CA, 92631, (714) 992-0223

Anadex Inc., 9825 DeSoto Ave., Chatsworth, CA, 91311, (213) 998-8010

Axiom Corp., 1014 Griswold Ave., San Fernando, CA, 91340, (213) 365-9521

Centronics Data Computer Corp., 1 Wall St., Hudson, NH, 03051, (603) 883-0111

C. Itoh Electronics Inc., 666 Third Ave., New York, NY, 10017, (212) 682-0420

Data General Corp., 15 Turnpike Rd., Westborough, MA, 01581, (617) 485-9100

Dataproducts Corp., 6200 Canoga Ave., Woodland Hills, CA, 91365, (213) 887-8000

Data Royal, 235 Main Dunstable Rd., Nashua, NH, 03060, (603) 883-4157

Datasouth Corp., 4216 Stuart Andrew Blvd., Charlotte, NC, 28210, (704) 523-8500

Digital Equipment Corp., 1 Iron Way, Marlborough, MA, 01752, (617) 493-4622

DIP Inc., 745 Atlantic Ave., Boston, MA, 02111, (617) 482-4214

Eaton Printer Prods., Technical Ind'l Pk., Riverton, WY, 82501, (307) 856-4821

Epson America Inc., 23844 Hawthorne Blvd., Torrance, CA, 90505, (213) 378-2220

Facit Data Products, 66 Field Point Rd., Greenwich, CT, 06830, (203) 622-9150

General Electric Co., GE Drive, Waynesboro, VA, 22980, (703) 949-1000

Heath Co., Benton Harbor, MI, 49022, (616) 982-3200

Infoscribe, 2720 S. Croddy Way, Santa Ana, CA, 92704, (714) 641-8595

Integral Data Systems, Milford, NH, 03055, (603) 673-9100 ·

Integrex Inc., 233 N. Juniper, Philadelphia, PA, 19107, (215) 627-0966
Lear Siegler Inc., 714 N. Brookhurst St., Anaheim, CA, 92803, (714) 774-1010
Malibu Elecs., 2301 Townsgate Rd., Westlake Village, CA, 91361, (805)
    496-1990
Mannesmann Tally Corp., 8301 S. 180th St., Kent, WA, 98031, (206) 251-5500
MPI, 4426 S. Century Dr., Salt Lake City, UT, 84107, (801) 263-3081
Microtek Inc., 9514 Chesapeake Dr., San Diego, CA, 92123, (714) 278-0633
Okidata Corp., 111 Gaither Dr., Mt. Laurel, NJ, 08057, (609) 235-2600
Printek Inc., 1517 Townline Rd., Benton Harbor, MI, 49022, (616) 925-3200
Radio Shack, 700 One Tandy Center, Ft. Worth, TX, 76102, (817) 390-3011
Sanders Technology Inc., Columbia Dr., Amherst, NH, 03061, (603) 882-1000
Star Micronics Inc., 200 Park Ave., New York, NY, 10016, (212) 986-6770
TEI Inc., 5075 S. Loop East, Houston, TX, 77033, (910) 881-3639
Teletype Corp., 5555 Touhy Ave., Skokie, IL, 60077, (312) 982-2000
Telex Computer Products, 6422 E. 41 St., Tulsa, OK, 74135, (918) 627-1111
Texas Instruments, Box 225012, MS 84, Dallas, TX, 75265, (214) 995-6611
Wang Laboratories, 1 Industrial Ave., Lowell, MA, 01851, (617) 459-5000

19. PRINTERS, ELECTROSENSITIVE

Centronics Data Computer Corp., 1 Wall St., Hudson, NH, 03051, (603)
    883-0111
Radio Shack, 700 One Tandy Center, Ft. Worth, TX, 76102, (817) 390-3011
Texas Instruments, Box 225012, MS 84, Dallas, TX, 75265, (312) 982-2000

20. PRINTERS, HIGH-SPEED LINE

Centronics Data Computer Corp., 1 Wall St., Hudson, NH, 03051, (603)
    883-0111 [dot matrix]
C. Itoh Electronics Inc., 666 Third Ave., New York, NY, 10017, (212)
    682-0420 [chain; drum]
Datagraphix, P.O. Box 82449, San Diego, CA, 92138, (714) 291-9960
    [various types including laser]
Data Printer Corp., 99 Middlesex St., Malden, MA, 02148, (617) 321-2400
    [chain; drum]
Dataproducts Corp., 6200 Canoga Ave., Woodland Hills, CA, 91365, (213)
    887-8451 [band]
Houston Instrument, One Houston Square, Austin, TX, 78753, (512) 837-2820
    [electrostatic]
Mannesmann Tally Corp., 8301 S. 180th St., Kent, WA, 98031, (206) 251-5500
    [dot matrix]
Okidata Corp., 111 Gaither Dr., Mt. Laurel, NJ, 08057, (609) 235-2600
    [dot matrix]
Printronix Inc., 17421 Derian Ave., Irvine, CA, 92713, (714) 549-7700
    [dot matrix]
SSI Inc., 2841 Cypress Creek Rd., Ft. Lauderdale, FL, 33309, (305) 979-1000
    [band]

Sperry Univac, Box 500, Blue Bell, PA, 19424, (215) 542-4213
[laser]
Trilog Inc., 17391 Murphy Ave., Irvine, CA, 92714, (714) 549-4079
[dot matrix, color]

21. PRINTERS, INK-JET

Applicon Inc., 32 Second Ave., Burlington, MA, 01803, (617) 272-7070
IBM, 1133 Westchester Ave., White Plains, NY, 10604, (914) 696-1900
PrintaColor Corp., P.O. Box 52, Norcross, GA, 30071, (404) 448-2675
Siemens Corp., 240 E. Palais, Anaheim, CA, 92805, (714) 991-9700

22. PRINTERS, NLQ DOT-MATRIX

Amperex Inc., 230 Duffy Ave., Hicksville, NY, 11802, (516) 931-6200
Anacom General Corp., 1116 E. Valencia Dr., Fullerton, CA, 92631, (714)
992-0223
Centronics Data Computer Corp., 1 Wall St., Hudson, NH, 03051, (603)
883-0111
Digital Equipment Corp., 1 Iron Way, Marlborough, MA, 01752, (617)
493-4622
Epson America Inc., 23844 Hawthorne Blvd., Torrance, CA, 90505, (213)
378-2220
Integral Data Systems Inc., Milford, NH, 03055, (603) 673-9100
Malibu Elecs., 2301 Townsgate Rd., Westlake Village, CA, 91361, (805)
496-1990
Mannesmann Tally Corp., 8301 S. 180th St., Kent, WA, 98031, (206) 251-5500
Qantex/North Atlantic, 60 Plant Ave., Hauppauge, NY, 11788, (516) 582-6060
Sanders Technology Inc., Columbia Dr., Amherst, NH, 03061, (603) 882-1000

23. PRINTERS, THERMAL

Alphacom Inc., 2323 S. Bascom, Campbell, CA, 95008, (408) 559-8000
Apple Computer Inc., 10260 Bandley Dr., Cupertino, CA, 95014, (408)
996-1010
Gulton Industries, Gulton Ind. Pk., East Greenwich, RI, 02818, (401) 884-6800
Houston Instrument, One Houston Square, Austin, TX, 78753, (512) 837-2820
Texas Instruments, Box 225012, MS 84, Dallas, TX, 75265, (214) 995-6611
Trendcom, 480 Oakmead Parkway, Sunnyvale, CA, 94086, (408) 737-0747

24. PRINT-SPOOLING HARDWARE

Compulink Corp., 1840 Industrial Circle, Longmont, CO, 80501, (303)
651-2014 ["Sooper Spooler"; for printers with standard serial or parallel
inputs]

MicroCompatible, 151 6th St., Atlanta, GA, 30357, (404) 874-8366
   ["CUE"; parallel/serial interface; drives several printers at once]
Practical Peripherals, 31245 LaBaya, Westlake Village, CA, 91362, (213)
   706-0339 ["MicroBuffer II"; fits a slot in the Apple II]
Prometheus Products, 45277 Fremont Blvd., Fremont, CA, 94538, (415)
   490-2370 ["Versabox"; parallel/serial interface]
Quadram Corp., 4357 Park Dr., Norcross, GA, 30093, (404) 923-6666
   ["Micro Fazer"; for any printer driven from a parallel port]

25. SOFTWARE, GRAPHIC

Apple Computer Inc., 10260 Bandley Dr., Cupertino, CA, 95014, (408)
   996-1010 ["Apple Business Graphics" for charts & graphs on the Apple II
   and ?II]
Avante-Garde Creations, Box 30160, Eugene, OR, 97403, (503) 345-3043
   ["Ultraplot" for charts & graphs on the Apple II]
Borland Ltd., 69 Upper Georges St., Dublin, Rep. of Ireland, ph. 1802514
   ["Microplot" implements Tektronix PLOT 10 graphics on Z-80/8080
   micros]
Business & Prof. Software, 143 Binney St., Cambridge, MA, 02142, (617)
   491-3377 ["Screen Director" allows slide-show-like presentations of charts
   and other graphics on the screen of an Apple II]
Cambridge Devel. Lab, 36 Pleasant St., Watertown, MA, 02172, (617)
   926-0869 [a variety of packages that support the firm's S-100 video boards]
Cavri Systems, 26 Trumbull St., New Haven, CT, 06511, (203) 562-4979
   [specializes in interactive computer/video on the Apple II]
Computer Station, 11610 Page Svce. Dr., St. Louis, MO, 63141, (314)
   432-7019 [Apple screen-dump utilities for various dot-matrix printers]
Context Management, 23864 Hawthorne Blvd., Torrance, CA, 90505, (213)
   378-8277 ["MBA" for the IBM P.C. and Apple ///]
Data Type, 2615 Miller Ave., Mountain View, CA, 94040, (415) 949-1053
   ["Graftalk" creates graphs & pictures on CP/M systems]
Hewlett-Packard, 19447 Pruneridge Ave., Cupertino, CA, 95014, (408)
   725-8111 ["Graphics/125" graphics package for the HP 125 computer]
Interactive Microware Inc., Box 771, State College, PA, 16801, (814) 238-8294
   ["Visichart" and "Scientific Plotter" for the Apple II]
Maxtek Inc., 2908 Oregon Court, Torrance, CA, 90503, (213) 320-6604
   [Plotting & image-generating packages for TRS-80, Heath, Superbrain]
Muse Software, 347 N. Charles St., Baltimore, MD, 21201, (301) 659-7212
   ["Dataplot" for the Apple II]
Osborne/McGraw Hill, 630 Bancroft Way, Berkeley, CA, 94710, (415)
   548-2805 ["Microfinesse", integrated financial forecasting and business
   graphics for the Apple II]
Penguin Software, Box 432, West Chicago, IL, 60185, (312) 231-0912
   [wide variety of graphics software/hardware for the Apple II]
Personal Software, 1330 Bordeaux Dr., Sunnyvale, CA, 94086, (408) 745-7841
   ["Visiplot" for the Apple II]
Robert J. Brady Co., Bowie, MD, 20715, (301) 262-6300
   ["The Graphics Generator", business and technical graphics for the IBM-PC]

SmartWare, 2281 Cobblestone Court, Dayton, OH 45431, (513) 426-3579
  ["Graf-Pak" dumps Apple graphics to various printers]
Sublogic Inc., 713 Edgebrook Dr., Champaign, IL, 61820, (217) 359-8482
  [2-D and 3-D image generation for the Apple II]
Tektronix Inc., P.O. Box 500, Beaverton, OR, 97077, (503) 644-0161
  [PLOT 10 and PLOT 50 graphics libraries for Tek graphics terminals]

26. SOFTWARE, SPELLING-VERIFICATION

Aspen Software Co., Box 339-W, Tijeras, NM, 87059, (505) 281-1634
  ["Grammatik" & "Proof Reader" for TRSDOS, CP/M, and the IBM-PC]
Datalab Inc., 617 E. University #250, Ann Arbor, MI, 48104, (313) 995-0663
  ["Proof/it" for Alpha Micro AM-100 computers]
Hexagon Systems, Box 397, Station A, Vancouver, B.C., V6C 2N2, (604)
  682-7646 ["Hexspell" for TRS-80 Models I and III]
Innovative Software, 1150 Chestnut Lane, Menlo Park, CA, 94025, (415)
  326-0805 ["Spellguard" for CP/M systems]
Microcomputer Inds., 1520 E. Mulberry, Ft. Collins, CO, 80524, (303)
  221-1955 ["Wordcheck" for Commodore PET w/ "WordPro" w.p.
  software]
Micro Pro International, 1299 4th St., San Rafael, CA, 94901, (415) 457-8990
  ["SpellStar" for use with "WordStar" w.p. on CP/M systems]
Oasis Systems, 2765 Reynard Way, San Diego, CA, 92103, (714) 291-9489
  ["The Word" for CP/M systems]
On-Line Systems, 3675 Mudge Ranch Rd., Coarsegold, CA, 93614, (209)
  683-6858 ["The Dictionary" for the Apple II]
Sensible Software, 6619 Perham Dr., W. Bloomfield, MI, 48033, (313)
  399-8877 ["The Sensible Speller" for the Apple II]

27. SOFTWARE, WORD-PROCESSING

Apple Computer Inc., 10260 Bandley Dr., Cupertino, CA, 95014, (408)
  996-1010 ["AppleWriter" for 40-column Apple II]
Charles Mann Assoc., 7594 San Remo, Yucca Valley, CA, 92284, (714)
  365-9718 ["Docuwriter" for 40-column Apple II]
Commodore Computer Systems, 681 Moore Rd., King of Prussia, PA, 19406
  ["Wordcraft 80" for the Commodore PET/CBM]
Computer Services Corp., 71 Murray St., New York, NY, 10007, (212)
  619-4000 ["Perfect Writer" for CP/M, Apple, TRS-80, Heath, North Star]
Datamont Inc., 9748 Cozycroft Ave., Chatsworth, CA, 91311, (213) 709-1202
  ["Write-On" for Apple II, Apple III, IBM-PC]
Designer Software, 3400 Montrose Blvd., #718, Houston, TX, 77006, (713)
  520-8221 ["Palantir" for CP/M systems]
Hayden Publishing Co., 50 Essex St., Rochelle Park, NJ, 07662, (201)
  843-0550 ["Piewriter/Formatter" for the Apple II, 40- and 80-column]
Hewlett-Packard, 19447 Pruneridge Ave., Cupertino, CA, 95014, (408)
  725-8111 ["Word/125" for the HP 125 computer]

IJG Computer Svce., 1260 W. Foothill Blvd., Upland, CA, 91786, (714)
946-5805 ["Electric Pencil" for TRS-80]

Info. Unlimited Sfwr., 281 Arlington Ave., Berkeley, CA, 94707, (415)
525-9452 ["EasyWriter" for Apple II, 40- and 80-column, IBM-PC]

InfoSoft Systems, 25 Sylvan Rd. S., Westport, CT, 06880, (203) 226-8937
["WpDaisy" for CP/M or I/OS operating systems]

Lexisoft Inc., Box 267, Davis, CA, 95616, (916) 758-3630
["Spellbinder" for CP/M]

Lifetree Software, Inc., 177 Webster St., Monterey, CA, 93940, (408) 659-3221
["Volkswriter" for IBM-PC]

LJK Enterprises, P.O. Box 10827, St. Louis, MO, 63129, (314) 846-6124
["Letter Perfect" for Atari and Apple II, 40- and 80-column]

Micro Pro International, 1299 4th St., San Rafael, CA, 94901, (415) 457-8990
["WordStar" for CP/M systems, the Apple II with CP/M, IBM-PC]

Muse Software, 347 N. Charles St., Baltimore, MD, 21201, (301) 659-7212
["Super Text II" for the 40- and 80-column Apple II]

NEC Home Elecs., 1401 Estes Ave., Elk Grove Village, IL, 60007, (312)
228-5900 [color w.p. software for NEC computers]

North Star Inc., 14440 Catalina St., San Leandro, CA, 94577, (415) 357-8500
["Northword" for Horizon and Advantage computers]

On-Line Systems, 3675 Mudge Ranch Rd., Coarsegold, CA, 93614, (209)
683-6858 ["Screenwriter II" for the Apple II]

Owl Software Corp., 1605 E. Charleston Blvd., Las Vegas, NV 89104, (213)
982-6243 ["Text Plus" for IBM-PC]

Peachtree Software, 3 Corporate Sq., #700, Atlanta, GA, 30329, (404)
325-8533 ["Magic Wand" for CP/M systems]

Professional Software, 166 Crescent Rd., Needham, MA, 02194, (617)
444-5224 ["WordPro Plus" for Commodore Computers]

Radio Shack, 1300 One Tandy Center, Ft. Worth, TX, 76102, (817) 890-3272
["Scripsit" for TRS-80]

SCION Corp., 8455 Tyco. Rd., Vienna, VA, 22180, (703) 827-0888
["Wordsmith" for CP/M or North Star]

Select Sys., 919 Sir Francis Drake Blvd., Kentfield, CA, 94904, (415) 459-4003
["Select" for CP/M-equipped computers]

SOF/SYS Inc., 4306 Upton Ave. S., Minneapolis, MN, 55410, (612) 929-7104
["The Executive Secretary" for Apple II]

Structured Systems Group, 5204 Claremont, Oakland, CA, 94618, (415)
547-1567 ["Letteright" for CP/M]

Texa Soft, 1028 N. Madison Ave., Dallas, TX, 75208, (214) 946-7912
["Versatext" for IBM-PC]

Vector Graphic, 500 N. Ventu Park Rd., Thousand Oaks, CA, 91320, (805)
499-5831 ["Memorite III" for Vector Graphic computers]

28. TERMINALS, GENERAL-PURPOSE

ADDS Inc., 100 Marcus Blvd., Hauppauge, NY, 11787, (516) 231-5400

Ann Arbor Terminals, 6175 Jackson Rd., Ann Arbor, MI, 48103, (313)
663-8000

Beehive International, Box 25668, Salt Lake City, UT, 84125, (801) 335-6000
CELCO, 70 Constantine Dr., Mahwah, NJ, 07430, (201) 327-1123
Data General Corp., 15 Turnpike Rd., Westborough, MA, 01581, (617)
  485-9100
Datamedia Corp., 7401 Central Hwy., Pennsauken, NJ, 08109, (609) 655-5400
Datapoint Corp., 9725 Datapoint Dr., San Antonio, TX, 78284, (512)
  690-7151
Digital Equipment Corp., 129 Parker St., Maynard, MA, 01754, (617)
  897-5111
Falco Products, 1286 Lawrence Station Rd., Sunnyvale, CA, 94086, (408)
  745-7123
General Terminal Corp., 14831 Franklin Ave., Tustin, CA, 92680, (714)
  730-0123
Harris Corp., 1025 W. NASA Blvd., Melbourne, FL, 32919, (305) 727-9100
Hazeltine Corp., Commack, NY, 11725, (516) 462-5100
Heath Co., Benton Harbor, MI, 49022, (616) 982-3200
Honeywell Info. Sys., 200 Smith St., Waltham, MA, 02154, (617) 890-8400
IBM, 1133 Westchester Ave., White Plains, NY, 10604, (914) 696-1900
Industrial Micro Systems, 628 Eckhoff St., Orange, CA, 92668, (714) 978-6966
Lear Siegler Inc., 714 N. Brookhurst St., Anaheim, CA, 92803, (714) 774-1010
Megadata Corp., 35 Orville Dr., Bohemia, NY, 11716, (516) 589-6800
Micro-Term Inc., 1314 Hanley Ind'l Ct., St. Louis, MO, 63144, (314) 968-8151
Perkin-Elmer, 360 Route 206 S., Flanders, NJ, 07836, (201) 584-1400
Ramtek Corp., 2211 Lawson Lane, Santa Clara, CA, 95050, (408) 988-2211
Tektronix Inc., Box 1700, Beaverton, OR, 97075, (503) 644-0161
Teletype Corp., 5555 Touhy Ave., Skokie, IL, 60077, (312) 982-2000
TeleVideo Systems Inc., 1170 Morse Ave., Sunnyvale, CA, 94086, (408)
  745-7760
Texas Instruments, Box 1444, MS 784, Houston, TX, 77001, (713) 494-5115
Transnet Corp., 1945 Route 22, Union, NJ, 07083, (201) 688-7800
Videx Inc., 897 N.W. Grant Ave., Corvallis, OR, 97330 (503) 758-0521
Wyse Technology, 2184 Bering Dr., San Jose, CA, 95131, (408) 946-3075

29. TERMINALS, HIGH-RESOLUTION GRAPHIC

Aydin Controls, 414 Commerce Dr., Ft. Washington, PA, 19034, (215)
  542-7800
California Computer Prods., 2411 W. LaPalma, Anaheim, CA, 92801, (714)
  821-2011
CELCO, 70 Constantine Dr., Mahwah, NJ, 07430, (201) 327-1123
Colorgraphic Comm. Corp., 2379 J. Glenn Dr., Atlanta, GA, 30341, (404)
  455-3921
Comdec Inc., Box 8050, Ann Arbor, MI, 48107, (313) 973-8422
Datamedia Corp., 7401 Central Hwy., Pennsauken, NJ, 08109, (609) 655-5400
Data Type, 2615 Miller Ave., Mountain View, CA, 94040, (415) 949-1053
Evans & Sutherland, 580 Arapeen Dr., Salt Lake City, UT, 84108, (801)
  582-5847
Harris Corp., Box 37, Melbourne, FL, 32901, (305) 727-4000

Hewlett-Packard, 3404 E. Harmony Rd., Fort Collins, CO, 80525, (303) 226-3800

IBM, 1133 Westchester Ave., White Plains, NY, 10604, (914) 696-1900

Intelligent Sys. Corp., 225 Technology Pk., Norcross, GA, 30092, (404) 449-5961

Ithaca Intersystems, Inc., 1650 Hanshaw Road, P.O. Box 91, Ithaca, NY, 14850. (607) 257-0190

Megatek Corp., 3931 Sorrento Valley Blvd., San Diego, CA, 92121, (714) 455-5590

Ramtek Corp., 2211 Lawson Lane, Santa Clara, CA, 95050, (408) 988-2211

Rockwell International, P.O. Box 4302, Anaheim, CA, 92803, (714) 632-3164

SCION Corp., 12310 Pinecrest Rd., Reston, VA, 22091, (703) 476-6100

Sigma Information Sys., 556 Trapelo Rd., Belmont, MA, 02178, (617) 484-2063

Tektronix Inc., P.O. Box 500, Beaverton, OR, 97077, (503) 644-0161

Three Rivers Computer, 720 Gross St., Pittsburgh, PA, 15224, (412) 621-6250

30. TERMINALS, TOUCH-SENSITIVE SCREEN

Ampex Corp., 401 Broadway, Redwood City, CA, 94063, (415) 367-2011 ["Touchterm 80" with integral IR touch/dele sensors]

Carroll Mfg. Co., 1212 Hagen St., Champaign, IL, 61820, (217) 351-1700 [terminal with integral IR sensors and kits to add touch-sensing to an existing terminal]

Datamedia Corp., 7401 Central Hwy., Pennsauken, NJ, 08109, (609) 665-5400 ["Excell 22T" with integral infrared touch sensors]

Elographics Inc., 1976 Oak Ridge Tpke., Oak Ridge, TN, 37830, (615) 482-4038 [transparent conductive-membrane faceplate attaches to any CRT]

Interaction Sys. Inc., 24 Munroe St., Newtonville, MA, 02160, (617) 964-5300 [capacitance-type faceplate attaches to your CRT screen]

Lear Siegler Inc., 714 N. Brookhurst St., Anaheim, CA, 92803, (714) 774-1010 [offers terminals outfitted with touch sensors from Interaction Systems on special request]

TSD Displays/Megadata Corp., 35 Orville Dr., Bohemia, NY, 11716, (516) 589-6800 [an echo-ranging approach using acoustic waves; terminals & add-on kits]

31. TERMINALS, VOICE-COMMAND

Infolink Corp., 1925 Holste Rd., Northbrook, IL, 60062, (312) 291-2900

Interstate Electronics Corp., Box 3117, Anaheim, CA, 92803, (714) 635-7210

Scott Instruments, 815 N. Elm St., Denton, TX, 76201, (817) 387-9514 [unit adds voice-recognition capability to the Apple II & TRS-80]

Threshold Technology, 1829 Underwood Blvd., Delran, NJ, 08075, (609) 461-9200

32. WORD PROCESSORS, DEDICATED

Datapoint Corp., 9725 Datapoint Dr., San Antonio, TX, 78284, (512) 699-7059

Exxon Office Systems, P.O. Box 10184, Stamford, CT, 06904, (800) 327-6666

Honeywell Info. Sys., 200 Smith St., Waltham, MA, 02154, (617) 890-8400

IBM, 1133 Westchester Ave., White Plains, NY, 10604, (914) 696-1900

Lanier Bus. Prods., 1700 Chantilly Dr. NE., Atlanta, GA, 30324, (404) 329-8000

Vydec Corp., 9 Vreeland Rd., Florham Park, NJ, 07932, (201) 822-2100

Wang Laboratories, 1 Industrial Ave., Lowell, MA, 01851, (617) 459-5000

Xerox Office Prods., 1341 W. Mockingbird Ln., Dallas, TX, 75247.

WORD PROCESSORS, DEDICATED

GLOSSARY

address—1) A location in memory. 2) To gain access to a particular memory location for the purpose of reading or writing data there.

algorithm—A step-by-step procedure by which a task can be accomplished or a problem be solved.

analog-to-digital converter—A device that converts the instantaneous value of a voltage into a digital code of some sort. For example, a 5-volt input might be converted to 101, which is the binary representation of five. A typical A/D converter will have 4-16 bits of precision and an arbitrary scale factor.

archival—Refers to the long-term, non-volatile storage of data. Information on magnetic tape lasts for approximately three years, while ten-year storage lifetimes are anticipated for the new optical discs.

ASCII—Short for American Standard Code for Information Interchange, a seven-bit digital code used to represent letters, numbers, and other characters in the computer.

backup—To transfer the contents of one storage volume to another as a precaution against equipment malfunction or operator error.

band printer—A high-speed printing device that uses fully formed type characters mounted on a rotating band. Printing takes place on a line-by-line basis.

bank-switched memory—A block of memory that can be switched in to temporarily replace an equivalent amount of computer RAM. Bank switching gives a computer access to more memory than it can address directly, but the process of switching a bank in or out increases the time necessary to read or write data.

bar code—A graphical means of representing statistical data like stock or part numbers. Wide and narrow black bars, separated by white spaces, encode the data in a form that can be quickly and accurately read by machine.

bar-code scanner—An electro-optical device that reads bar-code data. The scanner also performs error checking to ensure that the data have been correctly read.

baseband bus—A form of network in which digital data are exchanged between nodes over a length of coax cable. Contention (q.v.) usually is employed to determine which device has the right to transmit over the bus at any given time. Messages are broadcast to all nodes, but are accepted only by those nodes to which the messages have been addressed.

baud rate—A measure of the speed of serial data transmission. Dividing the baud rate by ten yields the transmission speed in characters per second.

bidirectional printing—The ability to print lines alternately left-to-right and right-to-left. Printing bidirectionally saves time and results in less wear on the print-head carriage mechanism.

bit—Short for binary digit, the smallest unit of digital information. Bits can have the value of 1 or 0, but no other. Information of any kind can be represented in the computer as a collection of bits.

bit-mapped display—If a direct correspondence exists between each pixel on the screen of a CRT and at least one unique bit in computer memory, the display is said to be bit-mapped. For black-and-white drawings, a one-to-one map is sufficient, but color or gray-level images require that multiple bits of storage be reserved for each pixel.

boilerplate document—Combining selected paragraphs from a set of standard paragraphs with a small amount of original information (names, dates, etc.) produces a boilerplate document. Contracts, business proposals and medical reports are a few of the documents that lend themselves to boilerplate composition. Word processors with boilerplate capability make document preparation especially easy.

bold printing—The ability to make certain letters darker than the surrounding text. Daisy-wheel printers produce bold letters by overstriking or shadow printing (q.v.).

bps—Abbreviation for bits per second, a measure of the rate at which data are being transmitted.

broadband bus—A network architecture in which the independent nodes converse over a common length of coax cable by means of RF modems. By converting digital data into analog signals of various high frequencies, the modems make possible the simultaneous transmission of several messages, each occupying a separate frequency band or channel. The broadband bus is therefore similar in operation to a cable TV system. Transmission rights on a particular channel are settled by contention (q.v.). Data, voice, and video information can all be handled by a broadband bus.

brush—In graphics, a blob of color that can be moved anywhere on the CRT screen by means of a joystick, mouse, or similar input device. As the brush moves, it leaves behind it a trail of color. Graphics software often provides brushes of various widths, which allow the user to literally paint on the screen.

bubble memory—A non-volatile form of storage based on mobile magnetic domains formed in a thin slab of garnet. The bubble memory is intermediate between semiconductor memory and magnetic disk in terms of cost per bit and storage density.

buffer—A block of memory, usually small, that functions as a temporary holding area for data being used by the computer system.

bus—The set of lines over which communication between the CPU and various other elements of a computer system (such as RAM or ROM) takes place. A bus can usually be segregated into three distinct sets of lines that carry control, address, and data signals. Also, the interconnecting cable in certain forms of network is known as a bus.

byte—A set of eight bits taken as a logical group. Each byte of data can have one of 256 possible binary values.

calligraphic display—Another name for a line-drawing display, that is, a system that generates all images as collections of smooth straight lines.

cartridge-disk system—A form of mass storage in which data are recorded on rigid disks coated with magnetic material. One or several of these disks may be mounted on a common spindle and housed within a protective cartridge. Since these cartridges can be physically removed from the disk drive, there is no problem with backup. However, contamination of the cartridge by dirt or dust is a potential problem.

chain printer—A high-speed line printer that uses solid type mounted on a revolving chain.

chaining—The linking together of files so that they can be processed as a group, one after the other, rather than separately.

channel—On a broadband-bus network, one of several independent frequency bands within which information is conveyed. Messages in different channels can be transmitted simultaneously over the same cable without interference. The intended recipient of a message must be tuned to the proper channel in order to receive it.

character—A letter, number, punctuation mark, or other symbol used as an element of text.

character generator—An integrated circuit responsible for converting a byte of data representing a character into a pattern of dots recognizable as that character. Electronic displays that use character generators require less memory to store a screen of text than bit-mapped displays. However, using a character generator severely restricts the types of graphics that can be displayed.

chip—Another name for an integrated circuit.

coaxial cable—A two-conductor electrical cable built so that one conductor completely encircles the other. Coax helps reduce the electrical interference generated by fast-rising digital signals.

color map—In graphics, a scheme whereby a limited number of bits can be made to do the work of more. If a bit-mapped display offers eight bits per pixel, and thus a range of 256 colors, an eight-bit-input/24-bit-output map would allow the user to choose any 256 simultaneous colors from a possible range of over 16.7 million. In addition, all of this would be accomplished without a threefold increase in display-memory capacity.

COM—Short for computer output on microfilm, the storage of textual data as tiny images on photographic film.

command-driven software—Programs that make little or no effort to guide the user with menus. Instead, command-driven software expects the operator to know what commands are available and when each is appropriate. Software of this type may be more difficult for the novice, but it allows the experienced user to proceed at a faster pace.

composite video—A signal composed of video information plus synchronizing pulses, which are needed to control raster scanning. In the case of color, three separate (red, green, and blue) video signals can be combined with sync pulses to produce composite video, but this limits the amount of picture detail that can be conveyed. Separate RGB color video is thus preferable.

computer—A machine capable of performing a virtually limitless number of functions. Each desired function—whether it be word processing, accounting, or graph plotting—must be specified by a set of instructions known as a program.

contention—A process by which nodes compete for the privilege of transmitting over a network. One of the more popular forms of contention is CSMA/CD (q.v.)

control character—A non-printing character produced by pressing the CONTROL key at the same time as one of the letter or punctuation keys. There are 32 different control codes with ASCII values from 0 to 31.

continuous form—Paper in the form of one long sheet that is pulled through a printer by tractors, pins, or rollers. Sheet boundaries may or may not be marked by perforations.

cpi—Abbreviation for characters per inch, a measure of how densely characters are printed on a line.

cps—Short for characters per second, a measure of how fast data are being printed or transmitted.

CPU—An acronym for central processing unit, that part of a computer dedicated to adding, subtracting, shifting, comparing, and otherwise manipulating data. In short, the CPU is where the actual business of computing is performed. In a microcomputer, the entire CPU will be contained in a single integrated circuit.

crash—1) A fatal collision between the read/write head of a hard disk and a speck of dust or other debris. 2) Program failure due either to operator error or an inherent flaw in the software.

CRT—Short form of cathode-ray tube, the most popular electronic display.

CSMA/CD—Short for carrier-sense, multiple-access with collision detection, a form of arbitration common on bus-oriented networks. Under this system, each node waits until the bus is silent before beginning a transmission. Since nodes act independently, it is possible for two to start transmitting at the same time, in which case a collision is detected and some form of evasive action is taken.

cursor—A small movable figure that acts as a pointer on a CRT screen. In word processing, the cursor is generally a blinking rectangle or underline character. In graphics, a small circular or cross-shaped cursor is common.

daisy-wheel printer—An impact printer capable of producing text of excellent quality at speeds ranging from 12 to 55 cps. The name is derived from the shape of the machine's type element, which resembles a flower with an abundance of slim petals.

data set—Another name for a modem.

decimal tabbing—A feature found on some word processors that automatically aligns a column of figures so that all decimal points lie on a straight vertical line, regardless of the number of digits to the left or right of any particular decimal. This is handy when financial or statistical tables are being prepared.

dedicated word processor—A machine whose sole intended function is the preparation of documents. If well designed, a dedicated word processor ought to be the easiest and most efficient way to work with words.

default—A parameter value used by a word-processing system in the absence of an explicit specification of some other value by the operator. For example, a common default value for the number of lines per page is 66. The operator does not have to specify the line density when he prints a document unless he wants a value other than 66, the default.

dictionary—A feature on many word processors that allows text to be automatically checked for spelling errors. On some systems, it may also be used to automatically hyphenate words that overlap the right margin. Dictionaries may comprise as many as 100,000 words.

digitizing tablet—A graphical input device that simplifies the job of feeding spatial data to a computer. Circuits in the tablet keep track of the position of a stylus, which the operator can move anywhere on the surface of the tablet. Pressing a button sends the current X and Y coordinates of the stylus to the computer.

directional constraint—In graphics, a limitation on the placement or motion of a point usually brought about by ignoring the X or Y coordinate furnished by an input device. For example, under a directional constraint a joystick might be able to move a cursor horizontally but not vertically. Directional constraints make horizontal or vertical lines easier to draw in some instances.

direct-view storage tube (DVST)—An electronic display similar to the CRT but with an inherent memory that eliminates the need for display refreshing. Once drawn, an image persists for up to an hour on the screen of the storage tube.

distributed control—A form of network management in which control is shared by the nodes of the network instead of being allocated to a single device. A distributed-control system does not fail catastrophically the way that a system with centralized control does when its control unit malfunctions.

dithering—The intermingling of dots of various colors to produce what appears to be a new color. The dots must be so small and closely spaced that the eye fuses them together. Dithering extends the range of colors that can be produced by an electronic display or hard-copy device.

DOS—An abbreviation for disk operating system, the software that controls the storage and retrieval of files on disk.

dot-matrix printer—A device that prints letters consisting of numerous tiny dots of ink. Dot-matrix printing is fast and economical, but the results are generally deemed not as attractive as text printed on a daisy-wheel printer.

draft quality—Refers to printed copy considered not suitable for correspondence, but good enough for most other purposes.

DRAW—Acronym for direct-read-after-write, a recording technique used with optical discs. The DRAW method results in fewer data errors, since information is checked immediately after being recorded. If errors are detected, the information is recorded again on a new part of the disc, and the bad sectors are ignored.

dumb terminal—Equipment of this sort performs two basic functions: It sends what the operator types on a keyboard to the computer, and displays the computer's response on a CRT or other display. Editing functions, if present, will be primitive, and the amount of internal memory is likely to be small.

edit—To modify or correct that which was done before. Both text and graphics can be edited by erasure, rearrangement, and replacement.

electronic mail—The process of sending, receiving, storing, and forwarding messages in digital form. Electronic mail may be addressed to just one recipient, or it may be broadcast to all stations in a network. The principal virtues of electronic mail are speed and convenience.

electronic publishing—The dissemination of information in machine-readable form. The best prospect for electronic publishing is the optical disc, which can hold one to two billion bytes of data, or more than half a million pages of text, per side.

electrosensitive printer—A device that prints letters by electrically zapping selected spots on the surface of a metallic-coated paper. The black-on-silver output of an electrosensitive printer is not pretty to look) at, but the machine is cheap and fast.

fanfold paper—One long, continuous sheet of paper, perforated at regular intervals to mark page boundaries, and folded fan-style into a stack.

fiber-optic cable—Also known as a light pipe. A fiber-optic cable conducts light around corners in almost the way that a hose conducts water. Light that enters one end of an optical fiber is internally reflected until it reaches the opposite end.

field—The set of even- or odd-numbered scan lines that makes up one half of a complete image, or frame, on an interlaced raster-scan CRT.

file—The fundamental unit of data storage. By issuing the proper commands in conjunction with a file name, it is possible to store, retrieve, or modify the contents of a file.

filling—In graphics, a software function that allows the interior of a closed polygon to be filled with a color of the operator's choosing.

firmware—Software imbedded in a ROM chip.

fixed spacing—The printing of letters at fixed horizontal intervals on a page. All letters, regardless of width, are placed the same distance apart (measured from center to center).

flip-flop—A simple digital memory device, the output of which can be either 0 or 1. The status of a flip-flop remains constant until some prescribed input signal flips it to the opposite state.

floppy disk—A popular form of mass storage consisting of a thin layer of iron oxide (which holds the data) deposited on a flexible mylar disk. A thin jacket protects the disk from dirt and abrasion. Floppy disks are available in single- and double-density versions with one or two sides.

font—A style of type. Each font represents characters slightly differently.

footer—Information printed at the bottom of a page—for example, chapter titles or page numbers may be placed in a footer. Most word processors can automatically print footers on each page of a document. A footer is not the same thing as a footnote, which appears only on a page where extension or clarification of a topic is required.

format—1) To specify margins, line spacing, justification and other factors that govern how text is printed on a page. 2) To prepare a soft-sectored disk for data storage.

form letter—A document consisting mainly of standard text into which selected pieces of personal information, such as a customer's name and address, have been inserted. The object of all this is to produce a seemingly personal and friendly sales letter. A form letters differs from a boilerplate document in that every recipient of a form letter gets basically the same information. In contrast, boilerplate documents are prepared specially for each client.

frame—The video image produced by one complete scan of the screen of a raster-scan CRT. If the scanning is done in an interlaced fashion, the frame is composed of two separate fields, which are traced out alternately on the screen.

frequency-shift keying (FSK)—A simple modulation scheme used on low-speed modems. Digital 1's and 0's are converted to sine waves of different frequencies, which can be transmitted over the telephone lines.

friction-feed—A paper-feed system that operates by clamping a sheet of paper between two rollers—one metal, the other rubber. As the rollers rotate, the paper is drawn into the printer.

full-duplex—Properly, this refers to communication that takes place in two directions simultaneously over the same link. Full-duplex is also used to describe the operation of a terminal that transmits data and relies on a computer to echo it back for display on the screen.

full-page display—A CRT screen capable of displaying 66 lines of 80-95 characters.

function key—A specially designated key which, when pressed, initiates some function on a word processor or graphics terminal.

global operation—In word processing, an operation performed throughout an entire file. A global replacement, for example, would replace every instance of some word in the file with a new word designated by the user.

half-duplex—Basically, this refers to two-way communication that takes place in one direction at a time over a common data link. Also, terminals that display the data they transmit on screen without relying on a computer to echo it back are said to be operating half-duplex.

halftoning—Using dot patterns of variable density to simulate gray levels on a display that is strictly black-and-white (i.e., that allocates only one bit of storage per pixel).

handshaking—An exchange of signals between sender and receiver designed to ensure that trhe sender transmits only when the receiver is ready to accept new data.

hard copy—Textual or graphical data that have been printed on paper or recorded on photographic film. Hard copy is so named because it is a tangible and permanent record of computer output.

hard disk—A rotating magnetic memory device that uses a rigid aluminum disk coated with a layer of iron oxide. Hard disks come in two styles: Winchester and removable-cartridge.

hardware—All the electronic and mechanical components that make up a computer system.

header—A short message posted at the top of each page of a document—for example, a name or title. Headers can be inserted automatically by most word-processing systems.

hot zone—On some word processors, a user-defined region beginning at the right margin of a page and extending about seven spaces to the left. If a word ends within the hot zone, the system automatically places the next character entered at the beginning of the next line. If a word begins before the hot zone and ends beyond the right margin, the operator will usually have to hyphenate it, though some systems will hyphenate automatically. Contrast this with word wrap.

ink-jet printer—A non-impact printer that forms characters by literally spraying ink onto a page.

integrated circuit—One of the rectangular plastic or ceramic devices with 8-40 pins that are so common inside a computer. Each integrated circuit is a complex marvel of engineering, containing anywhere from hundreds to hundreds of thousands of microscopic transistors.

interface—1) To join two different pieces of equipment together electrically. Proper interfacing requires that each device transmit signals compatible with the other. 2) A circuit that translates incoming and outgoing signals so that a device can communicate with the outside world in some standard fashion.

I/O—Short form of input/output.

joystick—A popular graphical input device. With the proper software, it is possible to move a cursor horizontally or vertically on a CRT screen simply by deflecting the arm of the joystick.

justification—Printing a page so that both the left and right margins are straight. This is accomplished by padding extra spaces between words to make all lines the same length. Either whole spaces or microspace increments may be added, depending on the software and the printer in use.

kilobyte—To those who value consistency in language, this ought to mean 1,000 bytes, but computer types persist in defining it as 1,024. This might be more palatable if everyone in the computer business, including ad writers, would stick to the 1,024-byte convention. As it is, one manufacturer's 256K memory board may be identical to another's 262K; the only difference lies in how the kilobyte is defined.

laser disc—Another name for an optical disc.

laser printer—An expensive, very-high-speed device capable of printing in excess of 20,000 lines per minute.

letter quality—A term applied to printed copy of the highest caliber, consisting of sharp, fully formed characters. Also known as correspondence quality.

light pen—Basically, a device to detect areas of illumination on the screen of a CRT. With the proper software, a light pen can be used to draw lines, erase features, make menu selections, etc.

line-drawing display—An electronic display on which images are represented as collections of smooth, straight lines. The principal line-drawing displays are the random-scan CRT and the direct-view storage tube (DVST).

line printer—A device that prints text on a line-at-a-time basis. Line printers are faster than serial printers, but not as fast as the laser or xerographic types.

liquid-crystal display (LCD)—A flat, low-power, solid-state device that forms images as collections of black dots on a white background. LCD devices capable of displaying several complete lines of text are currently available, and large-area LCD graphical displays are a future prospect.

local-area network—A system that allows computers and intelligent terminals in the same plant or office to communicate with one another and share common resources, like mass storage and printers.

logic seeking—The ability of a printer that works bidirectionally to seek out the shortest printing path. After a line has been printed, the logic-seeking function determines whether it would be faster to print the next line left-to-right or right-to-left.

loop—A form of network architecture. The loop is characterized by a data path that runs from terminal to terminal and forms a closed circle. A central controller usually regulates the flow of messages and data around the loop.

lpm—Abbreviated form of lines per minute, a measure of printing speed.

magnetic disk—One of the most popular forms of mass storage. Data are stored as magnetic-field reversals in a layer of iron oxide that coats the disk. Two types of magnetic disk, floppy and hard, are in common use.

magnetic tape—A widely used means of sequential data storage. Magnetic tape comes in a variety of styles, from the small cassettes of ¼-inch tape used to economically store programs and data, to 2400-foot reels of ½-inch tape used in archival storage.

mainframe—A very large computer that typically offers high-speed operation and extensive memory resources.

mass storage—A non-volatile form of memory with a storage capacity much greater than that of computer RAM. When necessary, files can be deposited in or retrieved from mass storage by a computer. Most mass-storage devices in use today are magnetic, but optical memories show great promise for the future.

memory—To be precise, computer memory is no more than a means to store and later retrieve data. Beyond this, it bears little resemblance to human memory, which is characterized by a complex set of associations linking the data stored. No helpful associations exist in computer memory, so in order to retrieve stored information, the user had better know beforehand exactly what he wants and where it can be found.

memory-mapped I/O—A technique whereby communications ports are arranged to look like memory to a computer. By writing to and reading from certain memory addresses, the computer is thus able to exchange data with the outside world. The addresses taken by a memory-mapped serial or parallel port cannot be used by RAM or ROM.

menu—An on-screen display of the options currently available to the user. Menus make a program easy to use because they provide step-by-step guidance.

menu-driven software—Programs that make extensive use of menus. Software of this type is relatively easy to use, especially for a novice.

microcomputer—A computer whose central processing unit (CPU) is contained in one integrated circuit, known as a microprocessor. Microcomputers have revolutionized the computing industry by providing powerful features at low cost.

microfiche—A 5x7-inch piece of photographic film containing the images of hundreds of pages of text. Microfiche can be read by means of an inexpensive magnifying and projecting apparatus.

microprocessor—A one-chip CPU.

minicomputer—A computer intermediate in size and performance between a microcomputer and a mainframe. Unlike a microcomputer, a mini does not use a single-chip CPU, but a collection of integrated circuits instead. Generally, a minicomputer will be faster than a microcomputer and have a larger amount of semiconductor memory (RAM).

modem—A device for converting digital data into audio tones, and vice versa. Modems allow computer data to be transmitted quickly and economically over the telephone lines.

modular constraint—In graphics, a limitation on the placement of images such that some or all points of an image are forced to lie on the intersections of an invisible grid.

monitor—A device consisting of a CRT and various electronic support circuits that can be used to display computer-generated text and graphics. A monitor is similar to a TV, but it lacks the RF circuits needed to pick up and detect commercial broadcasts.

mouse—This is a type of graphical input device found on a few computers. Rolling the mouse around on a desktop produces X-Y motion of a cursor on the CRT screen.

NLQ—The abbreviated form of near letter quality, a description applied to dot-matrix printers that form characters from large numbers of overlapping dots. If properly executed, this results in very legible text that compares favorably with letter-quality copy.

node—One of the points linked together by a network. Computers, intelligent terminals, printers, and mass-storage units are some of the devices likely to be found at the nodes of a network.

operating system—Software that controls the exchange of information between a computer and its peripherals, organizes and keeps track of data files, and does the countless "housekeeping" chores that keep a computer system running smoothly. One benefit of an operating system is that it provides a standardized environment in which an application program can work. Thus, two very different computers with the same operating system should be able to run the same user program with only minor modifications, if any.

optical character recognition (OCR)—The process of scanning printed text and converting it into digital data. OCR machines allow for the fast entry into a word processor of previously typed material.

optical disc—A high-density storage medium that holds promise as a means for archivally storing large amounts of computer data. Information is inscribed on the optical disc by a laser that burns a pattern of holes into a tellurium film on the disc's surface. Currently, the major drawback of the optical disc is that, once written, data cannot be erased.

PABX—Abbreviation for private automated branch exchange, which is to say, a private telephone system with automatic switching. PABX equipment provides telephone communications within an office or factory, and also links up with the public telephone system. Some forms of PABX handle data as well as voice.

paddle—A graphical input device consisting of a single potentiometer which the user actuates with a knob or lever. A paddle might be thought of as half a joystick, since it offers one degree of positioning freedom, whereas the joystick offers two.

pagination—The division of text into page units, usually performed automatically by a word processor.

parallel port—A communications interface in which all the bits of a word of data are transmitted simultaneously. Thus, in an eight-bit computer, eight lines would be needed to transmit data by the byte, that is, eight bits at a time. Usually two sets of data lines are used—one for incoming data, the other for outgoing. In addition to data lines, a parallel port will also contain handshaking lines to ensure that a sender transmits only when a receiver is ready to accept data. Transmission between two parallel ports is potentially faster than that between two serial ports, since the serial ports lose time converting words of data into a stream of bits, and vice versa.

parity checking—A scheme to detect single-bit data errors. Before being transmitted or stored, every data word has a special parity bit attached to it. If odd parity has been selected (even parity is also possible), the parity bit is adjusted so that the total number of 1's in the data word and parity bit is odd. For example, if there are three 1's in the data word, the parity bit will be 0, but if the data word contains two 1's, the parity bit will be 1. When the data word and parity bit are later received or fetched from storage, parity is checked. If it is not odd, at least one of the bits has been altered.

peripheral—Any auxiliary piece of equipment that works in concert with a computer. Typical peripherals include printers, terminals, and plotters.

personal computer—Generally, any small, low-cost microcomputer.

photomultiplier—An extremely senstive light detector with very fast response. The photomultiplier is one of the few vacuum-tube devices that have not been eclipsed by solid-state technology. Light pens used with high-resolution displays rely on photomultiplier tubes.

pin feed—A paper-feed system that relies on a pin-studded roller to draw paper, punched with matching holes, into a printer.

pixel—Contraction of the words picture element. A pixel is the smallest dot that can be displayed on a system's viewing screen.

plasma-panel display—A light-weight, flat, electronic display suitable for applications that demand portability and ruggedness. Dot-matrix letters and graphics are produced by selectively firing cells of a neon-based gas arranged in a grid pattern. The resolution of a plasma panel is inferior to that of a CRT.

plotter—An electromechanical device that draws diagrams under computer control. The movement of a mechanical arm, to which a fiber-tip pen is attached, produces lines on paper or drafting film.

point-plotting display—An electronic display that constructs all images out of sets of discrete points. The most important point-plotting display at the present time is the raster-scan CRT. Other point-plotting displays include the plasma panel and the LCD matrix.

port—In electronics, two or more signal lines carrying related information. A serial port can operate with as few as three lines, while an eight-bit parallel port will require at least 11, counting handshake and ground lines.

printer—Any machine that converts digital data into printed text.

print spooler—A device that very quickly accepts data from a computer, and then feeds it at a leisurely pace to a printer. In effect, the spooler acts as a repository for text waiting to be printed. Using a spooler allows a computer to dump text rapidly and get on with other work, instead of wasting time spoon-feeding a printer.

print wheel—Another name for a daisy-wheel type element.

program—A sequence of precisely formulated instructions that specify how a computer is to perform some task.

prompt—A message generated by a computer program for the guidance of an operator; for example, "INSERT DISK IN DRIVE B" or "TURN ON PRINTER."

proportional spacing—If the horizontal space allotted to a printed character is proportional to the width of that character, the spacing is said to be proportional. The alternative to this is fixed spacing.

ragged left—Refers to text printed with a straight right margin and an uneven left margin. Also known as flushed right.

ragged right—If the left margin of a page of text is kept straight, and the right margin is left uneven, the result is known as ragged-right (or flushed-left) printing.

RAM—An acronym for random-access memory, the semiconductor memory in which programs and data are stored. Any location (address) in RAM can be accessed independently of any other location.

random access—Refers to a memory device that allows data to be accessed independently of any other data in memory. Under random access, the time required to locate and retrieve a piece of information is always the same, regardless of where in memory that information is stored.

random-scan CRT—All images produced on this type of electronic display are constructed of smooth straight-line segments. Solid surfaces cannot be represented, except as wire-frame diagrams (q.v.).

raster—The zig-zag pattern traced by the electron beam of a CRT used in a point-plotting display system.

raster-scan CRT—The most versatile electronic display. Raster scanning constructs all images—whether they be points, lines, letters, or solid surfaces—out of numerous, tiny dots.

read—To extract data from storage.

refresh—To repeatedly cause an image to be traced on the screen of a CRT. Doing this often enough (say, 60 times a second) gives the appearance of a steady display with no trace of flicker. If refreshing were stopped, the image would quickly fade away.

resolution—The number of dots per inch produced by an electronic display or hard-copy device. Higher resolution (more dots per inch) means that finer details can be depicted. It also means that curves and diagonal lines will appear smoother and more realistic on a point-plotting display.

RF—Abbreviation for radio frequency, the general term for a broad spectrum of electromagnetic radiation ranging in frequency from ten thousand to 40 billion cycles per second. Radio-frequency radiation has been used primarily for the purpose of communication.

RF modem—Similar in concept to a conventional modem (q.v.) except that the transmission frequencies employed are much higher. This allows data to be sent at a higher rate. RF modems transmit not over the phone lines but over broad-band-bus networks, where they allow as many as 50 different transmissions to be broadcast simultaneously over the same coaxial cable.

RGB video—A method of conveying color video information that uses separate red, green, and blue video signals instead of a composite. Usually, the sync signals are also separate. Color monitors with RGB inputs are capable of resolving much more detail than their low-cost composite-video counterparts.

ring—A form of network architecture in which every node connects to two others to form a chain. The beginning and end of this chain are then connected together, thereby producing a closed ring. Network control is distributed, and the right to transmit over the network is determined by token-passing (q.v.).

ROM—Read-only memory. The contents of ROM can be addressed and read by a computer, but they can never be changed. The principal purpose of ROM memory is to store programs that will be used by the system, such as a language or an operating system.

RS-232C—A standard type of asynchronous serial port.

rubber-band line—In graphics, a line that appears to stretch between a fixed point of origin and a movable endpoint. The illusion of elasticity is created by redrawing the line several times a second so that it always keeps up with the movable endpoint. A rubber-band line can be repositioned any number of times until it lies just where the operator wants it. Hitting the proper key then freezes the line in place.

scaling—The process of changing the size of an image. For instance, scaling by a factor of two multiplies all dimensions of an image by two.

scanner—Another name for either an OCR machine or a bar-code reader.

screen dump—The process of transferring the contents of the block of memory containing screen data (either graphical or textual) to a printer or other hard-copy device. A screen-dump program is unnecessary if the hard-copy device has a video interface, since all screen data can be extracted from the system's video output.

scroll—To shift every line of text on a video screen up or down by the same increment. This shifting is performed repeatedly until the desired spot in the text has been reached. If the scroll is upward, a new line must appear at the bottom of the screen as an old one disappears at the top. On some systems, it may even be possible to scroll text horizontally so that extra-wide documents can be viewed.

sector—On an optical or magnetic disk, one of several equal segments into which a circular track of data is divided. Files are retrieved by reading the sectors that have been allocated to them by the operating system.

sequential access—Used in reference to a memory device that retrieves information in the order in which it was stored. Cassette tape is a common example of sequential-access memory. The time required to find a particular piece of information using sequential access depends on the position of that information in memory.

serial port—An interface between two digital devices that transfers data bit by bit over a single wire. If the port is bidirectional, two wires are used: one carries outgoing data, the other incoming data. A serial port is slower than a parallel port, since the individual bits of a word are transmitted one after another rather than simultaneously.

serial printer—A machine that prints one character at a time.

shadow-mask CRT—A color CRT with three electron guns and a screen containing red, green, and blue phosphor dots. The shadow mask ensures that each electron beam strikes only dots of the proper color.

shadow printing—On a daisy-wheel printer, a bold character can be printed by backing up the printhead to within 1/120 inch of its previous position and restriking. The slight amount of misregistration between the initial impression and the overstrike produces a fatter, bolder character.

single-sheet feeder—A device to automatically feed individual cut sheets of paper to a daisy-wheel printer.

smart terminal—A CRT terminal with enough native intelligence to allow extensive editing of text before transmission, the storage of multiple pages of text, and various other amenities not found on a dumb terminal.

software—Another name for a program, or sequence of computer instructions. Software can exist in various physical forms—reversals in a magnetic field on a floppy or hard disk, high and low voltages in semiconductor memory, tiny burned-out holes on an optical disk—but the characteristic that it retains in all physical forms is its ability to be interpreted by a computer as information of a special kind: instructions. Software is usually purchased on disk, but it is important to keep the distinction clear between the software and the package it comes in.

star—A network configuration consisting of a central controller and satellite terminals, which connect to the controller to form a star pattern. If the controller fails, the whole system collapses.

storage tube—See direct-view storage tube.

streamer—A tape deck that operates at a continuous high speed (30-100 inches/ second) rather than starting and stopping between separate blocks of data. Streaming tape decks are useful for Winchester backup, among other things.

TDM—Short for time-division multiplexing, a process that allows several different messages to be transmitted alternately on the same communications link.

Short segments of several multiplexed messages are interleaved in successive time slots. Suppose that two separate messages, an alphabetical sequence and a numerical one, are being transmitted. The multiplexed signal might look like (1,a,2,b,3,c,4,d. . .) or (1,2,a,b,3,4,c,d. . .). The recipient of a particular message must pick out the relevant bits and pieces at the proper times.

terminal—A device that enables an operator to communicate with a computer. The operator enters commands and data by means of a keyboard, and views computer output on the terminal's CRT or storage tube. Some terminals provide printed output instead of an electronic display.

thermal printer—Though not of much use in word processing, thermal printers are fast and silent. They print by burning dot patterns into special paper.

token-passing—A popular means of arbitration in ring networks. The digital token, a code that confers the right to transmit on its holder, is passed around the ring in some prescribed order. Only the node currently holding the token can transmit; the rest just listen. Tokens are sometimes employed with bus-oriented networks, too.

touch-sensitive screen—An accessory that mounts on the face of a CRT and allows a user to communicate with his computer simply by touching words or images that appear on the CRT screen.

track—On an optical or magnetic disk, one of several circular bands in which data can be stored. A 5.25-inch floppy magnetic disk may comprise 35-96 tracks, while a 12-inch optical disc generally has 54,000. On magnetic tape, the tracks are fewer in number (usually nine) and they run lengthwise.

tractor-feed mechanism—A pair of pin-studded belts that rotate in unison and pull paper, punched with complementary holes, into a printer.

transformation—In graphics, one of the modifications that can be made to the placement or size of an on-screen image. The three basic transformations are rotation, translation, and scaling.

translation—The movement of an image to a new position on the screen. Under translation, every point in the image moves in the same direction with the same speed at any given instant. In other words, translation is movement without rotation.

UPC—Short form of Universal Product Code, a bar-code system widely used by supermarkets in the United States.

utility—A program, usually relatively short, that performs some function useful to system maintenance or operation, such as disk copying or memory testing.

video digitizer—A device that converts the signal from a video camera into digital form and stores it in memory, where it can be analyzed or modified by the computer.

vidicon—The tube inside a TV camera that converts the image of a scene into an electrical signal.

volatile—Refers to any form of memory that loses data when the power is turned off. Semiconductor RAM is the chief example of volatile memory.

wild-card character—A unique character which, when used as part of a name, is interpreted by the system as being a match for any other character. Thus, if a word processor is directed to search for "Fred*", it might locate "Freddy" as well as "Frederick" if both were present in the file.

Winchester disk—A special type of hard disk that is hermetically sealed against contamination by smoke, dust, pollen, cracker crumbs, etc. The disk is therefore not removable, but the system is very reliable and compact.

wire-frame diagram—A method of representing a surface or solid object. The wire-frame diagram contains lines, often arranged as a mesh or lattice, that define the surface contours of an object. Wire-frame diagrams can be used on any type of display system; on a line-drawing display, they are the only way that a solid object or surface can be effectively represented.

word—A group of bits taken together as a logical unit. The word is the fundamental unit of data or program-instruction storage in a computer. Generally, larger word sizes are indicative of faster operation. Most microcomputers operate on eight-bit words, or bytes, of data, and some on 16-bit words. Minis have a 16- or 32-bit word size, and mainframes typically use 64-bit words.

word wrap—On some word processors, when a word overlaps the right margin, the entire word is automatically removed from the line it was in and placed at the start of the next line. Subsequently typed letters follow the wrapped word on the new line. Like a hot-zone (q.v.), word wrapping makes it unnecessary for the operator to terminate each line manually with a carriage return.

write—To place data into storage.

xerographic printer—A very-high-speed, expensive printing machine that functions very much like a xerographic copier.

INDEX

NOTICE